Transcultural Modernisms

Publication Series of the Academy of Fine Arts Vienna
Eva Blimlinger, Andrea B. Braidt, Karin Riegler (Series Eds.)
Volume 12

Transcultural Modernisms

Model House Research Group

Fahim Amir
Eva Egermann
Moira Hille
Jakob Krameritsch
Christian Kravagna
Christina Linortner
Marion von Osten
Peter Spillmann
(Editors)

Sternberg Press

On the New Publication Series

We are pleased to present this new volume in the publication series of the Academy of Fine Arts Vienna. This book, published in cooperation with our highly committed partner Sternberg Press, successfully embodies the series' new concept, which is now devoted to central themes of contemporary thought about art. The volumes in the series comprise collected contributions on subjects that are the focus of discourse in terms of art theory, cultural studies, art history, and research at the Academy of Fine Arts Vienna and form the quintessence of international study and discussion taking place in the respective fields. Each volume is published in the form of an anthology edited by staff members of the Academy of Fine Arts Vienna. Authors of high international repute are invited to write contributions dealing with the respective areas of emphasis. Research activities such as international conferences, lecture series, institute-specific research focuses, or research projects serve as the points of departure for the individual volumes.

We should like to thank the editors, in particular Christian Kravagna and Moira Hille, project leader Marion von Osten, and the authors for their outstanding conceptual, scholarly, and artistically innovative work, the graphics team of Surface for the new layout design, and Martina Dattes (Academy of Fine Arts Vienna) for her editorial supervision and thorough support of the series. Special thanks go to Sternberg Press for its constructive and creative partnership with the Academy of Fine Arts Vienna.

The Rectorate of the Academy of Fine Arts Vienna
Eva Blimlinger, Andrea B. Braidt, Karin Riegler

Editors: Moira Hille, Christian Kravagna, Marion von Osten
Translation: Erika Doucette, Emily Lemon, Sam Osborn
Copyediting: Emily Lemon, Erika Doucette, Gabrielle Cram
Proofreading: Charlotte Eckler
Design: Surface, Frankfurt am Main/Berlin
Photo editing: Christina Linortner, Peter Spillmann
Webdesign and programming: Peter Spillmann, Michael Vögeli
Printing and binding: Generál Nyomda Szeged

ISBN 978-3-95679-012-6

This book is part of the research project
Model House-Mapping Transcultural Modernisms
http://www.transculturalmodernism.org
Supported by WWTF - Vienna Science and Technology Fund

Sternberg Press
Caroline Schneider
Karl-Marx-Allee 78
D-10243 Berlin
www.sternberg-press.com

Contents

With Animals

In China

From Casablanca to Be'er Sheva

And Crip

Epilogue

CIAM IX Aix en Provence (1953

habitat

Habitat

learnin

CIAM VI Bridgewater (194

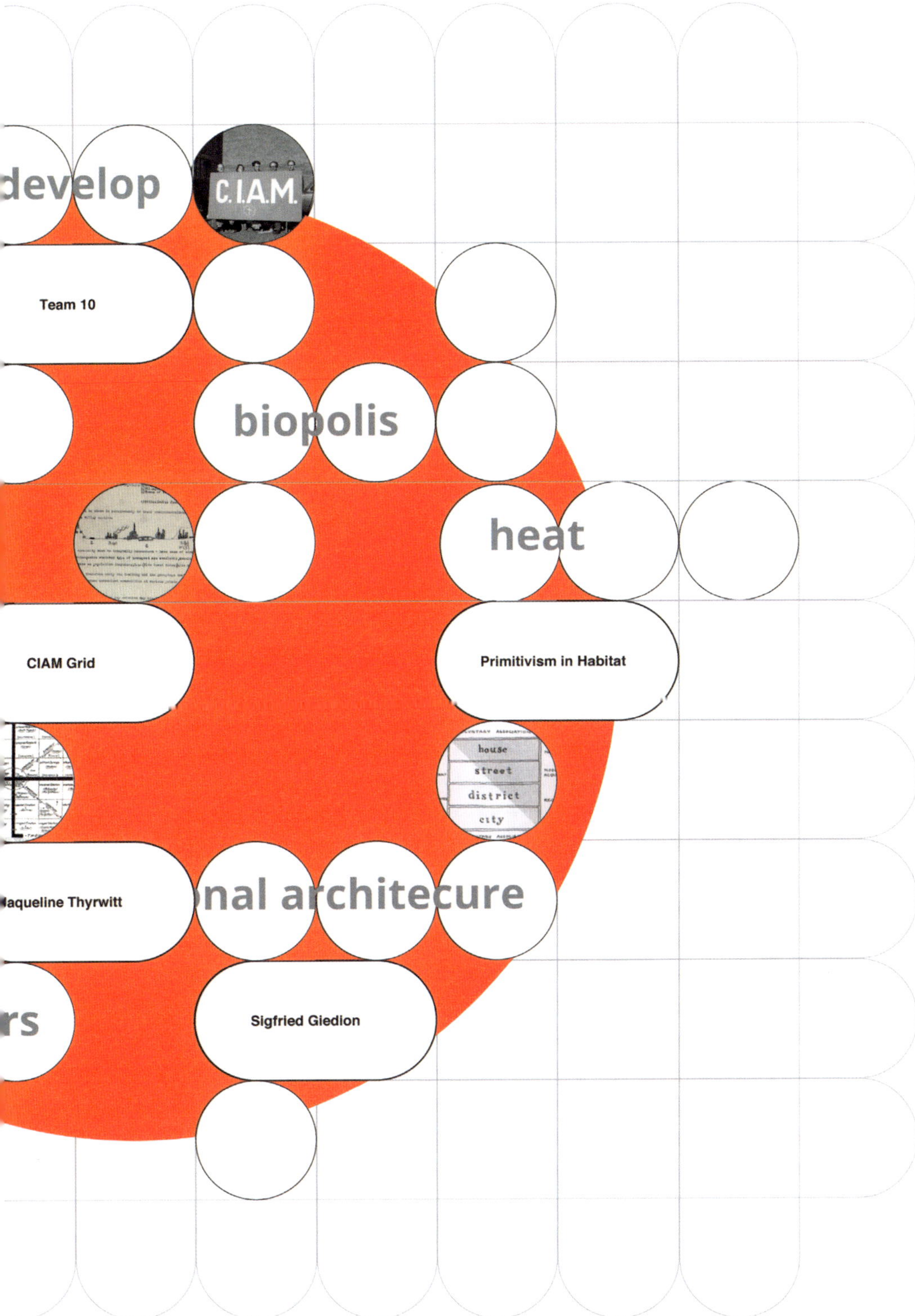
develop
C.I.A.M.
Team 10
biopolis
heat
CIAM Grid
Primitivism in Habitat
house
street
district
city
aqueline Thyrwitt
nal architecure
rs
Sigfried Giedion

Introduction

Marion von Osten

This publication is an outcome of the research project *Model House–Mapping Transcultural Modernisms*, which investigated and mapped out the network of encounters, transnational influences, and local appropriations of an architectural modernity manifested in various ways in housing projects in India, Israel, Morocco, and China that served as exemplary standard models, not only for Western societies. Based on three case studies of modernist architectural projects realized in the era of decolonization, the project covered specific social relations and the transcultural character of building discourses at the height of modernism. Rather than building on the notion of modernism as having moved from the North to the South—or from the West to the rest of the world—the emphasis in *Model House* was on the exchanges and interrelations among international and local actors and concepts, a perspective in which "modernity" is not passively received, but is a concept in circulation, moving in several different directions at once, subject to constant renegotiation and reinterpretation.

At the beginning of the research project, we were concerned with the question of how the travel and building practices of both Western and non-Western architects within colonial and postcolonial contexts set transnational knowledge transfers in motion. Thus, the project studied the mutual migration of discourses, people, and practices across geographical space. At the same time, the experimental methods of the researchers—a team of artists, architects, and humanities scholars—allowed the project to compare the local, social, political, and discursive conditions under which the building projects were realized, on the basis of different approaches in terms of material as well as forms of interpretation. Throughout the project there was an ongoing exchange by publishing the research findings and other documents on a website and database especially conceived for the project. These processes made it possible to examine whether the concrete local contexts produced specific methods, results, or even crises for the modernist planning certainties. Moreover, the assumption that spaces/places are characterized by the constant interaction of many different actors under unequal conditions lead *Model House* to employ a praxeological approach, which initially grasps everything as action, i.e., perceiving of everything that exists as being endowed with agency. The built environment is not simply something that is built and inhabited, but that is formed through and in interaction with the given political, social, technological, and economic conditions, public discourses, concepts, and artistic and scientific production. Thus, the basic question of the research team was formulated in a deliberately open way: who or what builds a city or a city district?

Against this background, in his doctoral research project, philosopher Fahim Amir expands on the notion of transculturality by including dimensions of nonhuman agency in architecture and urban planning, which have thus far been neglected. Conceptual questions concerning the agency of nonhuman animals as "other actors" in both the production of metropolitan and post/colonial spatiality and in the traces and manifestations of animality found in images and discourses surrounding architectural modernism, such as in Le Corbusier's early writings or in the planning discourse on Chandigarh, have provided new insights into the significance of nonhuman actors for modern planning discourse. Moreover, the interwovenness of modern architecture discourse and nonhuman animals as former co-dwellers is strongly linked to discourses on biopolitics, epidemics, and hygiene, as Nádia Farage shows in her examination of the modernization of Rio de Janeiro. On the one hand, the erasure of nonhuman animals and rural practices from public view in the modern city at the beginning of the twentieth century, which continues to this day, mirrors processes of "class-making" and the introduction of new forms of industrial production, but as Farage highlights, on the other hand, it also shows how new movements of resistance and solidarity were formed between human and nonhuman animals.

Politics of segregation and erasure that also constituted social movements are reflected in artist Eva Egermann's interview with Susan Schweik, in which she speaks about the Ugly Laws in modern city policies and the City Beautiful Movement in the United States, which had radical effects on disabled and homeless persons as well as on international planning ideologies. In the interview with Rob Imrie, the question of architecture as an enabling practice entails a critique of the normative approach to the human body within architecture. Since Eva Egermann's doctoral research also focused on bodily difference in the context of architectural modernity and the spaces where disability/ableism intersect with urban planning, the *Model House* research collective was also able to address space as a form of representation of social structures, as a product of power relations and of social, economical, and cultural discourses and practices.

With this conceptual framework, current approaches from Postcolonial Studies, such as the idea of a multiple or "entangled" modernity, are not simply applied to the discourse of modern architecture, but are also expanded upon through adding other perspectives from ideology critique or queer perspectives on the production of space. This methodological openness enabled us to bring specific urban planning models into conversation with one another and to explore potential connections or differences. Simultaneously, inquiring about the actors and agency involved in architecture and urban planning also opened up perspectives that could account for counter-narratives, resistance, and unruliness.

In the course of the research process, particularly with the focus on the concrete building projects in China, India, and Israel, the research team was confronted with the question of how to grasp and describe the transformation from a colonial modernity, in which European architects had once played a formative role, to a modernity of independence along with its actors. Some building projects adopted colonial building methods or a modernist vocabulary of forms—as in the case of Chandigarh—but in their realization employed local methods of building and materials that were based on manual labor. And, at the same time, as the examples from China and Morocco show, there was also a synthesis of regional architectural traditions and the modern language of form. Can approaches to postmodern thought perhaps already be found at the height of modernity, during the era of decolonization? How did this paradigm shift correspond with the postcolonial condition and its actors—and did it, or did they, bring it about?

The increased global interest in local, vernacular forms of building in modern architecture since the end of the Second World War, and a turn toward the use, everyday practices and self-building of the inhabitants themselves, and toward the relation and relationships between the private and public spheres seem to indicate a change in perspective. Issues of vernacular architecture and regionalism were central issues of debate within the *Congrès International d'Architecture Moderne* (CIAM) in the 1950s or in UN chartas on housing. These discourses were also popularized through Bernard Rudofsky's famous 1964 exhibition "Architecture without Architects" at the Museum of Modern Art, New York. As a result, a number of regionalist concepts that utilized vernacular architecture and regional building traditions in various ways emerged around the globe. However, as the conversation with architecture historian Felicity D. Scott shows, the discourse on the vernacular within building practice had many outcomes and interpretations. It was used for very different planning concepts and highly diverse practices. It became a style or basis for "climate sensitive" approaches in modernist housing programs. On colonial grounds references to the vernacular had bio-political implications and served colonial apartheid politics. In postwar Britain it affected non-plan movements that celebrated the self-builder and local building practices. Thus one result of the transdisciplinary research process was the specification of the contextual framings, in which the vernacular functioned as an agent with very different outcomes.

A case study conducted by architect Christina Linortner in collaboration with her research fellows, historian Jakob Krameritsch and artist Eva Egermann, investigates postwar urbanist projects of various actors in China that employ notions of the premodern, the regional, and the vernacular. These typologies and practices had been a subject of interest for modernist architects such as Margarete Schütte-Lihotzky and Werner Hebebrand in their travels to China in the 1950s. The interview with architectural historian Duanfang Lu, whose theoretical basis strongly refers to Linortner's research, highlights how modernity grappled with different histories, cultures, nationalities, and ethnicities, while also pointing to the intertwined relationship between modernity, scarcity, and the built environment, specifically after the *Great Leap Forward* in China. The article by the architect Chunlan Zhao argues that the *gan-da-lei* housing in the new town of Daqing, which was derived from a local vernacular housing typology, has metaphorically gained a double meaning: as a basic living unit and as a working method, it represented both past traditions and Mao's imperative to "build the country through thrift and hard work."

A second case study conducted by artist and writer Marion von Osten in collaboration with artist Peter Spillmann focused on "cultural-specific housing projects for Muslims" developed by Michel Écochard under French colonial rule in Casablanca, Morocco, which also had an impact on new town programs in Israel after 1948, such as the model neighborhood in Be'er Sheva. This study raises the question as to which shifts in meaning can be traced when a building typology—in itself a vernacular-modern synthesis—travels from a specific location and political conditions to another political context/territory. While the patio house in Casablanca consciously claimed to Arabize modern planning by creating housing for the colonized working class that segregated them from the colonial city center, the Israeli adaptation transformed a similar concept of the patio house into a desert climate-specific, regional approach. Nonetheless, both projects share similar biopolitical implications, as they were both built to accommodate a large influx of people. Housing programs were seen as measures for governing the arriving populations who were mainly non-European in both cases. In the interview with Jerusalem architect and curator Zvi Efrat, he demonstrates how the search for new typologies and models in architecture and urban planning was associated with the historical project of Zionism and nation building in Israel. However, in addition, the new "models" also express a specific architectural practice in which social questions are reduced to new design concepts.

The third case study conducted by artist Moira Hille, in research collaboration with philosopher Fahim Amir, applies a praxeological perspective in their analysis of the construction of the new city Chandigarh as a Euro-Asian enterprise in independent India. Against this background, architect, urbanist, and historian Vikramāditya Prakāsh's article shows that the building process of this large new town as part of the nation building process in India also created divisions between specific religious groups and separated the rural and the modern population. Furthermore, in a script for the video *Around Chandigarh*, Moira Hille traces the history of architect Minnette De Silva, the representative of India and Ceylon at the CIAM Conference in Aix-en-Provence in 1953. De Silva established a regional, modern-architecture approach combining local handcrafts and skills with modern construction methods and the use of local materials, allowing for the construction of modern, low-price houses. In the interview with architectural historian Anoma Pieris, it is once again clear that this regional approach is not easily comparable with other regionalisms, such as the UN proclamation of that time, and that De Silva's translocal approach took ideas from the modernist revaluation of traditional crafts in addition to taking into account the social-political aesthetics of the colonial/postcolonial domestic sphere.

In this book, modernism is not presented as a universalist and/or European project, but as marked by cultural transfers and their global localization and translation. Thus, as art historian Christian Kravagna points out in his article, a central theoretical precondition for the project at large was how the distinct meaning of the transcultural can be described as a concept and compared to other concepts that have been used to understand phenomena of cultural change within situations of culture contact. In reference to the historical focus of the *Model House* research project, namely the period of decolonization in the mid-twentieth century, Kravagna produces a historical perspective on the term and the meanings of transculturality by examining a range of theoretical models that developed between the 1920s and 1970s. The many ways in which the notion of the transcultural is "loosely" used or the belief that transculturality might describe a world where difference is dissolved harmoniously are critically examined in the interview with art historian Monica Juneja. Moreover, Kravagna's finding that the formation of transcultural thinking often took place in transdisciplinary milieus where scholarship, art practice, and political movements mutually transform one another has greatly informed the experimental layout of the research project itself.

From the very beginning, the *Model House* project facilitated and intensified the exchange between researchers from different disciplines and the integration of a multiplicity of text forms, media, and aesthetic practices. The research-based digital database, which is represented in this publication in the form of screenshots, was an important conceptual tool for exchanging, collecting, and analyzing ideas within the project. Designed and conceptualized by artist Peter Spillmann, in collaboration with the historian Jakob Krameritsch and the programmer Michael Vögeli, the database and website not only enabled but also constantly visualized the research process and its different steps. The result of this art- and design-based methodology was the creation of a polylogical and multiperspectival narration by a number of different speakers as well as visual and textual materials. The potential of this dialogical method is not in the publication of information but, in the sense of Dipesh Chakrabarty, in describing the project of modernism from the perspective of a series of localized events and specific actors, instead of continuing to tread the heroic path of universalism. By mapping and publishing first insights into self-generated online cartographies, a collective process was set in motion that resulted in the "Habitat Chart," a collective output, which architect Gabu Heindl reflects on in her article in this publication. With her epilogue and the other contributions to this book, the reader will not simply find a historical reevaluation of modernist projects under postcolonial conditions but also inquiries about the consequences of this project's research-based approach in addition to contemplations related to contemporary design practices and the responsibility of architects, designers, and planners today.

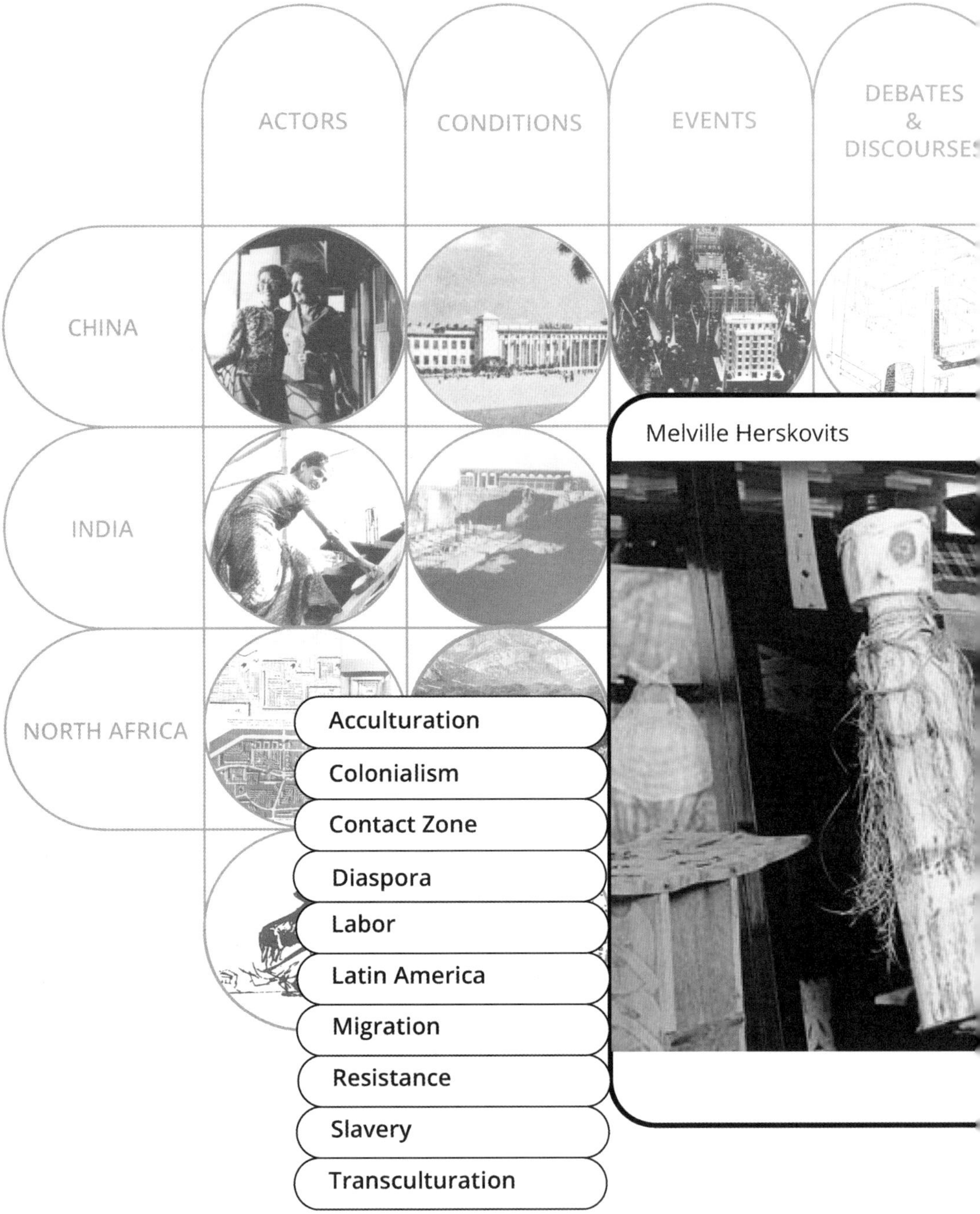
ACTORS
CONDITIONS
EVENTS
DEBATES & DISCOURSES
CHINA
INDIA
NORTH AFRICA
Melville Herskovits
Acculturation
Colonialism
Contact Zone
Diaspora
Labor
Latin America
Migration
Resistance
Slavery
Transculturation

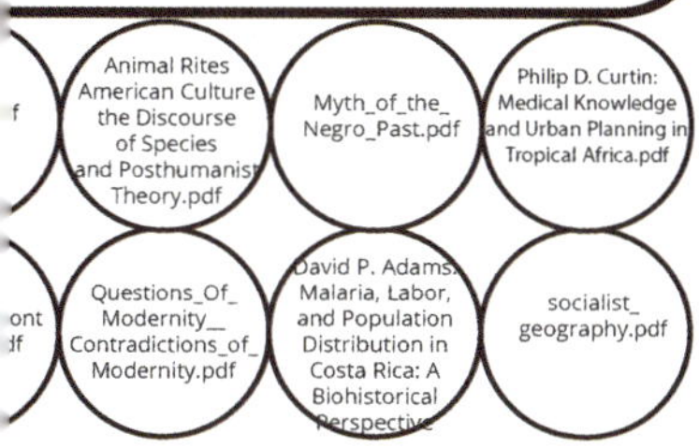

Transcultural Beginnings

Understanding Transculturalism

Monica Juneja and Christian Kravagna in Conversation

Christian Kravagna: In German-speaking countries, even within academic circles, we are often told that philosopher Wolfgang Welsch was the one to introduce the term "transculturality" in the 1990s. This supports the idea that it is a very new concept within cultural discourse. However, as we are both well aware, the term "transculturation" has been in use at least since 1940 through the work of Fernando Ortiz, and since around the 1920s, theories of transculturality have also played a key role in attempts to overcome the concept of "race" and notions of culture based on nation/ethnicity. What are your historic-theoretical points of reference for addressing transculturality? Could it be that all that is left for German-speaking scholars is to simply acknowledge its delayed arrival (and, on top of that, that a German philosopher has been accredited with introducing the term)? Or would you say that, within this discursive context, there were other precursors of the current approach to transculturality?

Monica Juneja: Though it might seem a truism, it must be observed that transculturation or the transcultural as an analytic approach inevitably builds on the groundwork of theoretical approaches of the past few decades, often indirectly—the linguistic-cum-cultural turn, gender studies, postcolonial studies—whose insights it responds to, refines and takes in different directions. The term itself, "transculturation" does indeed go back to the anthropologist Fernando Ortiz in his study of the sugar and tobacco cultures in colonial and postcolonial Cuba. While Ortiz saw this as a unidirectional process that entailed an initial loss followed by the emergence of something new, the transcultural in its present usage has become a concept and a perspective that is multidirectional and multivalent. In Ortiz's understanding—and this was an important observation—the explanatory potential of transculturation went beyond that of acculturation, in that it helped reconceptualize processes of adaptation as transformation. Furthermore, his analysis directs our attention to the nexus between objects and practices. In recent years, the transcultural has become a buzzword of sorts, used by a range of scholars in different, not always consistent ways and framed by diverse disciplinary contexts; this calls for a certain critical distance. At times the term is loosely used to stand for "cross-cultural" or "intercultural" in other contexts to denote a sensitivity to differences and the competences required within a multicultural society (e.g., in the case of fields designated as "transcultural" nursing or psychiatry); in German historical writing of the late twentieth century it was used as an adjective to qualify civilizational entities beyond the frontiers of Europe ("transkulturell vergleichende Geschichtswissenschaft") – here too, it is important to critically question the historical underpinnings of these taxonomic entities in the first place.

The definition proffered by Wolfgang Welsch has been generally regarded as a major theoretical landmark in that Welsch deployed transculturality as a heuristic device to critique the conceptualization of culture ascribed to Herder and the Enlightenment—i.e., a view of culture as a closed, internally cohesive, and linguistically homogeneous sphere—which, according to Welsch, is "untenable" today as it is no longer commensurate with the experience of modern societies. "Transculturality," he writes, "is a consequence of the inner differentiation and complexity of modern cultures." This makes it a more appropriate concept in his view than intercultural or multicultural, both of which sustain a hermetic and fixed idea of culture instead of transcending it. Finally, Welsch considers the traditional Herderian view of culture as "normatively dangerous," and hence the transcultural—equated automatically with the cosmopolitan or the syncretic—is seen as a political and ethical corrective to ethnocentrism and xenophobia.

While the perspective of the Heidelberg Cluster "Asia and Europe in a Global Context" shares Welsch's critique of a bounded notion of culture, it departs from Welsch's position in some significant ways. To begin with, Welsch's critique of existing notions of culture as obsolete is premised on the assumption that border crossings and cultural mixing are unique attributes of modernity. This is an approach which he shares with other cultural anthropologists who seek to spotlight the radical break that contemporary globalization has effected with the past by obscuring earlier historical forms of mobility and connectedness that have been characteristic of cultures over centuries, pre-dating the advent of modern communication and global capital. Secondly, Welsch conceives of transculturality as stasis, as a characterization of culture, and of the multiple identities of those who inhabit it. His analytical model does not address issues of processuality. And finally, his normative approach, which sees transculturality simply as an ethical corrective and postulates an opposition between "folklore" or "rhetoric" and the "real" syncretic substance of cultures, stands in the way of historicizing ethnocentric notions of culture as ideological constructs, which are equally embedded within and products of transcultural processes and exist in a constant state of tension with alternative positions, fueling virulent conflicts. I will return to this point while answering your last question.

Our understanding, while it draws upon insights of previous scholarship, views transculturation as denoting a process of transformation that unfolds through extended contacts and relationships between cultures. The concept can be used to refer both to a concrete object of investigation as well as an analytical method. The discursive category of "culture," as it emerged in the social sciences in tandem with the modern nation, was premised on the notion that life worlds of identifiable groups were ethnically bound, internally cohesive and linguistically homogeneous spheres. Culture, applied as a conceptual category to societies, past and present, invariably existed in tension with unruly and contradictory trends generated by mobility and extended contacts that have characterized regions and societies over centuries. The terms "transculture/transculturality" are an explicit critique of this notion, for the prefix "trans-" enables emancipation from the concept. Transculturality is about spatial mobility, circulation or flows, an insight drawn from studies of globalization, but is neither synonymous with nor reducible to these. It focuses on processes through which forms emerge in local contexts within circuits of exchange. Contact, interaction, and entanglement make the transcultural a field constituted relationally, so that asymmetry, as one attribute of relationships (together with categories such as difference, non-equivalence, dissonance), is an element that makes up this field. This attention to uncovering the dynamics of those formations both in the past and the present constituted through regimes of circulation and exchange distinguishes our understanding from that of Welsch—our research projects go back to antiquity and extend into the present. In other words, our research aims to investigate the multiple ways in which difference is negotiated within contacts and encounters, through selective appropriation, mediation, translation, re-historicizing and rereading of signs, alternatively through non-communication, rejection or resistance, or through a succession/coexistence of any of these. Exploring the possible range of transactions built into these dynamics works as a safeguard against polar conceptions of identity and alterity, equally against dichotomies between complete absorption and resistance, which characterize certain kinds of postcolonial scholarship, or more recent studies of cultural difference such as Hans Belting's *Florence and Baghdad: Renaissance Art and Arab Science* (2011), which, while seeking to write a connected history of perspectival vision, ends up dealing with Asia bringing in a form of cultural essentialism through the backdoor.

CK: In my research on the early history of theories of transculturality, I mainly focused on the "Black Atlantic." Here, the beginnings of Transcultural Studies can be traced back to the early twentieth century. I have hardly done any work on Asia. In which contexts can early ideas of Transcultural Studies be found there?

MJ: Theoretical approaches in different areas of study are embedded in and shaped by historical processes and identity formations of the concerned actors. Individuals and communities living in the diaspora, often in contexts marked by racism and other asymmetries of power, provided some of the earliest impulses for transcending existing disciplinary frameworks to theorize histories of slavery and a shared past that could not be contained within the boundaries of the present-day nation states. In a number of Asian contexts, on the other hand, disciplinary formations in the humanities—such as history and art history—were shaped by anti-colonial nationalism so that disciplines came to be closely tied to identity formations around the nation: the nation was thus the unit of analysis; a narrative of its unique achievements, past and present, explained purely from within, was transmitted through disciplines and institutions—the university, the museum, and the heritage industry. All these left little space for transcultural frameworks. While Postcolonial Studies—in the Indian context Subaltern Studies—brought in fresh and critical voices, which questioned the narratives of national solidarity by shifting the focus to the margins and repressed voices, their framework continued to be determined by the territorial frontiers of the nation state. More recently, historians have written about "connected" or "entangled histories," or have framed their subjects of study as being connected by bodies of water—the Indian Ocean, the South Pacific; anthropologists now focus on diasporas, mobility, and porous boundaries; art history, on the other hand, has by and large remained assiduously tied to a paradigm that precludes insights into cultural dynamics and entanglements, which question narratives of cultural purity and originality. Institutional structures prevailing in Western universities have maintained the boundaries between the area studies and the "mainstream," which has been a major hurdle to investigations adopting a transcultural approach. It is therefore not surprising that the critical edge of perspectives such as the Black Atlantic is rare in an Asian context. More recently, however, writings on globalization, migration, and modern media—mainly authored by scholars of Asia located in the West—have hailed a world without boundaries, marked by global flows (Appadurai), which, in a sense, involve a rejection of localized bounded cultures, thereby providing an initial impulse to transcultural studies—as has been done in the first phase of our Cluster. Yet here too, our research has brought us to a point where transcultural studies can refine the analysis of flows by looking more closely and critically at the dialectic between the dissolution of certain boundaries and the reaffirmation of other kinds of difference, of how de-territorialization is invariably followed by re-territorialization. Moreover the challenge now is to find a language to theorize the complex morphology of flows, to supplement macro-perspectives by descending into the thicket of localities—urban and rural, past and present, central and at the margins—in which the dynamics of actual encounters involving a host of actors become more clearly evident and meaningful.

CK: In the "Europe and Asia Cluster," there are researchers from different regions and different traditions of thought working in collaboration. This implies

a setting that already entails a process of negotiating concepts and terms. Are there different conceptions of transculturality within the Cluster and if so, do you consider them to be based on something other than differences in region and/or traditions of thought? Is there an "internal" debate on the term and its meaning within the Cluster? Or is there a kind of general approach to transculturality that is agreed upon for this project? Within the Cluster, what disciplines are considered to be forerunners or innovators for transcultural thought?

> MJ: While it is true that the Cluster brings together researchers with different regional specializations—European and Asian studies—their primary concern in seeking a common platform is to be able to overcome the hermetic isolation of their disciplines, which have left their mark on the local material they study. The result is a large, grey area of unasked questions and unstudied links; an equally large range of anomalies that refuse to fit into the existing explanatory patterns; and, most irritatingly, a vicious circle where the angle and selection dictated by a "nation state default mode," which itself has not been subjected to scrutiny, leads to results that, in turn, fortify the unproven assumptions on the basis of which they had been gained in the first place. Transculturality thus becomes a heuristic tool, an analytical mode rather than a theoretical given: its explanatory potential needs to be elaborated and substantiated by empirical research. The focus of our research is not on the existence of the transcultural per se but on its dynamics—which then requires linguistic and cultural competences across departments and regional specializations. Each of these necessarily implies certain disciplinary understandings, practices, and canons, which then have to stand the test of critical rereadings and fresh questions. Our Cluster has not sought to set up a separate new framework of Transcultural Studies outside of existing fields, rather to draw upon the competences of these fields as an indispensable asset for a transcultural approach. Having said this, however, there is a constant need to negotiate inner differences—one example has been the different ways in which disciplines—anthropology, Indology, or art history—define the concept of culture. An "avant-garde," if we so wish to term it, can be identified less in terms of a discipline per se, but rather can be found in areas of scholarship and subjects, which individual scholars or groups have defined innovatively and boldly across disciplines—studies of migration and diasporas across time, of transregional literary public spheres, studies of cosmic kingship in pre- and early modern Eurasian regions, or studies of slavery, to name a few.

CK: My own research has shown that there is a remarkable relationship between transculturality and transdisciplinarity (Fernando Ortiz uses literary parables; Édouard Glissant is a poet and theoretician; Melville Herskovits

draws on the artistic protagonists of the New Negro Movement). Have you made similar observations?

MJ: Yes, indeed, a transcultural framework requires the synergetic interaction of disciplines. As an art historian, I am drawn to certain conceptualizations of literary phenomena that highlight the tension between national belonging and the need to make the world your canvas. The study of migrant objects also involves grappling with their translation into different media—image, text, political treatise, or myth.

CK: There are several different concepts of culture as a process of amalgamation and translation (syncretism, creolization, hybridity), which were initially created to address certain regional and historical situations (the Antilles in Glissant, Cuba in Ortiz, Brazil in Arthur Ramos and Gilberto Freyre, etc.), all of which had close ties with colonialism. In recent years, these situated terms have been "globalized" and many of the authors who played a key role in the development of transcultural thought have commented on this process. For instance, Édouard Glissant has stated that "the whole world is becoming creolized"; and Stuart Hall has also made similar statements. Do you think we can now speak of a kind of globalization of the transcultural? If so, would this also mean discounting the link between transculturality and "contra-modernity" (Homi K. Bhabha) or "counter-culture of modernity" (Paul Gilroy)? In other words: is it important to distinguish between different conceptualizations of transculturality and their use?

MJ: Transcultural Studies owes its formative impulses to concepts such as "hybridity" or "creolization," which, at the time they were formulated, sensitized us to border crossings and cultural mixing. Together with their "globalization," these concepts have, however, suffered dilution from inflationary usage. The explanatory power of hybridity, for instance, remains limited by the presupposition, implicit in the term's indelible biologist overtones, of "pure" cultures, which then somehow blend or merge into a "hybrid" that is treated as a state beyond enunciation or articulation. This and other terms, such as creolization or métissage, often end up as theoretical straightjackets into which experiences of global relationships can be accommodated without further investigation of the processes and agents involved—and thus at the cost of the precision necessary for grasping their specificity and dynamics. In that sense, I would argue against the conflation of transcultural with these terms. A transcultural perspective, premised as it is on an understanding of culture that is in a condition of being made and remade, does not take historical units and boundaries as given, but rather constitutes them as a subject of investigation, as products of spatial and cultural displacements. Units of investigation are constituted neither mechanically following the territorial-cum-political logic of modern nation states nor according to civilizational or cultural categories drawn up by the universal histories of the nineteenth century, but are continually defined as participants in and as contingent upon the historical relationships in which they are implicated. As such, transculturality is not just another metaphor or umbrella term for "cultural flows," "hybridity," or any cognate deployed to capture exchanges that transgress cultural, linguistic, and material boundaries. As understood here, it rather operates on a different register and highlights the procedural character of a broad variety of phenomena, including flows, entanglements, and other forms of circulation, and confronts us with the challenge of finding a precise language to capture the morphology of the relationships built into these phenomena.

CK: The correlation between transculturality in modern architecture and decolonization is one of the central themes in our research project *Model House–Mapping Transcultural Modernisms*. During the era of decolonization, the West exported models of modernist architecture to the colonies, where they underwent processes of transcultural appropriation and transformation. In part, the same thing happened in the early reception of Transcultural Studies within the Euro-American context (e.g., Ortiz, Glissant). They are involved in political projects. Based on your research, do you also see this connection between transculturality and decolonization?

MJ: Decolonization is per se a transcultural project, however, viewing it through this lens allows you to transcend binaries of different kinds: those in which culture is seen as flowing from high metropolitan centers to absorptive colonial peripheries, where colonies are evacuated of agency through asymmetries of power; or even in cases where colonies have recast and reconfigured models exported to them, the matrix remains the colonizer-colony binary. A transcultural view allows you to locate these processes in a global context that transcends this opposition and views cultural phenomena as multi-sited interactions. One example of this approach is Partha Mitter's study of modernism in South Asia, which he plots on a global scale that looks beyond the bipolar model of colonial agency that introduced modernist art as part of its civilizing mission and the nationalist Indian response to it. I have worked on the architectural history of the central governmental complex of New Delhi after it was declared the new capital of India in 1912. This work showed that classicizing architecture was very much part of a multi-pronged transcultural relationship that connects European capital cities with others, such as Washington DC, Pretoria, and Canberra. In these cases, architects from the European continent migrated to Chicago, and then Peking, creating a classicizing mold for capital cities. This phenomenon can be fully grasped when a model is transplanted to and translated within multiple sites. Its location within a different matrix, and the close examination of the complex local negotiations involved, allow us to understand and theorize the proliferation of multiple translations.

CK: During a discussion at the International Congress of Art Historians in Nuremberg, art historian Horst Bredekamp called for an end of postcolonialism. Only when postcolonialism (and the "guilty conscience" it instills in "us") is finally a thing of the past, will we be able to approach research on global art history in an unfraught manner. Although radically phrased, Bredekamp is not alone in his opinion. Parul Mukherji has critically noted that more and more congresses (also in English-speaking contexts) are tending towards a transcultural paradigm in place of postcolonial perspectives. The critical issue regarding this trend is the loss of the political. So, would this mean that transculturality is just an academically sanctioned version of postcolonial critique?

MJ: While I share the view that the practice of disciplines is an ethical undertaking, ethics is not something that can be reduced to ascribing "blame" or "guilt" in absolute terms to individual scholars. In this sense, postcolonial perspectives are more about a methodological critique of existing disciplinary practices being complicit with asymmetries of power rather than about imputing responsibility to individual scholars of succeeding generations for acts of colonial violence and appropriation. Viewed in this light, Horst Bredekamp's stance looks at the issue from a perspective of political correctness that reduces academic pursuits to a matter of good and evil. And transcultural practice certainly has a lot to do with ethics—indeed, by questioning the underpinnings of disciplinary formations, taxonomies, and research protocols, it takes us into the heart of an ethical question—about our role as producers of knowledge and how this knowledge has shaped institutions. To take the example of art history: the discipline has ended up separating individual objects, has reorganized them into genres, hierarchies, and neat chronological sequences; it uses the category of style as a convenient tool for coordination and stabilizing endless mobility and metamorphoses of objects and forms. The idea of stylistic development implies a scheme that is not only artificially maintained by attending to a geographic location as self-contained; more than that, the idea itself is inevitably like a biological, evolutionary construct applied to culture, where it does not belong and where it operates by creating centers and peripheries and by suppressing human agency and the circulation of material objects. Reminding ourselves that the discipline itself as a product of history is the first ethical responsibility we share.

A contentious issue of the present—which I think Bredekamp is referring to but which has also evoked discussions elsewhere—is the question of objects appropriated in different historical contexts of the past from cultures across the world, which now are present in the displays of Western museums. What are the ethical issues involved here? Does the circumstance that the British Museum hardly possesses any objects of "British" art make it less of a "national" museum and rather a "universal" museum, as James Cuno has termed it? Here, too, we need to make a distinction between the institutional processes of creating a museum and the stories the objects themselves narrate. The institution itself is an enterprise implicated in nation-building—nationalist sentiment, however, is not stable and unchanging over time but historically formed. Museums of the nineteenth century were formed by contexts of the nation and empire—in this sense, the British Museum does not need to possess "British" objects to qualify as "national"; its collection is about and part of the nation's history of collecting through different means from across the globe—and the transactions involved here—archaeological enterprises, gifting, warfare, and the art market—need to be made transparent. In today's context, nations cultivate a self-image that is not identical with that of the nineteenth or early twentieth century: so, if reunified Germany seeks to bring together its collections of non-European art in a museum of the world, housed behind the restored façade of an erstwhile Prussian castle, this is also a nationalist enterprise of the present, to claim a cosmopolitan character for the nation, which would come as a corrective to the past. However, the objects themselves tell their own stories, which resist efforts to contain them in established narratives: for instance, how does the presence of non-European objects in the heart of the metropolis make us rethink master narratives about "Western" heritage, here, for instance, housed in museums that are a stone's throw away from the Humboldt Forum? Critical stances are not a monopoly of postcolonial writing alone—and transcultural perspectives will stand the test of acceptability only by living up to ethical imperatives of criticality and bringing to light fresh histories and understandings of culture, which disciplinary practices of the past have ended up suppressing.

CK: "Asymmetry" is a key concept within the Cluster's research program. Does this focus on asymmetries (of vectors, of power relations), as supplements to "flows," serve as a methodological tool to circumvent what I would call "happy transculturalism" which has become increasingly popular (particularly in art history)? (Though German-speaking art history barely knew what to do with the transcultural paradigm only a few years ago, it currently appears to be perfectly content with perceiving anything and everything as transcultural.)

MJ: Among the many "loose" usages of the notion of the transcultural is the romanticizing belief that we inhabit a world where difference is harmoniously dissolved, where connectivity and mobility imply a fortunate cosmopolitanism and emancipatory potential. In fact, this belief underlies Welsch's definition of transculturality as an important ethical corrective to ethnocentrism, wherein he dismisses all assertions of difference or rejections of cosmopolitan identities as "folklore" or "rhetoric" as distinct from the "real," syncretic substance of cultures, one "which favors coexistence rather than combat." Yet no serious scholarship can work with this opposition between "substance" and "rhetoric"—the latter is not inseparable from a transcultural relationship. A closer look at transregional circulation and communication invariably brings forth a vast amount of material making assertions of difference—cultural, ethnic, linguistic, and religious, which become central to the construction of identities. There is no dearth of examples from across the globe to show that a shared language created through the experience of migration and exchange, the very intensity of entanglement, precipitates a concern with the generation of difference. In fact, the language of sharing itself, taken as given, can occlude the contestations and the means, at times violent, through which groups negotiated their differences. The strength of a transcultural method that examines the varied and often contradictory processes of relationality would lie in analyzing the workings of such rhetoric, its translation into social and cultural practice, and the modes of resistance against it, rather than dismiss it as politically reprehensible. To take a concrete example: warfare presents us with the paradox of bringing together men (and in specific historical contexts entire families) of different ethnicities, religious faiths, and linguistic identities (often fighting across these lines), thereby promoting, in the long run, the practice of cosmopolitan exchange and at the same time of producing discourses of irreconcilable alterity, articulated through innumerable textual and visual representations, and practices such as iconoclasm or looting. Another example: in today's world of contemporary art where cultures are said to share a common, unbounded notion of art that cuts across national and cultural divisions, we encounter a new divide between those who enjoy access to authoritative knowledge about art, share the values of autonomy and transgression ascribed to it, and those who do not. This boundary cuts through a transnational and connected art world: it is often produced by fissured constellations within the locality and can generate conflict, controversy, and censorship, which in turn become global issues. The Danish cartoon controversy, the destruction of the Bamiyan Buddhas, the assaults on the Indian artist M. F. Husain, or the forced detention of Ai Weiwei are all examples of conflagrations that have erupted within fractured public spheres where today's global vocabularies about autonomous, interventionist art do not find a uniform resonance. Here, a transcultural view goes a long way in helping us grapple with the complexity of global phenomena that generate their own forms of exclusion and violence. Asymmetries are therefore one among a whole complex of relationalities that a transcultural perspective takes upon itself to investigate.

Transcultural Beginnings
Decolonization, Transculturalism, and the Overcoming of Race

Christian Kravagna

When we take a critical look at the history of modernity today and attempt to approach the phenomena of transcultural modernism from a post-Eurocentric perspective, we usually operate with a dynamic notion of culture that we have borrowed from Postcolonial Studies, critical migration and Diaspora Studies, critical anthropology, and parts of globalization theory. It is clear that several of the terms used to examine classical modern conceptions of culture have become part of our language through works published since the early 1990s. Against the backdrop of economic globalization and sociopolitical debates on migration and multiculturalism, critiques of a nationally defined conception of culture and of the idea of separate and ethnically distinct cultural spheres, which especially modern ethnology propagated, made themselves heard toward the end of the twentieth century. While conservative authors such as Samuel Huntington responded to these developments with warnings of a "clash of civilizations,"[1] thereby operating with the essentialist notion that each culture is a distinct entity unto itself, others opted for a more precise examination of the transitions, exchanges, constellations, and mutual exchange of cultural traits and practices, not only in the current era of globalization but also throughout the history of modernity, colonialism, and decolonization. Arjun Appadurai has analyzed the process of cultural globalization as a complex dynamics of diverse "flows" and "scapes," emphasized the global production of locality, and brought attention to transnational identity-scapes.[2] Homi K. Bhabha has focused on the "in-between of culture" and on the hybridization processes that are part of cultural practices and the production of culture, which he presents as counter-movements to the sharp boundaries drawn between the cultures of the colonizers and the colonized, and has recognized a postcolonial "contra-modernity" within these processes.[3] Mary Louise Pratt has historically examined "contact zones" as sites of agency, power relations, and resistance along colonial borders.[4] James Clifford has countered anthropology's fixation on a static and place-bound conception of culture with a paradigm of "routes," advocating for a particular emphasis to be placed on "traveling cultures."[5] With the concept of the "Black Atlantic," Paul Gilroy radically severed the link between culture and territory; he examined the marks left by the slave trade, colonialism, and diasporic cultural movements on the Atlantic, in which he sees a "counterculture of modernity."[6]

1 Samuel Huntington, *The Clash of Civilizations* (New York: Simon & Schuster, 1996).
2 Arjun Appadurai, *Modernity at Large: Cultural Dimensions of Globalization* (Minneapolis, MN: Minnesota University Press, 1996).
3 Homi K. Bhabha, *The Location of Culture* (London: Routledge, 1994).
4 Mary Louise Pratt, *Imperial Eyes: Travel Writing and Transculturation* (London: Routledge, 1992).
5 James Clifford, *Routes: Travel and Translation in the Late Twentieth Century* (Cambridge, MA: Harvard University Press, 1997).
6 Paul Gilroy, *The Black Atlantic: Modernity and Double Consciousness* (London: Verso, 1993).

Recalling that these (and numerous other) widely read volumes were published in the 1990s, one could be inclined to situate the emergence of transcultural studies at a time when—to adhere for a moment to a common historical narrative—globalization came after the division of the world into two parts in the decades of the Cold War. However, tracing the history of transcultural thought further back, an increasing number of variations on writings of this kind can be observed to arise between the two world wars. The idea here is not to pinpoint the very first theory of transculturality, but instead to locate the early development of transcultural studies within the historical-political contexts from which they emerged, and their connections with decolonial movements, antiracist thought, and new, post-ethnic notions of cultural identity, as well as with nation-building processes. A review of the most important publications from the American context shows that the era in which transcultural studies began appearing in Brazil, Cuba, Mexico, and the United States was the same era when the fascist systems in Europe emerged as the climax of the race ideologies that had been developing since the eighteenth century. The modern Western conception of culture is founded on the notion that a people, nation, and/or race are the bearers of culture and that it is necessary to demarcate boundaries between cultures and races in order to ensure "purity," and to dominate or even annihilate purportedly inferior races. Each of the contributions to early transcultural thought discussed in the following are based on an earnest, if at times problematic, attempt to overcome race as a determining factor of culture. Gilberto Freyre in Brazil, Fernando Ortiz in Cuba, José Vasconcelos in Mexico, and Melville J. Herskovits in the United States have, each in their own way, endeavored to decouple race from culture, to view the boundaries between European, Amerindian, and African cultures as permeable and, instead of distinguishing between cultures or races, to acknowledge and closely examine their hybrid forms, even downright propagating such hybrid forms as a means of undoing racist orders of domination. The set of problems that arise from these theoretical approaches, both on a political and social level, can also be read as an aftereffect of slavery and its abolition.

Of the entire American continent, the country with the largest African population and, in 1888, the last to abolish slavery, was Brazil. The liberation of the Black population and the transition from empire to republic in 1889 not only brought about fundamental changes in the country's social order and economic relations of production; with it also emerged a question of Brazilian national identity. One of the earliest political responses was the so-called *embranquecimento*, an immigration offensive with the goal of intensifying immigration from Europe to accelerate the modernization of Brazil by shoring up the white labor force. This policy of "whitening" arose from the European notion that progress was inextricably linked to the white "race." In the earlier decades of the twentieth century, and in opposition to this concept of white superiority, numerous scholars and artists developed Brazilian identity concepts based on the sexual and cultural mixing of European, African, and Amerindian elements, which had been going on for hundreds of years. Alongside psychologist Arthur Ramos's research on Black cultures, which began in the 1920s and wherein he studied and observed, among other things, "the merging of African deities with Christian saints and the divinities in the Indian theology,"[7] within the "syncretic" religious notions and practices of Candomblé, the work of sociologist Freyre had a particularly strong impact on Brazil's post-ethnic identity model as well as on international transcultural research. Following in the footsteps of German-American anthropologist Franz Boas, who had supervised his doctorate in New York, Freyre continued to decouple cultural analysis from biologically determined racial dispositions by underscoring the importance of historical, economic, and social factors. Although the notion of race remains present in Freyre's work, he speaks out against a determinist interpretation thereof and against the notion of racial superiority or inferiority. In his book *Casa Grande e Senzala (The Masters and the Slaves)*, first published in 1933, Freyre describes the "formation of an agrarian, slave-holding and hybrid society,"[8] which, since the very beginnings of Portuguese colonization, had witnessed the ongoing intermingling of ethnic groups and mutual influence, both in terms of spiritual and material culture. Freyre underscores the ability of the Portuguese colonizers to overcome the climate conditions in the tropics and their willingness to forge sexual and family bonds with Indian and African women as conditions for the "success" of colonization in Brazil, and attributes the strength of Brazilian society and the beauty of its culture to its hybridity: "the contact of European culture with that of the aborigines was smoothed by the oil of African mediation."[9] Freyre describes the influence of the African slaves' eating habits on the Europeans, or of the Black nurses' stories on white children's imaginations, and speaks of Christianity in the masters' houses as influenced by the "superstitions" of the slave hut. Freyre's valorization of the African components of Brazilian culture played a formative role in forging a new national self-conception that recognized African and Indian blood in the veins of every Brazilian, leading to the repeal of discriminatory laws.

Later, Freyre was rightly accused of sugarcoating the colonial violence that shaped relations during slavery. Upon this basis, he euphemistically proclaimed

7 Arthur Ramos, *The Negro in Brazil* [1939], trans. Richard Pattee (Washington, DC: The Associated Publishers, Inc., 1951), 94.

8 Gilberto Freyre, *The Masters and the Slaves: A Study in the Development of Brazilian Civilization*, trans. Samuel Putnam (Berkeley: University of California Press, 1986), 3.

9 Ibid., 78.

10 Lourdes Martínez-Echazábal, "Mestizaje in Latin America," in *The Creolization Reader: Studies in Mixed Identities and Cultures*, eds. Robin Cohen and Paola Toninato (London: Routledge, 2010), 257–65. On a critique of the sexist and anti-Semitic facets of Freyre's writings, cf.: Jeffrey D. Needell, "Identity, Race, Gender and Modernity in the Origins of Gilberto Freyre's Oeuvre," *The American Historical Review* 100, no. 1 (February 1995): 51–77.

an "ethnic democracy" in Brazil, with equal rights for all population groups, which was exposed as a national myth that had served to obscure social inequality for many decades to come.[10] Nonetheless, the positive value Freyre placed on the creativity generated within processes of "miscegenation" (*mestiçagem*) and processes of cultural hybridity gained widespread appeal in the 1930s, for example among US American researchers and Black civil rights activists who faced racial segregation (Jim Crow Laws) within their own social contexts.[11] From today's perspective, perhaps the most remarkable thought in Freyre's interpretation of the conditions under which the Brazilian or "Luso-tropical" society emerged is found in an argument he uses to explain the Portuguese colonizers' adeptness in terms of adaptation and integration. Because the Portuguese were what he terms "bicontinental" even before their American expansion, the category race always carried little significance for Portugal. The geographic and climatic proximity to Africa and the long history of Moorish presence had made the Portuguese into a "people existing indeterminately between Europe and Africa,"[12] which, by integrating Islamic religious elements into its culture, for example, had developed the capacity to merge opposing elements. To whatever extent this may be true or false, it is relevant for the concepts of transculturality that later developed in that it assumes the existence of a culture (and population) that has always been mixed, thereby undermining the ideologies of cultural separation and racial purity that were predominant throughout the first half of the twentieth century. Although Freyre uses this concept to argue that Brazil's colonial practices were markedly different from those of other colonizers, in particularly the British, but also the Spanish, thereby fostering a "Luso-Brazilian" brand of nationalism, his ideas are nonetheless indicative of conceptions of culture and identity that later emerged. For instance, Édouard Glissant distinguishes between the creolization of "composite cultures" of the Americas, particularly in the Caribbean, where the creolization process is more recent, from "atavistic" forms of culture where identity is derived from a singular common root, pointing out that the latter underwent creolization long before.[13]

Between the 1920s and 1940s, the main problem characteristic of the research in this field is the overcoming of race. From today's perspective, it is not easy to comprehend the difficulties that scholars, even those who were politically antiracist, faced in devalorizing the concept of race within social and cultural science. The protagonists discussed here differ from one another, both in terms of their academic biographies and of the extent of progress they made regarding their own perceptions of race. For instance, Freyre and Ortiz both made radical transitions over the course of their careers, from early studies concerned with the "decadence," lack of physical vigor (Freyre), and criminality (Ortiz) of certain groups, to employing social and economic models of explaining modes of behavior and cultural practices. As we have already seen, despite the radical revaluation of processes of mixing and the valorization of culture, Freyre's ideas about the sexual union between members of different ethnic groups still strongly rely on the concept of race. This is reminiscent of Mexican philosopher and politician José Vasconcelos, who, in 1925, announces the end of racial difference through the *mestizaje* and proclaims the emergence of a universal "synthetical" race in his book *La Raza Cosmica*. What had already come to pass in Latin America would later spread throughout the world—the disappearance of all known races through their fusion into a singular "cosmic race" that combines all the better attributes of the former races. A new aesthetic era of humanity would emerge from Latin America, under the sign of love, beauty, and creativity, bringing the era of rationality and racial/cultural purity to an end. "What is going to emerge out there is the definitive race, the synthetical race, the integral race, made up of the genius and the blood of all peoples and, for that reason, more capable of true brotherhood and of a truly universal vision."[14] Regardless of the fact that his project may appear merely utopian and esoteric, or in part rely on former notions of evolutionist race theory, the context in which Vasconcelos formulates his ideas is the Mexican revolution, which the author actively participated in. As a minister between 1921 and 1924, he worked on democratizing the educational system as a component in the process of restructuring Mexican society. One significant difference from Freyre's identity model of *mestiçagem* and hybrid culture in Brazil is that Vasconcelos's approach is explicitly transnational and aimed at a Latin American racial and cultural synthesis. Viewed within the context of the struggle against contemporary forms of US imperialism on the American continent, throughout his entire essay, the leitmotiv of Latin America serves as an antithesis to the Anglo-Saxon concept of segregation and hierarchical racial and cultural orders, examples of which he sees in white supremacy and the US segregation policy.

Cuban concepts of transculturality, of which Fernando Ortiz is the most prominent theorist, were developed within the political and economic context of a postcolonial Cuba facing the threat of neo-colonialism. In 1933, Ortiz himself had been a consultant for the short-lived revolutionary government under Grau San Martín and had written *Contrapunteo Cubano del tabaco y el azúcar (Cuban Counterpoint. Tobacco and Sugar)*, published in 1940, during the Batista dictatorship, which had catered to the economic interests of the United States who in turn gave the regime its support. The fact that Ortiz founded the "Cuban Alliance for a Free World" shortly after his book was published

11 Henry Louis Gates Jr., *Black in Latin America* (New York: New York University Press, 2011), 12–58.
12 Freyre, *The Masters and the Slaves*, 4.
13 Édouard Glissant, *Poetics of Relation*, trans. Betsy Wing (Ann Arbor: University of Michigan Press, 1997).
14 José Vasconcelos, *The Cosmic Race/La raza cósmica* [1925], trans. Didier T. Jaén (Baltimore: Johns Hopkins University Press, 1997), 20.

is a clear indication of the anti-imperialist direction of his analyses of Cuban history, economy, and society in *Cuban Counterpoint* and his other works. In 1906, as a young scholar still largely influenced by biological concepts of race and evolutionary models of history, he published his first book *Hampa afro-cubana: los negros brujos* (*Afro-Cuban Underworld: The Black Sorcerers*), an anthropological study of criminality, a treatise on Afro-Cuban "backwardness" and "deviance." He later takes up a sociological approach that emphasizes the importance of cultural and economic rather than biological factors for progress. In his works to follow, however, he still focuses on the backwardness of Cubans and how to overcome this predicament. Although Ortiz at first utilizes a European-Western notion in regards to the kind of "civilization" Cuba must achieve, he soon develops a deep appreciation for regional popular cultures and begins writing about Cuban folk music and its African influences, among other things.[15]

In *Cuban Counterpoint*, Ortiz writes about the economic, social, and cultural development of Cuba from its colonial beginnings up to the time the book was written. He depicts the history of Cuba as an interplay between tobacco and sugar, which function as actors whose historical contexts constitute counterpoints that have contributed to shaping Cuban society and culture. The sugar economy had been bound up with capitalism from the onset (investments, machines, credits, banks, etc.), unlike tobacco: "the child of the savage Indian and the virgin earth is a free being."[16] The difference between tobacco and sugar is intensive versus extensive cultivation, quality versus quantity, individuality versus uniformity. Sugar requires energy, machines, labor divisions, creates time pressure, since it has to be processed within a short time, as well as intermittent "jobs" for many. Sugar consumes and destroys the land, because more energy (forests) and means of transport (railways) are needed in order to produce a greater volume. Tobacco requires knowledge instead of machines, careful attention and selection of soil, light, and leaves, offers regular jobs for few, and prospers in smaller agricultural units.

Tobacco and sugar also bring different cultures with them. The one is simple, rural, and folkloristic; the other an urban high culture influenced by Europe. Tobacco generated an independent middle-class; sugar brought about the extremes between master and slave, the rich and the working class. "In the history of Cuba sugar represents Spanish absolutism; tobacco the native liberators."[17] Sugar not only brought slavery and is the reason that the slave trade and slavery persisted in Cuba for so long, it also stands for the deprivation of freedom in general, for Cuba's status as a colony, and its economic backwardness even after colonialism—"keeping Cuba in the economic status of a colony."[18] Ortiz's descriptions of the sugar industry are reminiscent of the current economies of transnational corporations. "As though the whole country were one huge mill, and Cuba merely the symbolic name of a great center controlled by a foreign stockholders' corporation."[19] Ortiz refers to the development of class-consciousness among the tobacco workers in the nineteenth century, emphasizing in particular the public readings that took place in the tobacco workrooms. While the noise in the sugar mills made communication impossible, and the old "work songs" of the slaves could no longer be heard, the silence of the tobacco workrooms made them well suited for readings that were also used to promote local political propaganda. "They worked with tobacco leaves and book leaves."[20] Within this branch of industry, the first workers' unions were founded, newspapers printed, and the tobacco workers provided the strongest support for the revolutionary struggle for Cuban independence.

In the section "On the Social Phenomenon of 'Transculturation' and Its Importance in Cuba," Ortiz introduces the term transculturation.[21] He himself deems it a "neologism," and a "substitute for the term *acculturation*, whose use is now spreading."[22]

> *Acculturation* is used to describe the process of transition from one culture to another, and its manifold social repercussions. But *transculturation* is a more fitting term. I have chosen the word *transculturation* to express the highly varied phenomena that have come about in Cuba as a result of the extremely complex transmutations of culture that have taken place here, and without a knowledge of which it is impossible to understand the evolution of the Cuban folk, either in the economic or in the institutional, legal, ethical, religious, artistic, linguistic, psychological, sexual, or other aspects of its life.[23]

The true history of Cuba is the history of its interconnected transculturations. The indigenous, Spanish, African (here, Ortiz mentions many and makes some distinctions based on cultural relativism), European, Jewish, and Asian groups, who settled on the land bit by bit, had been uprooted and had to adapt to a "new syncretism of cultures," "faced with the problem of disadjustment and readjustment, of deculturation and acculturation—in a word, of

15 Fernando Coronil, "Introduction to the Duke University Press Edition: Transculturation and the Politics of Theory: Countering the Center, Cuban Counterpoint," in *Cuban Counterpoint: Tobacco and Sugar* [1947] (Durham, NC: Duke University Press, 1995), ix–lvi, here specifically xviii.

16 Fernando Ortiz, *Cuban Counterpoint: Tobacco and Sugar* [1947] (Durham, NC: Duke University Press, 1995), 56.

17 Ibid., 71.

18 Ibid., 80.

19 Ibid., 64.

20 Ibid., 92.

21 Ortiz traces the transculturation of tobacco (consumption) from a social and ritualistic phenomenon among the indigenous population to its demonization by the colonizers and the first appropriation by the slaves from Africa, to its medical and economical uses in Europe, which were oriented on status, distinction, and profit.

22 Ibid., 97.

23 Ibid.

transculturation."[24] Ortiz writes: "this vast blend of races and cultures overshadows in importance every other historical phenomenon."[25]

> I am of the opinion that the word *transculturation* better expresses the different phases of the process of transition from one culture to another because this does not consist merely in acquiring another culture, which is what the English word *acculturation* really implies, but the process also necessarily involves the loss or uprooting of a previous culture, which could be defined as a deculturation. In addition it carries the idea of the consequent creation of new cultural phenomena, which could be called neoculturation.[26]

Similar to Freyre in Brazil, Ortiz was also later criticized for his *cubanidad* construction of identity, with which all ethnic and cultural differences could be overcome. However, the professed equality through mixing had not eradicated social inequality. Bronisław Malinowski, a leading anthropologist of his time, whose later work focused on the processes of "culture contact," enthusiastically adopts the new term "transculturation" and declares acculturation as "ethnocentric" in his introduction to the Spanish edition from 1940—wherein he seeks to appropriate Ortiz's decidedly historical approach as belonging to the functionalist school of thought he represented. Malinowski recognizes the "moral connotation," which problematically implies that the "primitive" (must) adapt to Western culture, and highlights the heuristic advantages of transculturation, which describes a mutual exchange of cultural traits, a process through which new realities—"original and independent"—emerged.[27]

The fact that acculturation need not always be understood as a one-sided process when applied to cultural transformation in situations of contact is demonstrated in the works of US American anthropologist Melville J. Herskovits, one of the pioneers of African American Studies. In the late 1920s, Herskovits began researching Black cultures in the Americas and their connections to Africa, and was in contact with his senior "colleagues" Freyre, Ramos, and Ortiz in the 1930s and 1940s, adopting certain terms they had developed, including Ramos's syncretism.[28] While Freyre's and Ortiz's studies on cultural contact and mutual transformation are instrumental for the development of post-ethnic concepts of national identity, Herskovits's research is embedded within the context of racial discrimination in the United States. Unlike Freyre's and Ortiz's early works, which still use a biologistical and evolutionist framework, Herskovits, coming from the "anti-racist" school of Franz Boas,[29] detaches culture from the idea of racial determinism from the very beginning. This goes so far that young Herskovits makes even the slightest trace of cultural difference between African Americans and white Americans disappear in his earliest essays. In 1925, he writes about his observations of life in Harlem "of the African culture, not a trace," consciously avoiding anything suggestive of a link between genetics and culture, since this had been the predominant idea behind race theory in the United States.[30] Therefore, when Herskovits holds that African Americans showed "complete acculturation" to (white) US culture, it is indeed to be understood in the sense of assimilation. However, when Herskovits speaks of "acculturation" in his later texts, the term has taken on greater complexity and comprises many of the meanings Ortiz subsumes under the term transculturation. As a member of a committee set up by the Social Science Research Council in 1935 to outline "acculturation studies," Herskovits defines the term in a *Memorandum for the Study of Acculturation* as follows:

"Acculturation comprehends those phenomena which result when groups of individuals having different cultures come into continuous first-hand contact, with subsequent changes in the original cultural patterns of either or both groups."[31] Upon further specification, the difference between the terms is addressed: "under this definition, acculturation is to be distinguished from culture-change, of which it is but one aspect, and assimilation, which is at times a phase of acculturation."[32] In his field studies in Western Africa, Suriname, Brazil, and the Caribbean, Herskovits develops a refined instrument for studying cultural transfer, the adoption and appropriation of cultural elements in situations of contact under conditions of colonial rule and slavery within the African American context. Melville Herskovits's historical significance can be attributed to his book *The Myth of the Negro Past*, published in 1941, which was highly controversial at the time of its publication both within anthropology as well as in a broader discourse on US race relations. Herskovits demonstrates the perpetuation of African elements in the linguistic, religious, social, and cultural practices of Blacks in the Americas. In terms of method, he focuses on ethnohistory and formulates a critique of structural functionalism, which conceives of the present as the only temporal axis.

24 Ibid.
25 Ibid., 99.
26 Ibid., 102–3.
27 Bronisław Malinowski, "Introduction," in *Cuban Counterpoint: Tobacco and Sugar*, ed. Alfred A. Knopf [1947] (Durham, NC: Duke University Press, 1995), lvii–lix.
28 Kevin A. Yelvington, "The Invention of Africa in Latin America and the Caribbean: Political Discourse and Anthropological Praxis, 1920–1940," in *Afro-Atlantic Dialogues: Anthropology in the Diaspora*, ed. Kevin A. Yelvington (Santa Fe: School of American Research Press, 2006), 35–82.
29 In 1910, Boas had already identified the US American "race problem" as mainly being a problem of racial prejudice. Franz Boas, "The Real Race Problem," *The Crisis*, no. 1 (December 1910): 22–25.
30 Melville J. Herskovits, "The Negro's Americanism," in *The New Negro: Voices of the Harlem Renaissance*, ed. Alain Locke (New York: Touchstone, 1997), 359. For a detailed account of Herskovits's intellectual biography, see Jerry Gershenhorn, *Melville J. Herskovits and the Racial Politics of Knowledge* (Lincoln: University of Nebraska Press, 2004).
31 Robert Redfield, Ralph Linton, and Melville J. Herskovits, "A Memorandum for the Study of Acculturation," *Man: A Monthly Record of Anthropological Science*, no. 35 (October 1935): 145–46.
32 Ibid., 146.

His extensive data and examples thus refute the popular myth supported by racist sciences whereby African American population groups had lost their culture through uprooting and enslavement, or willingly given it up in the face of the "superiority" of their masters' white culture. The scientific mainstream around Herskovits interpreted differences in Black lifestyles and forms of expression as mere "degenerations" of white civilization resulting from African Americans' racially-based "inability." On the contrary, one of the central statements in Herskovits's book on the contemporary debate concerning race vs. culture, reads: "Culture is learned, not inborn [...] the factor of race does not enter."[33]

"Retention" and "reinterpretation" present the two processes whose respective relationships to one another allow for a description of the dynamics of transformation in cultural contact, whereby these relationships can take thoroughly different forms: from an insistence on old elements, to "borrowings" from new ones, as well as their reinterpretation in particular aspects (language, belief, art), depending on the conditions under which they occur.[34] Herskovits's empirical studies debunk distorted images presented by the myth of the "Negro past" as arguments for legitimizing racial suppression in the United States. At the close of the first chapter, he defines the political meaning of a scientific examination of the history and presence of African cultural elements in the United States: "To give the Negro an appreciation of his past is to endow him with the confidence in his own position in this country and in the world which he must have, and which he can best attain when he has available a foundation of scientific fact concerning the ancestral cultures of Africa and the survivals of Africanisms in the New World."[35]

African American intellectuals and activists largely welcomed Herskovits's research, as it often provided them with the empirical data for their own interpretation of African American culture. *The Myth of the Negro Past* appeared as part of a study on race relations in the United States, commissioned by the Carnegie Foundation and headed by Swedish economist Gunnar Myrdal, entitled *An American Dilemma*, which dealt with the contradiction between the "American Creed" (freedom and equal opportunity) and the reality of racial discrimination.

If one emphasizes the positive reception of these anthropological studies on the transculturality of African American religions, songs, dances, stories, language use, etc., it is necessary at this point to address a structural problem within the history of research on transculturality, for: similar studies were conducted simultaneously, or perhaps even earlier, by Black researchers, whose work did not receive the same recognition. One of the reasons these researchers have largely remained forgotten can certainly be attributed to the fact that, in comparison to white scholars, they faced more difficult conditions in terms of research and publishing. Manuel Querino (1851–1923), who is considered the first Black historian in Brazil, and who was also active as an artist and politician, had to fight for the abolition of slavery before he (without any connection to the university) could conduct his research on Afro-Brazilian religious and popular cultural practices, including Bahian customs and cookery.[36] Today, when authors establish that several of Freyre's arguments for his model of Brazilian identity were taken from Querino, they also point out that the same Black researcher was also an activist in the autonomous organization of workers and in the Afro-Brazilian struggle for equal rights, thus by no means in a situation where Freyre's *democracia racial* had actually been put into practice.[37] Herskovits's research also benefitted from his collaborations with Alain Locke, Zora Neale Hurston, W.E.B. Du Bois, and the latter's connections to Western Africa as well as his own research on the "American Negro."[38] These are but two examples from the immediate context of the contributions discussed in this article that address the beginnings of the analysis and theory of transculturality within the American context. Each of these contributions has, in its own right and with a more or less lasting effect, played a part in forging a new understanding of culture and in overcoming "race" as a scientific paradigm and category of political order. Though some of the arguments may seem problematic from a historical perspective, the approaches cited here were nonetheless significant contributions to an early transnational discourse on decolonizing the notion of culture.

33 Melville J. Herskovits, *The Myth of the Negro Past* (Boston, MA: Beacon Press, 2005), xxi.
34 Ibid., chap. 4.
35 Ibid., 32.
36 E. Bradford Burns, "Manuel Querino's Interpretation of the African Contribution to Brazil," *The Journal of Negro History* 59, no. 1 (January 1974): 78–86.
37 Gates Jr., *Black in Latin America*, 40–58.
38 Christian Kravagna, "The Trees of Knowledge: Anthropology, Art, and Politics. Melville J. Herskovits and Zora Neale Hurston – Harlem ca. 1930," *Unsettling Knowledges, Transversal*, no. 1 (2012), http://eipcp.net/transversal/0112/kravagna/en.

Literature

Appadurai, Arjun. *Modernity at Large: Cultural Dimensions of Globalization*. Minneapolis: Minnesota University Press, 1996.

Bhabha, Homi K. *The Location of Culture*. London: Routledge, 1994.

Boas, Franz. "The Real Race Problem." *The Crisis*, vol. 1 (December 1910): 22-25.

Burns, E. Bradford. "Manuel Querino's Interpretation of the African Contribution to Brazil." *The Journal of Negro History*, vol. 59, no. 1 (January 1974): 78-86.

Clifford, James. *Routes: Travel and Translation in the Late Twentieth Century*. Cambridge: Harvard University Press, 1997.

Coronil, Fernando. "Introduction to the Duke University Press Edition: Transculturation and the Politics of Theory: Countering the Center, Cuban Counterpoint." In Ortiz, Fernando. *Cuban Counterpoint: Tobacco and Sugar* [1947]. Durham, NC: Duke University Press, 1995.

Freyre, Gilberto. *The Masters and the Slaves: A Study in the Development of Brazilian Civilization*. Translated by Samuel Putnam. Berkeley: University of California Press, 1986.

Gates, Henry Louis, Jr. *Black in Latin America*. New York: New York University Press, 2011.

Gershenhorn, Jerry. *Melville J. Herskovits and the Racial Politics of Knowledge*. Lincoln: University of Nebraska Press, 2004.

Gilroy, Paul. *The Black Atlantic: Modernity and Double Consciousness*. London: Verso, 1993.

Glissant, Édouard. *Poetics of Relation*. Translated by Betsy Wing. Ann Arbor: University of Michigan Press, 1997.

Herskovits, Melville J. "The Negro's Americanism." In *The New Negro: Voices of the Harlem Renaissance*. Edited by Alain Locke, 353-360. New York: Touchstone, 1997.

Herskovits, Melville J. *The Myth of the Negro Past*. Boston, MA: Beacon Press, 2005.

Huntington, Samuel. *The Clash of Civilizations*. New York: Simon & Schuster, 1996.

Kravagna, Christian. "The Trees of Knowledge: Anthropology, Art, and Politics. Melville J. Herskovits and Zora Neale Hurston – Harlem ca. 1930." *Unsettling Knowledges, Transversal*, no. 1 (2012). Published by eipcp – European Institute for Progressive Cultural Policies. Accessed April 1, 2013. http://eipcp.net/transversal/0112/kravagna/en.

Malinowski, Bronisław. Introduction to *Cuban Counterpoint: Tobacco and Sugar* [1947], by Fernando Ortiz, lvii-lix. Durham, NC: Duke University Press, 1995.

Martínez-Echazábal, Lourdes. "*Mestizaje* in Latin America." In *The Creolization Reader: Studies in Mixed Identities and Cultures*. Edited by Robin Cohen and Paola Toninato, 257-265. London: Routledge 2010.

Needell, Jeffrey D. "Identity, Race, Gender, and Modernity in the Origins of Gilberto Freyre's Oeuvre." *The American Historical Review*, vol. 100, no. 1 (February 1995): 51-77.

Ortiz, Fernando. *Cuban Counterpoint: Tobacco and Sugar* [1947]. Durham, NC: Duke University Press, 1995.

Pratt, Mary Louise. *Imperial Eyes: Travel Writing and Transculturation*. London: Routledge, 1992.

Ramos, Arthur. *The Negro in Brazil* [1939]. Translated by Richard Pattee. Washington, D.C.: Associated Publishers, Inc., 1951.

Redfield, Robert, Ralph Linton, and Melville J. Herskovits, "A Memorandum for the Study of Acculturation." *Man: A Monthly Record of Anthropological Science*, vol. 35 (October 1935): 145-48.

Vasconcelos, José. *The Cosmic Race. La Raza Cósmica* [1925]. Translated by Didier T. Jaén. Baltimore: Johns Hopkins University Press, 1997.

Yelvington, Kevin A. "The Invention of Africa in Latin America and the Caribbean: Political Discourse and Anthropological Praxis, 1920–1940." In *Afro-Atlantic Dialogues: Anthropology in the Diaspora*. Edited by Kevin A. Yelvington, 35–82. Santa Fe: School of American Research Press, 2006.

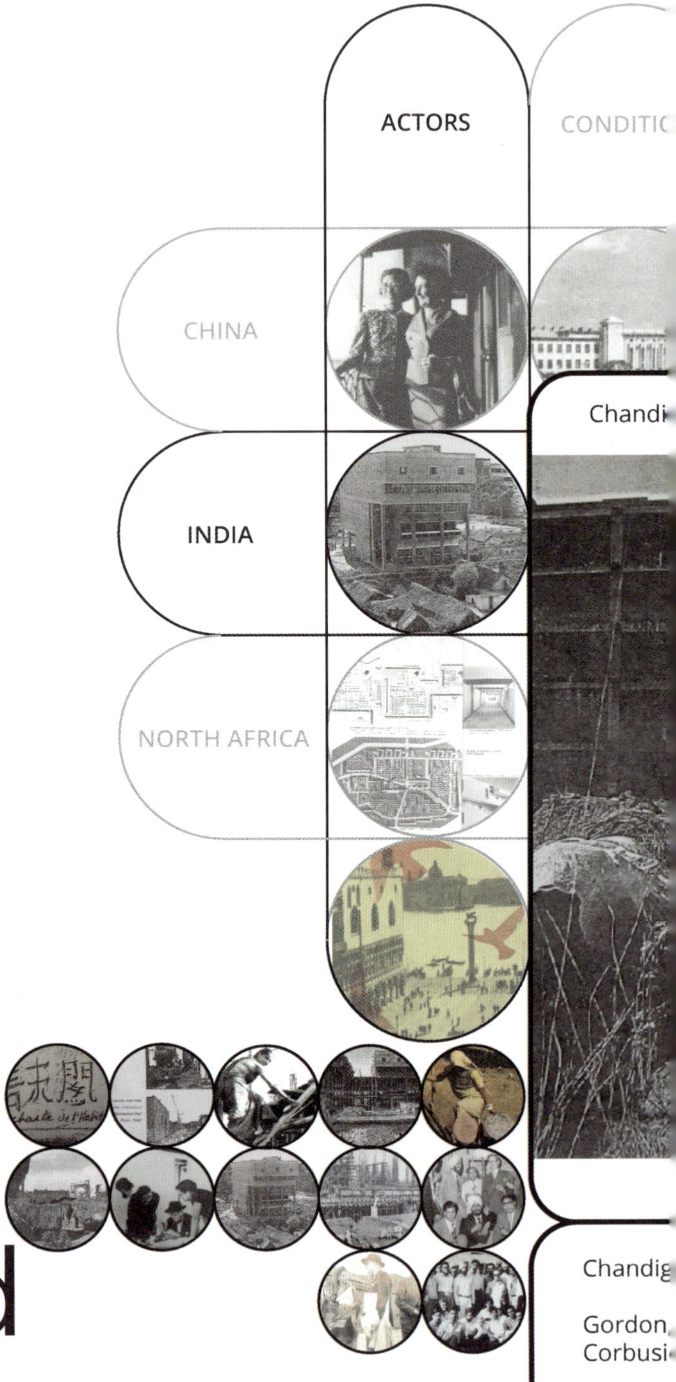

Chandig

Gordon,
Corbusi

© Gord
Le Corb
Issue.

Around Chandigarh

EVENTS | DEBATES & DISCOURSES | CONCEPTS | ART & RESEARCH | THEORIES

ing and Construction Site ×

▼

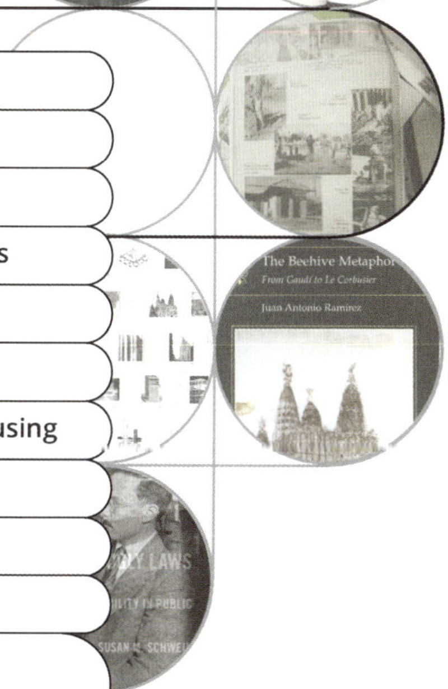

- Access
- Chandigarh
- City Planning
- Disabling Spaces
- India
- Labor
- Low Budget Housing
- Modernization
- Standards
- Village
- Vernacular Modernism

uction Site

Kilian (1990): Chandigarh Forty Years after Le
tura and Natura Quarterly: ANQ, special Issue.

st, Kilian (1990): Chandigarh Forty Years after
tectura and Natura Quarterly: ANQ, special

The Many Names of Chandigarh
An Index for Heritage Planning

Vikramāditya Prakāsh

At a time of unprecedented globalization and urbanization, one cannot *not* heed the clarion call to "save" Chandigarh, to create a manifesto and a legislation to conserve what Chandigarh stands for. But what does it stand for? There is many a great claim that can be made in the name of Chandigarh. Chandigarh was made, after all, as *the* aspirational city of postcolonial India, a modernist utopian "tabula rasa," designed by Le Corbusier, arguably the most prodigious architect of the twentieth century. Yet there are so many other claims addressed by so many other names that can be made in the name of Chandigarh. Such other claims, by the ineluctable logic of "distinerrance," must necessarily remain lost in the fog of history—ever present as potential claimants, and yet inevitably in the shadow, secondary and derivative, of the city's given names, its great claims: India – Tabula Rasa – modernism – Le Corbusier.

India, Tabula Rasa, modernism, Le Corbusier are, of course, in themselves metonyms, shorthand names for larger claims, that are in the end unverifiable. Who really does speak for "India," or "modernism," or even "Le Corbusier"? Metonymy functions by clearing a ground for itself, by keeping other claimants out of the center it claims. It makes other claims, derivative, orbital, peripheral. These derivative peripherals, orbiting around the center, are what in fact make the center, that give it a presence where there isn't any, that make a there for it where there isn't one. An abstraction, *in essence*, is not present as itself. It is made present only by its derivations, its manifestations, its impure multiplicities, at least once removed from itself.

The following praxeological reading is conceived as a listing of the multitude of those other possible name claims for Chandigarh—proxies, as it were—here remembered as a kind of act of historic preservation, restorative in content and restitutional in intent. It is enumerative and performative, and telescopes repeatedly across time, seeking the provenance and posterity of alter-claims and proxies. This essay (*essayer* in French: to try, to try out) of course does not ipso facto transform, or claim to transform, the "ground" realities as it were; i.e., it cannot undo that authoritative grounding, verification of grand abstractions that is the making of Chandigarh. There is, nevertheless, in such an essay, the aspiration of outlining a strategy of historic preservation, a framework for rethinking the past as the reimagining of another possible future, a future that is somewhat more inclusive and perhaps a little less servile to, a little less derivative from, its singular, special past.

Claim I: The Nation

The oft-repeated primary aspiration for Chandigarh was to verify the *naissance* of the new nation, i.e., to literally make in stone (*verificare* in Latin: literally "make into stone") that great claim called "India." Jawaharlal Nehru was the synecdochal client of Chandigarh as the first Prime Minister of the Indian nation recently claimed as an act of independence from colonial rule. He is oft quoted, with no ultimate source to verify its provenance, as having said: "Let this be a new city, unfettered by the past, a symbol of the nation's faith in the future." The city, and in particular its Capitol Complex with its self-conscious modernist staging of the institutions of state—the Assembly, the High Court, and the Secretariat—was created as one of the key identifiers of this Nehruvian vision. Nehru's vision for India was developmentalist, but today, early in the twenty-first century, the Nehruvian state is under siege, routinely vilified in the neo-liberal push to globalize. In the uncertainties of globalization, in the midst of the incessant ins and outs of the flight of capital, is born the call for Chandigarh's preservation, a once futurist, developmentalist vision now to be protected from the vicissitudes of capital (masquerading as the effect-of-time) through embalming. But even this restricted frame of preservation as protection must also stage the question of the Nehruvian legacy with all its attendant derivatives. Such as:

1. Although framed by the staging of the nation-state, Chandigarh in fact was a consequence of quid pro quo logics of the colonial partitioning of British India along religious lines. Ostensibly meant to protect the Muslim minority (about thirty percent at the time), the colonial authority's acceptance of the demand for a separate Muslim state was a derivative of the colonial project that was justified as the waiting room of history, i.e., the "white man's burden" of preparing a primitive people for enlightenment and self-governance, until they were ready for it.[1] By this logic, the making of Pakistan, specifically as a Muslim state, was an act of premature birthing, a guarantee that had to be instated to safeguard a "not-yet-ready" people. Only the two Muslim dominant states that were directly under British rule—Punjab and Bengal—were partitioned. And since Calcutta (now Kolkata), the colonial capital of Bengal, was included in the new India, Lahore, the old Mughal capital of Punjab was "given" to Pakistan by the colonialist logics of identitarian belonging (Mughal = Muslim = Pakistan). Chandigarh thus was made as India's "New Lahore."

2. But as India's New Lahore, Chandigarh was conceived in a rigorously secularist mold, i.e., as "Not Lahore," to negate the colonial-religious identitarian logics of the Partition. Modern architecture thus functioned as a proxy for decolonization as secularism in Chandigarh. Reciprocally, Pakistan in the early 1960s also began the construction of its own modernist capital, Islamabad, whose master plan was designed by Doxiadis, and a state assembly in Dhaka, designed by Louis Kahn—both of which can be construed as acts of defiance against their "not-yet-ready" mandate—in this case modern architecture functioning as a proxy for decolonization, as Westernization. By the early 1970s, however, India had successfully supported the

repartitioning of Pakistan with the creation of Bangladesh. And by the 1980s, both Pakistan and Punjab were reeling under religious violence, with the Taliban gaining ground in Pakistan and a Sikh demand in Punjab for an autonomous religious state resorting to terrorist tactics, learned from the Reagan-trained *mujahedin* in Afghanistan.

3. Although birthed by the Partition, there is no memorial or public account of the Partition in Chandigarh—or Punjab, or Pakistan, or Bangladesh for that matter. There is a "Martyrs' Memorial" on the Capitol Plaza in Chandigarh that is still incomplete and whose provenance and symbolic purpose remains un-established.[2] The larger consequences of the Partition are also still unresolved in postcolonial India and in South Asia in general.[3]

4. A limited number of Sikh and other refugees from Pakistan were given preferential homes in Chandigarh (at market prices with generous loan terms), but as a named city Chandigarh was rigorously denied any identity as a refugee-resettlement city.[4] The refugees were either allotted vacated Muslim homes (erasure by substitution) or resettled in new colonies, developed in particular in and around Delhi.[5] These new colonies stood in for and did the actual work of resettlement that should have been a part of Chandigarh's core brief. As proxy Chandigarhs, these colonies were called:
   a. Lajpat Nagar
   b. Rajinder Nagar
   c. Nizamuddin East
   d. Punjabi Bagh
   e. Rehgarpura
   f. Jungpura
   g. Kingsway Camp (later Guru Teg Bahadur or GTB Nagar)

5. The decision to make a new city rather than selecting an existing city as a capital was designed to force continuity, an elision, between the "birth" of a new nation and the "birth" of a new city. Some of the other cities that were considered and rejected to enable the Chandigarh elision were:
   a. Ludhiana
   b. Amritsar

1 Dipesh Chakrabarty's phrase in his book *Provincializing Europe: Postcolonial Thought and Historical Difference* (Princeton: Princeton University Press, 2000). See Introduction for the "waiting room of history" argument.

2 Most of the "program" for Chandigarh was based on what was "lost" with Lahore. But there was no Martyrs' Memorial in Lahore, so that suggests that with this one the Capitol may in fact have been intended to mark the martyrs of the Partition.

3 This is, of course, an infinite topic ranging from Kashmir to Abbottabad, for which I don't have room in this essay.

4 From the "Randhawa Papers," Chandigarh Archives.

5 Ibid.

c. Ambala
d. Patiala
e. Shimla

6. Although framed as the aspiration of the new nation, Chandigarh was in fact required only as the administrative capital of the State of Punjab. The State of Punjab, an abstraction in its own right, was made to align faithfully with the staging of the nation-state. This "made-to-align"-ment quickly proved to be fissiparous and unstable. Misalignments, there before the Partition, quickly asserted themselves, in particular the demand for an autonomous Punjabi Suba. By stressing linguistic identity as the basis of state formation, the Punjabi Suba movement had in fact challenged the colonialist religion-based partitioning of Punjab. The Nehruvian vision struggled between linguistic-based regional formations and a centralized, abstract identity based on the nation.[6] By 1965, following the assassination of Punjab's pro-Nehru Chief Minister, this alignment came undone. To maintain peace, the State of Punjab was divided into Punjab and Haryana; and Chandigarh, now a contested capital, was sublated into a Union Territory administered directly by New Delhi that simultaneously also hosted two state administrations. The Secretariat, the Assembly, and the High Court were divided in the ratio of 60:40 between Punjab and Haryana respectively. Chandigarh's urban area today is sometimes referred to as the "Tri-State Region."

Claim II: Tabula Rasa

Like the "nation," nature as "tabula rasa" is an impossible abstraction, verified by the discourse of physical geography. The site for Chandigarh was selected purposefully by aerial reconnaissance by P. L. Verma and P. N. Thapar, the Chief Engineer and Chief Administrator respectively encharged with building Chandigarh. From 15,000 feet only the geographical/ecological advantages of the site were highlighted—a gently sloping plain at the Shivalik foothills irrigated by intermittent rivers. This rigorously geographical reading of site, the site abstracted as nature, provided the alibi that verified it (*verificare*) as a "tabula rasa." Tabula rasa as raw nature requires the erasure of the historic specifics of the pre-existing inhabitants of the land. It points to the inherent epistemic violence resident in what we might retrospectively recount as a strictly ecological reading of site. Ecology without the sociality erroneously imagines deruralization as the responsibility only of restoring the rural to nature. The nation in fact occupies nature through such an abstraction. The land was acquired by the Nehruvian state using eminent domain.

In the United States, where I teach, as in most parts of the Western world where the rural is erased and fully converted to the urban, deruralization can possibly be theorized as the responsibility to restore nature. In India, and in most of the developing world, deruralization is the process of the incomplete displacement of an agro-rural sociality that remains inadequately converted into or accounted for in the new urban. Urbanization in this sense is more accurately and more ethically named "deruralization." More than urbanization, deruralization requires a better accounting to its rural not-tabula rasa:

1. Extensive pottery and other artifacts dating back to the second and third millennium BCE were found during construction excavations on site, suggesting the possibility of a significant unexcavated city or town beneath the Chandigarh site.[7] The Associate Director of the local Government Museum insists that the planning of Chandigarh directly derives from that of Indus Cities such as Mohenjo-Daro. The original names of Indus cities are unknown, because their script remains inconclusively deciphered. The civilization is named after the present name of the river system that formed its backbone: the Indus. Recent remote sensing archaeology also suggests that another river, the Ghaggar, was central to this civilization. The Ghaggar's running dry in the middle of the second millennium BCE was most likely the central cause that led to that civilization's abandonment. Chandigarh is located at the very "neck" of the Ghaggar, the point where it emerges from the Himalayas to begin its doomed journey across the plains. Given the contemporary Indian penchant for renaming cities based on their "origins," Chandigarh perhaps, one day may conceivably be renamed the "Ghaggar city."

2. Chandigarh was so named purportedly because of a village that existed on site with a temple dedicated to the goddess Chandi. The location and history of this village is both disputed and the subject of mythology.

3. By modern Hindu mythology, Chandi is one of the many names of *THE* goddess, or Devi, or the Female Principle. Unlike the male gods of the Hindu pantheon, who are many, with many an *avatar* or manifestation, Devi is the only female god whose many forms and corresponding names are a property of the varied characters known by different names that she assumes as the equivalent feminine counterparts to the various male gods. In all her forms, Devi is always just herself, different only *in names*. Some of Devi's other names, by the substitutional logics of Devi's names, also therefore substitutable prefixes for Chandigarh, are:
   a. Durga
   b. Parvati

6 The Indian Constitution, like that of the United States and other modern nations, struggles to balance the powers and identity of the Center and the States. The history of postcolonial India can be read as the indexing of this struggle.

7 A major Indus city lies beneath a mammoth mound in Ropar, a mere thirty kilometers from Chandigarh.

   c. Uma
   d. Gauri
   e. Himvati
   f. Jagatmata
   g. Bhavani
   h. Kali
   i. Shakti

4. "Garh," the suffix, can mean simply "place," but it usually, particularly in the local language Panjabi, denotes a "fort," a securitized territory, usually atop a hill. Fatehgarh, Hoalgarh, Lohgarh, Keshgarh, and Anandgarh are examples of local Punjabi towns that were formerly forts.

5. As per the original master plan of Chandigarh, the city was to be "protected" by the controlled periphery six kilometers wide on average. This protection was enshrined in the Chandigarh Periphery Control Act of 1952. The periphery, however, was breached when Punjab was subdivided in 1965. The periphery, like land created by erased fort falls, then became the site for new cities peripheral to the "old" city, like Panchkula and Mohali. Together, Panchkula, Chandigarh, and Mohali constitute the "Tri-City Region."

6. Chandigarh is a mere 100 kilometers from Kurukshetra, the haloed mythical battlefield of the Mahabharata, where the Gita is said to have been revealed in dialogue between Lord Krishna and Arjuna. Savitri Prakash, my mother and a self-studied authority on the Gita, has suggested that Chandigarh may have been the city, Virata, where the Pandavas spent the thirteenth year of the fourteen-year exile, when they were required to live anonymously.

7. The archival record shows that there were at least sixteen villages—none called Chandigarh—existing on the site where Chandigarh was laid out.[8] And so by the official logic of naming, the names of any one of these other villages could also have been the name of Chandigarh. Chandigarh's sixteen other possible names were:
   a. Mehla Majra
   b. Ram Nagar
   c. Sehzadpur
   d. Kalibar
   e. Hamirgarh
   f. Nagla
   g. Kanji Mijra
   h. Dalher Jattan
   i. Gurdaspur
   j. Kailar

k. Saini Majra
l. Rurki Parao
m. Kheri
n. Bajwara
o. Shahpur
p. Fatehgarh Kanthala

8. Every one of these sixteen villages was bulldozed and their land seamlessly integrated into the secular grid delineating the sectors of the city. They are not visible in the urban fabric anymore; they have been erased, the site rigorously deruralized.

9. If one had wanted to, one could have preserved the names of the erased villages by making them the names of the following sectors based on the sites of their erasure:
a. Sector 3 - Mehla Majra
b. Sector 6 - Ram Nagar
c. Sector 8 - Kalibar
d. Sector 12 - Sehzadpur
e. Sector 14 - Kanji Mijra
f. Sector 19 - Nagla
g. Sector 20 - Kheri
h. Sector 22 - Rurki Parao
i. Sector 23 - Bajwara
j. Sector 24 - Kailar
k. Sector 25 - Saini Majra
l. Sector 26 - Hamirgarh
m. Sector 28 - Dalheri Jattan or Gurdaspur
n. Sector 31 - Kanthala
o. Sector 34 - Fatehgarh
p. Sector 38 - Shahpur

10. When the villages were bulldozed, the only structures that were left standing were the religious structures, the Hindu temples and the Sikh Gurdwaras.[9]

8 The number of villages on site, of course, depends on how you count. Gopal Krishan's superb documentation *Inner Space – Outer Space of a Planned City: A Thematic Atlas of Chandigarh*, Chandigarh Perspectives, 1999, Map-2, suggests that the number of villages could be counted as being twenty-four or even fifty-four, depending on the area you count as Chandigarh. I am taking sixteen as the villages that were erased when Phase I of Chandigarh was established by the Capital Project Team, 1949–65.

9 The Indian definition of secularism involves equality of all religions and is not anti-religion like say, the French definition, which requires radical separation of church and state.

These were seamlessly incorporated into the gridded fabric of the new city without any kind of visual priority, a part of the secularist framing of the city. In Sector 8, a Hindu Mandir and a Sikh Gurdwara share adjacent plots, in line with a row of private homes. Over time, however, both the Mandir and Gurdwara have grown exponentially, asserting their presence on the street and skyline, insisting on special zoning exceptions for themselves.

11. Oral history suggests that all the Muslims who lived in the villages where Chandigarh was made were massacred during the Partition by their neighbors. The villagers who were displaced by the making of Chandigarh were given new homes in the houses that were "vacated" by the Muslims. The Muslim mosques, however, it seems were not retained.

12. Oral history also suggests that the village of Burail has the reputation that its "Rajput" residents were the only ones from the area who went to the camp where the Muslims of its village were sheltered in 1947 and invited them to come back, assuring their safety. Since then, Burail has had a solid reputation as a haven for displaced Muslims. After 2002, after the Godhra massacres of Muslims in Gujarat, the Muslim migrant populations of Burail swelled significantly.[10] New Chandigarh has many new mosques.

13. When Chandigarh's Second Phase was built in the 1970s, three additional villages were slated to be deruralized. Through political negotiations these villages had to give up their agricultural land but were able to retain their village land and housing with the promise that they would be incorporated into the city. These were:
    a. Burail
    b. Attawa
    c. Khajeri

14. These three villages were incorporated into the fabric of Chandigarh with a *lal dora* (red thread) arrangement; i.e., the laws governing Chandigarh did not apply within the red lines delineating their boundaries. Burail, Attawa, and Khejeri's *lal doras* delineated a rectilinear boundary around the village, oriented to the cardinal directions, so that these villages stand out distinctly because of their orientation and because of the dense, "organic" massing of their urbanism, like a counterproposition to the unfolding order of the modernist, secularist sectors.[11]

15. The residents of these incorporated so-called "urban villages," however, complain that they were a part of Chandigarh "in name only," precisely because none of the laws of Chandigarh applied to them, so none of the services standard to Chandigarh were extended to them. Today the senior landowners of these villages are agitating for more formal building bylaws

and services, and they want to be a part of Chandigarh in name and in deed. Freed from any zoning regulations, these incorporated villages have today become super-dense agglomerations catering to the vital informal economy of Chandigarh.

16. Relatively speaking, these "urban villages" are at the high-end of the low-end real estate values, catering to the infinite cheap rental economy required by migrant workers and the new rural for urban migrants. These "urban villages" have been the staging grounds of the inflow of migrants into Chandigarh, accommodated by the informality of their regulations that allows unregulated dense growth.

17. Because of their density, these "urban villages" of Chandigarh, along with some of the "slums" in the periphery, also constitute the largest voting blocks of the city and dominate municipal elections. The village, or rural population of Chandigarh is, like in most Indian cites, the majority of the urban population. The urban modern self-image of the city, like most Indian cities, suffers as a consequence of this fact. The majority of Indian cities are rural.

The elected Chandigarh Municipal Corporation, however, does not enjoy its full constitutionally mandated power because the city, with its status as a "Union Territory," is primarily governed by an administration consisting almost entirely of civil servants appointed by New Delhi.

Claim III: Modernism

As the aspiration to establish an objective, universal language, born of the Enlightenment, modern architecture was the ideal claim to manifest the nation. Modernism was part of the technology without identity that was imported by the Nehruvian state as part of its secular framing: "the temples of modern India." In this sense, architectural modernism was part of the nation's project, along with the massive hydroelectric dams such as Bhakra Nangal, to occupy nature.

However, the time on task to convert the project into a city was the responsibility in the first instance of the officers of the Indian Administrative Services, of Punjab cadre, or in Punjab Administration by so-called "special appointment."

10 Oral history from site visit by author in March 2012.

11 The grid of Chandigarh is oriented North-East South-West to be better oriented to the mountains and to take advantage of the direction of the prevailing winds. All the villages, however, in time-honored tradition were oriented to the cardinal directions.

1. The oldest files in the archives refer to the anticipated city as simply the "Capital Project."[12] The brief to make Chandigarh in the mold of a Garden City was prepared by A. L. Fletcher, a Kerala cadre officer of the Indian (erstwhile Imperial) Civil Service, who was the first administrative officer in charge of the Capitol Project. Together with Verma and Thapar, Fletcher prepared a detailed "brief" of the Capital Project down to the relative densities, the types of houses, and their relative square feet. His conception of a modern city was based in part on his experience as an administrator in the modernizing of colonial Lahore early in the twentieth century and was, therefore, colonial in origin.[13]

2. Albert Mayer and Matthew Nowicki, the first Americans who prepared the core conceptual design for Chandigarh, worked from Shimla. Mayer was picked for the project by Nehru because he was already in India, in Uttar Pradesh implementing a "model village" scheme, inspired by Mahatma Gandhi. Mayer, a planner, brought in Nowicki as the architect on the project. Nowicki's death in 1949 precipitated the creation of a new team. By the time Le Corbusier and the rest of his European team were hired, the Capital Project had begun its implementation stage, and so a project site was needed as a staging platform for the project. The site maps show that "Chandigarh" was the name of a railway station that was chosen as the project site.

3. The Chandigarh Railway Station was conveniently located on the route from New Delhi to Shimla. New Delhi, the old colonial capital, was adopted as the seat of the postcolonial Indian national government. Shimla was the erstwhile "summer capital" of colonial India and was where the state government of partitioned Punjab was temporarily located after 1947 until the new capital city was built.

4. In their persistent search to escape the heat and dust of India, the British "Raj" had laboriously built a railway line that connected New Delhi all the way up to Shimla (elevation 7,100 feet). To reach that elevation they had to build a train for the narrow gauge—two feet six inches, rather than the "standard" four feet eight and a half inches gauge used in the plains. At Kalka, twenty-seven kilometers from the Capital Project Site, from the point where the Himalayas rise rapidly, the track shifts from the standard to the narrow gauge. Ten kilometers from Kalka, along the railway track, there was a railway rest house, one of the innumerable built by the colonial administration to service the needs of their officers traveling on their extensive rail network. This rest house was located next to a small temple dedicated to Chandi, and so the railway station giving access to the rest house was called, on maps, Chandigarh.

5. From the Chandigarh Railway's rest house (a standard British Public Works Department structure with high ceilings, banked rooms, and a shaded verandah) was the most convenient state guesthouse from where the officers and architects could visit the site with ease by jeep. This is where Le Corbusier made his first stage "modifications" to the Mayer plan. M. N. Sharma, the first of the Indian architects to join the "Capital Project," first met Le Corbusier and the rest of his team here.

6. The Kalka express, the only train that serviced this station in the 1950s, arrived a little after midnight. My father, Aditya Prakash, the last of the Indian architects to join the project, was received at this station in 1952, two years after construction of the city had begun, by Maxwell Fry even at this late hour. He recalled having to drive a considerable distance in a jeep over *kucha* dusty roads to reach the site. Later the Chandigarh railway station was shifted to its current location by building a special loop. The broad gauge terminus, however, has remained in Kalka.

Claim IV: Le Corbusier

As the largest built work of the most influential architect of the twentieth century, Chandigarh can be considered the epicenter of modern architecture.

1. Mulk Raj Anand, editor of *Marg*, an avid Nehruvian modernist, in the preface to Aditya Prakash's retrospective manifesto *Chandigarh: A Presentation in Free Verse*, recalled the atmosphere in the Chandigarh guesthouse:

   > In the little clearing in the jungle, by the barn-like refugee style hut, where Le Corbusier and his associate architects worked, the heavy perfume of the vegetation came into our nostrils. The mosquitoes buzzed in a conference as though to pass a resolution against the building of Chandigarh, as a few of us crowded around the pale sage with the big, black-framed glasses on his furtive eyes.[14]

12 These are the archives known as the "Randhawa Papers" held in the City Museum, Sector 10, Chandigarh.

13 William J. Glover, *Making Lahore Modern: Constructing and Imagining a Colonial City* (Minneapolis: University of Minnesota Press, 2007).

14 Mulk Raj Anand, "Conversation with Le Corbusier," in *Chandigarh: A Presentation in Free Verse*, published by Aditya Prakash, Chandigarh Administration, Chandigarh, date unknown: 6. Written on the twenty-fifth anniversary of Chandigarh's founding, this booklet was written by Aditya Prakash from his desk as the Principal of Chandigarh College of Architecture around 1974. It was illustrated with the famous gestural sketches of Sunirmal Chatterjee, professor of Drawing at the Chandigarh College of Architecture. Mulk Raj Anand, novelist, essayist, and founding editor of the journal *Marg*, traversed the Chandigarh site from its earliest days becoming close friends with all the architects, particularly Aditya Prakash.

2. An avid Nehruvian modernist, Mulk Raj Anand christened Chandigarh "the finest city of humanism," speaking in Le Corbusier's voice. For Anand, Chandigarh's new gods of modern India were the sun and air.

3. At the same time, Chandigarh, according to Mulk Raj Anand, could be understood as a modern village relearned from the villages on-site:

   > I asked 'Corb' whether he had been to see the villages nearby. Always reluctant to speak at length in English, he said: "Oui! – See this model I have made of the symbol on the walls of the villages. [...] You look—my sketch book." We all eagerly scanned as he turned the pages: Open Hand, camels, donkeys, village belles, turbaned peasants, snakes, doorways, corners, verandahs, trees, pipal leaves, all drawn with the free hand, in great profusion "I will make a plan which is simple," said Le Corbusier. "A big village. In burnt brick. I will bring in air. Keep Sun God in control. Garden in every house. Not Paris, London, New York—Chandigarh, new city."

4. Not Paris, not London, not New York, these other not-names of Chandigarh were documented by Le Corbusier, in which he overlaid the profile of the Chandigarh Plan on top of that of Paris. In another drawing, he contrasted New Delhi and Chandigarh.

5. Le Corbusier indexed Chandigarh-as-a-village in carefully calibrated design gestures at the Capitol, incorporating the bucolic landscape of the agricultural zone around Chandigarh into the symbolic map of the Capitol Complex as a privileged point of reference. The Capitol Complex was built on land that originally belonged to the village Kansal (the actual village was preserved and still thrives today.) At one point he also worked on a "village" to be attached to the governor's palace, his reading of the minimal dwelling, but this "village" in fact was intended to house servants and staff of the governor.

6. In Mulk Raj Anand's narrative, Pierre Jeanneret played the role of translator to Le Corbusier, a role that seemed to have been natural to him at the time:

   > Pierre Jeannert [sic] commented in French what I understood him to mean: 'Corb' believes in precise drawing for his pupils. Himself, he is for something more than drawing. He did not go to ecole or college. He has mastered his craft. So that he can forget it. He is a creative artist.

7. Jeanneret, Chief Architect of the Capital Project Office, faithfully followed the modernist creed in his own designs for the minimal dwelling with a clerestory ventilating a simple split plan with a small front and large back yard. For the most part, Jeanneret labored to fulfill the Le Corbusian vision, in particular by being the architect on site who painstakingly translated Le Corbusier's free-form designs sent from Paris into manageable construction

documents that could be executed on site with hand poured concrete. But in his own designs—the housing, the schools, the university—Jeanneret stepped out to explore the possibilities of an Indian modernism, informed by ways of building with local materials—exposed brick, with the occasional concrete and river rock—to suit the local climate. His best buildings work quietly and in place, austere yet subtle essays in the art of functionalism. His biggest errors—like Gandhi Bhawan—attempt to be heroic.

8. Jeanneret's best work, in this sense, was the furniture that he designed and that he set up the atelier to design to furnish the innumerable government buildings that were created by the Capital Project Office. Fifty years anon, this furniture is old and broken and sits in many a rubbish heap that the government of India perforce maintains as a record of its innumerable possessions. Stolen from such rubbish heaps, this furniture is being purchased for fabulous prices for collections all over North America and Europe as "original" pieces of modernist art.

9. In its own time, however, this so-called Jeanneret furniture was built to be used. It was designed so that it could be built cheaper than mass-produced furniture—industrial mass production being the coveted, but rarely achieved, fantasy of modernist furniture—by hand, by local craftsmen, using local materials. Jeanneret, in other words, was using his learning of how to build in India to design this furniture, which was mass-produced by hand.

10. Towards the end of his life, Jeanneret had moved to making furniture with local cotton and leather, suspended from chains, a whimsical summary of designs that were now quotations from the makeshift furniture of the informal sector. Jeanneret never married and rarely ventured far from Chandigarh. His occasional parties were attended mostly by fellow architects. His closest friend, however, was his driver Bansi, who not only drove him wherever he needed, but also, according to oral sources, took care of all his material and spiritual needs. Little is known of Bansi, as yet. Domestic help in India migrates from rural regions, often at great distance, and is subsequently forgotten by the archives.

11. When Jeanneret left Chandigarh, sick and soon to die, he packed everything he could, "official" drawings and all, and took them back with him to Switzerland. Today these effects constitute the invaluable Jeanneret Archives, held at the Canadian Centre for Architecture in Montreal.

12. Yet a significant portion of the signature Chandigarh modernism was designed by Maxwell Fry and Jane Drew alongside Pierre Jeanneret. For Fry and Drew, their work in Chandigarh was part of the general staging of environmentally and socially responsible architecture. Fry and Drew, however, left Chandigarh

after only three years. They published their work done in Chandigarh later as part of their book *Tropical Architecture in the Dry and Humid Zones* (1956), which made no special mention of the staging of Chandigarh as a postcolonial project. For them, modernism was simply a geophysical project.

13. There is a great photograph in the Chandigarh Architecture Museum that shows the Capitol Project Team. Set up in the manner in which colonial administrations were set up, in long rows organized very strictly according to hierarchy, the Capital Project team in fact consists of seventy-eight people:
    a. twelve men, sitting on the ground;
    b. eighteen men, one woman, sitting in the second row;
    c. twenty-five men, standing in the third row;
    d. twenty-three men, standing on a bench in the back row.

14. Jane Drew is the only woman present in the picture. U. E. Chowdhry was the only Indian woman architect working on the project. Chowdhry, however, was absent the day this historic photograph was taken. There were, of course, thousands of women, part of the migrant labor force, who worked on the construction sites.

15. Other than the four white Europeans, the names of the remaining seventy-five members of the Capitol Project Team have yet to be fully recovered from the archives. This does not include the administration, the contractors, and the workers who built the buildings.

Chandigarh today is a well-established brand name. Legal battles are fought for the right to use the Chandigarh name. There is a Chandigarh University, located in Mohali, and Mullanpur has recently won the right to be renamed "New Chandigarh." Bollywood films and local pop-songs claim to describe a distinct Chandigarh-type youth—both male and female—too sophisticated for the village and small town folks of Punjab, but not urbane enough like those in Bangalore and Mumbai. Numerous new townships are on the boards in the former peripheral lands of Chandigarh. Greater Chandigarh, as it is now called, includes Mullanpur (also known as New Chandigarh), Kharar, Banur, Zirakpur, and Derabassi. All these areas have master plans, prepared by Jurong Consultants of Singapore, developed in the last five years.

Chandigarh administration has twice prepared, and withdrawn, its dossier nominating Chandigarh for "World Heritage" status, worried about the ability of the city to grow in the fossilization criteria of World Heritage. Brasilia's World Heritage status in this case is precisely the model of what not to do for Chandigarh.

What then is "living heritage"? Heritage planning can be described as the process of "managing change with a conscionable view to past." The management of change prepares for a future that must remain, at least partly, by definition unknown. In helping prepare for a future that is uncertain and partly, by definition, unknown, the ethical responsibility of the historian, I would argue, is not to fictionalize a singular past as authoritative metonymy, but to aspire to the ethical indexing of the past in a defined set of registers. In the present case, I have begun the process of laying out the "living field" that I believe should define the architectural heritage of this important city.

Literature

Chakrabarty, Dipesh. *Provincializing Europe: Postcolonial Thought and Historical Difference*. Princeton: Princeton University Press, 2000.

Glover, William J. *Making Lahore Modern: Constructing and Imagining a Colonial City*. Minneapolis: University of Minnesota Press, 2008.

Gopal, Krishan. *Inner Spaces, Outer Spaces of a Planned City: A Thematic Atlas of Chandigarh*. Chandigarh: Chandigarh Perspectives, 1999.

Prakash, Aditya. *Chandigarh: A Presentation in Free Verse*. Chandigarh: Marg Publications, 1980.

From Around a Modern House

Moira Hille

In this article, the term "transculturation" functions as a theoretical and practical tool which, according to Fernando Ortiz, with an awareness for the hierarchical and unequal power relations present therein, enables transcultural encounters to be conceived as a process of mutual interactions.[1] The term "transculturation" "refers to a multidirectional and endless interactive process between various cultural systems that is in opposition to unidirectional and hierarchical structures determined by the principle of origin that is always associated with claims for cultural authority."[2] The analysis here focuses on two modernist projects that were planned, but never realized. Both will be discussed in relation to transculturation and analyzed as actors within the modernist architecture discourse of the 1950s, with particular attention to transfers, interconnections, appropriation, and resistance.

The starting points are Le Corbusier's plan of the Museum of Knowledge in Chandigarh and architect Minnette De Silva's concept for a film about a dancer, also from the 1950s. What these two projects have in common is that, while a rough draft exists for each, neither was ever fully formulated.

Both of the architectures—here, architecture refers not only to buildings, but to constructions at large, thereby encompassing both the museum and the film—allow for a debate on knowledge production with a focus on depicting underrepresented actors, relations and references, conflicts and forms of knowledge within modernist architecture projects of the 1950s. This framework allows us to examine and critically assess each project's perspective and possibilities in regards to critical knowledge production. The architectures will also be analyzed as "built" displays that cast images of manifold influences, enabling us to study the actual sites where knowledge has been gathered and catalogued.

From this perspective, architectures are not simply built or inhabited; rather, they are founded upon political, social, technological, and economic conditions, powers, and struggles. This implies viewing the project of modernity through the lens of its manifold influences and deconstructing the concept of universalism by grasping it as a network of references and relations. In the *Model House* project, we respond to this network of connections and transcultural influences by mapping out structures, thereby rendering the "dialogical relations between specific places and times" visible "and thus creat[ing] chronotopical forms of narration in the sense of Bakhtin."[3] This not only enables a dialogue between seemingly unrelated concepts and considerations, but also

1 For more on the term transculturation and Fernando Ortiz, see Christian Kravagna, *Transculturation*, 2012, http://www.transculturalmodernism.org. See also Kravagna's contribution to this book.

2 Felipe Hernández, Mark Millington, and Iain Borden, eds., *Transculturation: Cities, Spaces and Architecture in Latin America* (Amsterdam: Rodopi, 1998), xi.

3 Fahim Amir, Eva Egermann, Moira Hille, Johannes Köck, Jakob Krameritsch, Christian Kravagna, Christina Linortner, Marion von Osten, and Peter Spillmann, "Model House–Mapping Transcultural Modernisms," *Texte zur Kunst*, no. 82 (June 2011): 147.

a focus on practices rather than on representation. Montage, a figure employed in modern cinema as well as in archives and museums, can be used to perform a textual analysis "around Chandigarh." Using both these projects and artistic research as a basis,[4] I will discuss four images related to the projects, in order to open up a conflict, both between the Museum of Knowledge and the film, and also between the photographs and their captions.[5] After all, it is only "when we take not just the 'flipside' of images into account, along with their comments, stamps, and cryptic abbreviations, but rather the entire context of their production and circulation, will their promise to represent reality be saved."[6]

De Silva's and Le Corbusier's practices both connect cinematic and visual production and architectural practices, not only in their architectural conception, but also in the filmmaking and photographic practices and in the visual material accompanying the built works. While Le Corbusier visually stages his architectures, the material depicting De Silva's houses is largely documentary. Here, the focus is often placed on the workers constructing and the people living in De Silva's houses—similar to her film project about a dancer in a village. In contrast, the visual representations of Le Corbusier's works, which he helped create, focus on presentations or demonstrations of the architecture's functionality.

The following is an encounter of the two. – **CUT** –

There is an image in *The CIAM Discourse on Urbanism 1928-1960* of a group of people sitting in rows.[7] The caption tells us that the image is from the CIAM congress 1946 in Bridgwater, England. The image is very small and the people depicted can only be identified with the help of a legend. The same image appears in another publication—in the biography of De Silva.[8] The image is about ten times as large as in the previous publication. Names are listed under the photograph, partly handwritten, since they had become more and more illegible from repeated reprinting. The size of an image does not necessarily correspond to a thematic focus, but has to do with agreements between the author and the publisher, financial matters concerning printing, etc. The viewer glances over the image. There are seventy-six people sitting in four rows in front of a bright brick wall. Thirteen women are present. Most of them are there with their husbands, some have architecture firms with their partners. Two of the women have their own architecture firms; one of them is Minnette De Silva. She represents India/Ceylon at the congress and is sitting in the first row, like all the other women, with the exception of Mrs. Wiener and Mrs. Stam-Beese, who are standing in the back rows. Minnette De Silva is wearing a sari, her hands are resting on her legs, which are crossed. She is sitting between Walter Gropius and Cornelis van Eesteren and, like most everyone, is looking into the camera. On her far right, at the end of the row is Le Corbusier. Jane Drew is sitting next to Gropius, and behind her Maxwell Fry; both were involved in planning Chandigarh. Jane Drew and Sigfried Giedion make up the middle of the first row. Margarete Schütte-Lihotzky sits to the left of De Silva in the front row. The image reads very differently in each of the publications. In the CIAM book, it documents a meeting and focuses on the star architects of European and US American modernity by giving more space to the names than the image itself. In the De Silva publication, the image shows an important historical event, in which she is the main protagonist and the center of attention. – **CUT** –

In 1953[9] and 1997,[10] De Silva mentions that she is planning, and respectively, had planned, a film about a dancer in a village.[11] The broad outline she describes is the structure, a kind of architecture we can use to examine the relationship between architecture, bodies, and representation in De Silva's practice.
De Silva was born in Sri Lanka between 1916 and 1918 into a Burgher/Sinhalese family and died in 1998, just one week before the first volume of her autobiography *The Life & Work of an Asian Woman Architect* was published, which had originally been planned as a two-volume publication. For most of her life, she lived in Kandy, a hill country in Sri Lanka, which belonged to the category "upper country." While the lower countries had already been conquered by the colonial powers in the early sixteenth century, the British took over power in Kandy in the first half of the nineteenth century. De Silva was an architect, an architecture theorist, and taught architecture history. She was the first Sri

4 Artistic research is understood here as an ongoing discussion since the 1950s, but it has increased particularly within the last two decades. The discussion is concerned with critically reassessing the binary between science and art as well as critiquing the politics of knowledge, research, and institutions. Here, artistic research is used as a method that links up to other approaches and projects "that have used techniques of artistic—which is to say dialogical, experimental, actor-related, or even agitorial—research to analyze and present historical-contemporary colonialities to produce a specific knowledge that exhibits rather than conceals the tortured materiality of objects and the practical logic of the institutions to which it owes its existence." See Tom Holert, "Artistic Research: Anatomy of an Ascent," *Texte zur Kunst*, no. 82 (June 2011): 56.

5 "So, montage is conflict. As the basis of every art is conflict (an 'imagist' transformation of the dialectical principle). The shot appears as the cell of montage. Therefore it also must be considered from the viewpoint of conflict. Conflict within the shot is potential montage, in the development of its intensity shattering the quadrilateral cage of the shot and exploding its conflict into montage impulses between montage pieces. As, in a zigzag of mimicry, the mise-en-scène splashes out into a spatial zigzag with the same shattering." Sergei Eisenstein, "The Cinematographic Principle and the Ideogram," in *Film Form*, ed. Jay Leda (New York: Harcourt, 1977), 28–44.

6 Hito Steyerl, *Die Farbe der Wahrheit. Dokumentarismen im Kunstfeld* (Vienna: Turia & Kant, 2008), 34.

7 Eric Mumford, *The CIAM Discourse on Urbanism 1928–1960* (Cambridge, MA: MIT Press, 2000).

8 Minnette De Silva, *The Life & Work of an Asian Woman Architect* (Colombo: Smart Media Productions, 1998).

9 Ibid., 257.

10 Susan Reed, interview with Minnette De Silva on August 27, 1997 (unpublished manuscript).

11 Parts of the following were taken from previously published texts on http://www.transculturalmodernism.org.

Lankan woman to be trained as an architect and the first Asian woman to be elected as a member of the Royal Institute of British Architecture (RIBA). From 1946 to 1956, she was the CIAM delegate for India and Ceylon. Beside her regular journeys to Europe, she traveled to Greece, Iran, Pakistan, Afghanistan, and India in the 1960s and started teaching architecture history in Hong Kong in the 1970s. She occupies a very important discursive position in the debates around modernist architecture and architecture history. In 1953, she published an essay in *Marg Magazine* about the first house she planned, the "Karunaratne House" (1947–1951), for which she outlines a concept and a building practice of "Modern Regional Architecture." She focuses on notions of traveling discourses, which avoid developing theories and practices that create exclusions based on identity, operating instead with the notion of transnational and transcultural understanding.
Her autobiography, published in 1998, is a collection of photographs, drawings, notes, and stories, which are presented in a somewhat nonlinear way. Her awareness of the intersection between postcoloniality, ethnicity, gender, and heteronormativity is illustrated in the title of her book: *Life & Work of an Asian Woman Architect*. Experiences of being exoticized in 1940s postwar London as an "exotic visitor from another planet," "romanticized" by Le Corbusier when "he was greatly attracted by his first live contact with *l'Inde*,"[12] not being taken seriously as an architect in Sri Lanka, being refused as a "daughter of the nation" because her parents were from different castes,[13] and falling out of heteronormativity by living alone and unmarried, choosing to concentrate on production rather than reproduction, and the effect these experiences had on her life and work are described with a feminist attitude in her autobiography.[14] The book is reminiscent of a collage and, as such, of her architecture. Her narratives rotate around terms such as modern and traditional, regional and international, skilled and unskilled. Like in her book, De Silva created a collage of her activities and the products of her activities as an architect, theoretician, teacher, ceramist, weaver. Overall, the book appears to be an elaborate collection. The second volume of the autobiography was never published; the manuscript, along with the rest of her archives and collection, has since been lost. – **CUT** –

The following scene is meant to visually establish the house as the stage, as the setting of negotiations between bodies, movement, representation, house, home, and gender.
Place:
Karunaratne House, Kandy.[15]
Sound:
At first, the sound fades out, placing the full attention on the image. As the sound recedes into the background, the images come to the fore until the sound takes over once again, taking the house out of the private sphere and into a more public sphere, e.g., the village.

Setting:
The camera enters a house through an open door. The house is old and empty; it seems like nobody has taken care of it for ages. The camera looks around. It is a modern house, built in the late 1940s. It is obvious that the camera is part of a moving body. The camera follows the steps as it follows the subjective gaze. After looking around (it is either the living room or the entrance hall, there are big windows on one side of the room, stairs that lead to the lower ground of the house, one wall is colored in a dark yet intense red, there is a huge rectangular hole in one wall, it appears that it was once made to make a picture fit inside, through the windows a garden is conjecturable, the grass looks wild), the camera starts to be affected by the architectural lines, the lines and streams caused by architecture, as well as the lines and streams caused by the time based cracks on the walls and the ground.
Camera:
There is a slow fade-in, as the camera, in a hovering motion, gently sweeps across the entrance area/upper living room in slow motion. The view follows, the camera continues onward, toward the upper stage, observing all the walls, cautiously, slowly, exactly.
Voice-Over:
The voice-over begins while the camera continues to follow the lines and cracks.
It is the fifteenth of October in 1954. My name is Minnette De Silva. I am writing a letter to Basil Wright: "I wonder whether you remember meeting me in London. We talked about a film of Ceylon and you said you would be interested ... I said I would get in touch when more details were worked out. The story is well on its way to completion: I have the broad outline worked out and there are two experts on Ceylon Culture and folk life working on the details. I am meeting various people to discuss the financial side of the film, being guided by your rough estimate of what an inexpensive color-film would cost. We are hoping Shell might finance us: do you know the people at that end? Or would any of the film people there be interested in this idea?
It is a purely indigenous film based on life in a village, with all the folk culture and living depicted, woven round the life of a young danseuse. She exists and is a lovely dancer and an interesting character. And, of course, this brings in the whole dancing clan too. This is just a bare sketch of the theme. I believe film companies are in need of 'exotic' film themes. This one is unique and with imaginative and poetic direction and photography could be a very beautiful film.

12 Minnette De Silva, *The Life & Work of an Asian Woman Architect*, 100.
13 On "nationalism and respectability" see Neloufer De Mel, *Women & the Nation's Narrative. Gender and Nationalism in Twentieth Century Sri Lanka* (Colombo: Social Scientists' Association, 2001), 103–04.
14 De Silva, *The Life & Work of an Asian Woman Architect*.
15 Minnette De Silva, "A House in Kandy," *Marg* VI, no. 3 (1953): 4–11.

Please write to me immediately to let me know your thoughts on this. First of all, whether you are seriously interested. Please keep this as private as possible. I am sending this letter and two other copies to various friends in the hope that one would forward it on. ... You gave me your address but it seems to be lost."[16]
The hand-held camera leaves the house through the front door, briefly looks up, then straight ahead toward the street. – **CUT** –

In 1935, De Silva's sister, Anil Marcia, and their friend, painter George Keyt, produced a dance piece, the first in which the history of Sri Lanka was performed. De Silva herself has an appearance as a tableau dancer. Focusing on Kandyan Dance, Susan Reed has extensively described the relationship between dance, decolonization, feminism, and nation-building. Until the 1940s, Kandyan Dance was performed only by men from certain castes in rural areas. During the struggles for independence, however, it became a significant site of struggle and conflict, also a site of feminist appropriation, where women challenged the Sri Lankan ideals of female purity and respectability by performing the dance. Though Kandyan Dance has been described as conservative, the historical absence of female dancers and feminist appropriations of the dance "provide[d] Sinhala women with open territory, the opinion of pushing boundaries of what is considered suitable dance for their gender."[17] I understand De Silva's use of the term "exotic" in her film description as a political term on multiple levels. For one, she appropriates the term by emphasizing it, treating this colonial mode of constructing a female other with irony, and using it to get funding from British film companies, as she is well aware of its currency on the postcolonial market. In addition, the "exotic" does not correspond with the image of women and the use of female bodies dictated by national ideals of "modesty, restraint, and submissiveness" in 1950s Sri Lanka. What's more, the dancers' growing popularity also enabled criticism of the caste system to become more visible in media and politics. In this period of nation-building, an "exhibitionary order" was established,[18] especially for dance, which depoliticized the performances by relegating them to the aesthetic realm of national folklore. "As an expression and embodiment of 'culture', dance as a medium is especially well suited for displays of identity, combining music, dress, body, and movement to convey ideas of a group's distinctiveness."[19] Since De Silva and her siblings began taking dance lessons in the 1920s, her film and dance can be viewed as a critical examination of national traditionalisms and folklorisms. The fact that she does not draw clear boundaries between traditional and modern, regional and international, gives visibility to combinatory practices, which serve as a critical counterpoint to the construction of identities. Anoma Pieris identifies an architectural precarity within De Silva's work that goes against the grain of a notion of modernity that bases itself on national identity. "There was no attempt in her work of smoothing out the rough edges of the different approaches into a coherent aesthetic; in fact, its irregularities are its most salient feature. [...] We see the problem of post-coloniality exposed as a precarious balance of Eastern and Western cultures, not as an aesthetic synthesis."[20] The village in the film becomes a stage, or rather, is treated as a stage, a form of display that depicts references and relationships between movement and architecture, between the dancer and the village. The village is also significant as a point of reference for analyzing modernist housing settlements.[21] The medialization of modernist architecture itself was also a key point of reference and was often incorporated into the architecture.[22] De Silva's work also addresses the relationship between moving bodies and the surrounding architecture in a way that sets it apart from medializing architecture that only represents the interior or exterior of a building. It is important to add that De Silva's architectures were influenced by the idea of flexible spaces and architectures capable of adapting to the ever-changing needs of their inhabitants. – **CUT** –

There is a black-and-white photograph at the Le Corbusier Center in Chandigarh. Next to the image, a piece of paper reads "Le Corbusier with Minnette De Silva." In the 1950s, during the construction phase, Le Corbusier invited De Silva to Chandigarh. The caption doesn't correspond to the image. On the left side of the image, there is a man with his back to the camera, and Le Corbusier is standing in the middle and talking to a woman on his left. De Silva is not in the picture.[23] Archives and museums sort and organize photographs based on the information found on the back: year, place, persons depicted, photographer. The front of the photograph only exists on a symbolic level, as an iconic stimulus.[24] It is less about the truthfulness of whom or what we see, but rather about the way in which truths are produced through classifications and inscriptions. Minnette De Silva is often mentioned as a friend of Le Corbusier's, not as an architect or a consultant. Through the photograph that she is not in, she is also documented in the Le Corbusier Center Archive. – **CUT** –

The city of Chandigarh was divided by the European modern city planning principles of CIAM.[25] The layout of Chandigarh is based on the Modulor, a

16 De Silva, *The Life & Work of an Asian Woman Architect*, 257.
17 Susan Reed, *Dance and the Nation: Performance, Ritual, and Politics in Sri Lanka* (Madison, Wisconsin: University of Wisconsin Press, 2010), 206.
18 Susan Reed borrows this term from Timothy Mitchell.
19 Reed, *Dance and the Nation*, 5.
20 Anoma Pieris, *Architecture and Nationalism in Sri Lanka: The Trouser under the Cloth* (London: Routledge, 2012), 134.
21 See village architecture as an exhibition display at the 1954 UN Housing Exhibition in Delhi, http://www.transculturalmodernisms.org.
22 Beatriz Colomina, *Privacy and Publicity: Modern Architecture as Mass Media* (Cambridge, MA: MIT Press, 1994).
23 "Le Corbusier with Telly Tata in Bombay, mid-1950s." See Nicholas Fox Weber, *Le Corbusier: A Life* (New York: Knopf, 2008), 549.
24 Steyerl, *Die Farbe der Wahrheit*, 32.
25 Parts of the following were taken from previously published texts on http://www.transculturalmodernism.org.

measurement plan based on the human figure of a 1.83-meter-tall British man, transferring organic functionalism to urban space. The city center is positioned as the heart, while the capitol complex is at the head. Here, discourse on life and architecture converge in a way that renders them indistinguishable from one another. Chandigarh is thus not only a living or organic architecture based on a functionalist notion of production, but what we have here is a functionalist aesthetic that is not only modeled on the human body but also claims to be life itself. In 1950, Le Corbusier was invited to develop this new capital city and prefecture for the Indian Punjab, at the request of India's first prime minister, Nehru, after India gained independence in 1947. Within the Indian Independence Act, the partition into India and Pakistan (West and East) was executed with the idea of separating Muslims from Hindus and Sikhs and vice versa. Punjab was divided up between Pakistan and India, and the capital Lahore was given to Pakistan. Immediately after the new lines were established, about fifteen million people crossed the border. There are many reasons why Chandigarh was built: to build a new capital for Punjab, to resettle people, to attract capital, to rebuild an economy, to symbolize India's independence, to create a new bureaucratic center, since Shimla, the temporary capital, couldn't accommodate the full government machinery, as a strategy to deal with the material and psychological loss of Lahore and to build a counterpart to it, and also because city life had begun to appeal to the ordinary middle class or lower middle class Indian.[26]

As the capital of the states of Haryana and Punjab, Chandigarh was meant to be an administrative city. Marked by the main features of Western modernity and symbols of ancient India, Chandigarh afforded the possibility to stand through and with these two references against colonialism. Chandigarh was the official city planning project of Indian postcolonialism and within this undertaking, it had the mission to make the assumed break between colonialism and postcolonialism visible and push the old agricultural India to a new state of industrialization. Chandigarh was meant to foster the establishment of a new national confidence.

The plans for Chandigarh's capitol complex, largely drawn up by Le Corbusier, consisted of four buildings—the administrative office, the high court, the parliament, and the governor's palace, which was later redesigned as the Museum of Knowledge. According to Nehru, building a governor's palace on the capitol complex did not correspond to the democratic architecture that was fundamental to the idea of Chandigarh. These basic democratic principles were supposed to be manifested in the capitol complex. The idea had been to create a building that represented and symbolized democratic ideals, that would archive, collect, and represent all "human activities."[27] It was to be an *all*-encompassing archive in the capitol complex built on the site of the governor's palace.[28] The archive was positioned as the brain in the Modulor. Le Corbusier described the Museum of Knowledge as an "Electronic Laboratory for Scientific Decision"; a museum that "becomes practicable and capable of being used as soon as the overwhelming techniques of electronics intervene (pictures, sounds, words, colours, diagrams, etc...) manifested by magnetic tape recordings which I have called the 'Round Books,' that is to say audiovisual films."[29]

The concept for the Museum of Knowledge invites criticism on different levels—as a biopolitically oriented repository of knowledge, as the representational apparatus of a feigned democracy, or as a sculpturalization and monumentalization of technology. Within the Chandigarh project, the possibility of representing marginalized and underrepresented positions and influences is structured to the effect that its name inevitably questions the type of knowledge being presented. Because the museum does not actually exist, one may ask whose knowledge fails to be represented. This question closely corresponds to the initial demand for a place that collects documentation on all activities,[30] thereby building (and assuming the function of) a pool of knowledge rather than of an archive based on a hierarchy of knowledge.

Administrative officials eventually used a hierarchical and dominant concept of knowledge to justify why the museum had failed to be realized in the 1950s: "In a country like India, however, where 80 percent of the population depends on primitive agricultural techniques and where the literacy rate is abysmally low, Le Corbusier's idea sounded incomprehensible."[31] – **CUT** –

There is a magazine called ANQ in the library of the Chandigarh Architecture School.[32] Inside, there are photographs from the construction of Sector 34 in Chandigarh. The photocopies are black and white. Sector 34 is a commercial

26 For more on the role of Chandigarh see: Vikramāditya Prakāsh, *Chandigarh's Le Corbusier: The Struggle for Modernity in Postcolonial India* (Seattle: University of Washington Press, 2002).

27 P. L. Varma, "Corbusier's Brave New World: Personal Impressions," *Architecture + Design: Le Corbusier in India* (September–December 1987): 47.

28 See Jacques Derrida, "Dem Archiv verschrieben," in *Archivologie*, eds. Knut Ebeling and Stephan Günzel (Berlin: Kulturverlag Kadmos, 2009), 29–60. An archive/archeíon is the site where all knowledge is stored, and also the place that endows those in political power with the right to validate or demonstrate laws. "On account of their publicly recognized authority, it is at their home, in that place which is their house (private house, family house, or employees' house), that official documents are filed." (Derrida) As guardians, the archons have the power to interpret this archive, for the documents claim to be the law. To be guarded thus, in the jurisdiction of this stating the law, they needed at once a guardian and a localization. See also Jacques Derrida and Eric Prenowitz, "Archive Fever: A Freudian Impression," *Diacritics* 25, no. 2 (Summer 1995): 9–63.

29 Ravi Kalia, *Chandigarh: The Making of an Indian City* (New Delhi: Oxford University Press, 1987), 116.

30 With reference to Nehru's demands concerning the Museum of Knowledge, he only ever spoke of human activities, nonhuman activities were never mentioned. For more on nonhuman activities see Fahim Amir's contribution to this book.

31 Kalia, *Chandigarh: The Making of an Indian City*, 117.

32 Chris Gordon and Kilian Kist, *Chandigarh. Forty Years after Le Corbusier* (Amsterdam: Architectura and Natura Quarterly 40, 1993).

subcenter. In one picture, there is a high-rise concrete building, which was probably not meant to be a residential, but instead a commercial, office, or restaurant space. The building is surrounded by huts that are about one-fifth the size of the concrete building. The image is blurry, neither the structural engineering nor the materials used are really discernible. They do not look like they are made out of the same materials—bricks or cement—as the buildings under construction, but rather out of clay with thatched roofs. There is no information on how long or when these dwellings were there. There are no people in the photograph. Pictures from the construction of the capitol complex showing women, men, and donkeys became especially popular, and manual modes of production and their aesthetic became significant for Chandigarh. These images represented the production relations between modern architecture and manual labor, and representations of construction sites in general were very popular for the idea of the future and modernity, since "the very idea of 'reconstruction' called forth the hopes of architectural modernity. Where the war had hit, however, utopian city concepts had little chance of being enacted anywhere immediately after 1945."[33] This at least gave some visibility to the workers in their jobs, although their living conditions remained underrepresented. Though photographic documentations of the construction site and the representative buildings created a kind of visibility for the workforce, the workers' living quarters were declared illegal once the first buildings had been completed.[34] – **CUT** –

After the partition, around 30,000 construction workers built Chandigarh as Punjab's new capital, with around 5,000 people working on the construction site at a time.[35] Half of them were children and women. Though Chandigarh was meant to represent the modern city of the age of industrialization, it was built by hand; manpower cost less than machine power, and it included women-power, child-power, and donkey-power.[36] "On the manual labor of men, women, and children 'as innumerable as ants' with the leisurely aid of miniature donkeys and scorning the impatient hustle of machinery, the city is slowly taking form. The same old crazy scaffolding bamboo, tied with bits of strings, astonishingly gives birth to structures of sublime grace and impressive solidity."[37]

During the construction of Chandigarh, the notion of a modern architectural universalism is set in contrast to the use of regional and local materials. With their practices and methods, artisans and construction workers were an integral component of an architectonic modernity in Chandigarh; these practices and materials become modern, that is to say, components of modernity, so that any attempt to relegate these practices to a realm of anachronistic and outdated tradition, which is seen as precisely the opposite of modernity, is bound to fail.

From the very beginning, the villagers demonstrated resistance against the construction: "The people's resistance to displacement was formalised in the anti-Rajdhani (note: Rajdhani: lit. capital) committee that was formed in 1948.

The anti-Rajdhani committee had promised the government to launch a satyagraha involving over 30,000 people all over the state to stop the construction of Chandigarh. It does not seem as if this massive agitation ever took off the ground. What did was a series of protest actions at the village level involving the local people. [...] Yet the agitation was fairly influential. Not much work could be done between 1948 and 1951 [...] because of the agitation by the local villagers. People would not allow the survey of ground water or the construction of sheds from where the engineers might function."[38] – **CUT** –

I took a picture from the roof of the administrative office. The photograph shows part of the extensive capitol complex. There are trails leading in different directions that cut across the green areas that surround the capitol complex. There could be various reasons that the Museum of Knowledge remained a project that was never realized. However, precisely its absence enables us to use Chandigarh as an opportunity to pose questions of democratic participation, modern urban planning, and nation-states. While the construction of the museum is an issue that still crops up in political debates, a body of knowledge has long since been inscribed in the capitol complex's landscape. Paths have emerged that were never planned, but that people who work in Chandigarh use on a daily basis. Economic power relations and an unequal representation are inscribed in the compound. They connect the workers who live in the surrounding neighborhoods and villages since they cannot afford to live in Chandigarh with their jobs in the city. – **CUT** –

bell hooks writes: "Yet to ignore this standpoint [that centralizes the perspectives of poor and working-class folks] is to reproduce a body of work that is neocolonial insofar as it violently erases and destroys those subjugated knowledges that can only erupt, disrupt, and serve as acts of resistance if

33 Stanislaus von Moos, *Chandigarh 1956* (Zurich: Scheidegger & Spiess, 2010), 55.

34 Cf. Interview with Madhu Sarin on March 14, 2011 (Moira Hille): "So during the construction of Chandigarh the laborers built their huts, no one talked about it. It was natural; Chandigarh needed labor and the laborers needed huts. A trade union leader, maybe a member of the communist party, told me during my research that till 1959 no one talked about the huts. But when the buildings started being finished, they started to say: Oh, you can't build like this; this is illegal use of the land. Their vested interest will grab valuable land in the new city and so we must ask them to get lost. In 1959 they issued the first notice to remove the huts at their own cost within such and such time: If you don't, we will do it and we will forcibly remove and we will recover the cost from you." Chandigarh, http://www.transculturalmodernism.org. See also Madhu Sarin, "Beyond the Margins of Planning," in *Chandigarh. Forty Years after Le Corbusier* (Amsterdam: Architectura and Natura Quarterly 40 1993): 67-69

35 Parts of the following were taken from previously published texts on http://www.transculturalmodernism.org.

36 U. E. Chowdhury, "High Cost Housing and Interiors," *Marg* XV, no. 1 (1961): 26–28.

37 von Moos, *Chandigarh 1956*, 35.

38 Kavita Sharma, Chitleen K. Sethi, Meeta, and Rajivlochan, *Chandigarh Lifescape: Brief Social History of a Planned City* (Chandigarh: Government Press, 1999), 26.

they are visible, remembered. Documentation of a cultural genealogy of resistance invites the making of theory that highlights the cultural practices which transform ways of looking and being in a manner that resists reinscription by prevailing structures of domination. Subversive historiography connects oppositional practices from the past with forms of resistance in the present, thus creating spaces of possibility where the future can be imagined differently—imagined in such a way that we can witness ourselves dreaming, moving forward and beyond the limits and confines of fixed locations."[39] – **CUT** –

This montage reveals the correlation between various documents, plans, concepts, and narratives, instead of grasping them as singular events. The examples show cultural practices that resist a dominant language, a language that lays claim to and co-opts the notion of modernity for itself.
In the 1950s, CIAM questioned a universalist notion. Building prefabricated high-rises were not the answer, and architects began looking for inspiration across the globe. When Sigfried Giedion writes about the aesthetic dignity of vernacular modes of "self-building," he employs a colonial binary logic of the "primitives" and the West.[40]
In this context, we should reconsider De Silva's film and the scope of knowledge she negotiates therein. A scope of knowledge is produced that relates both to modernist architectures and to vernacular building practices. Accordingly, De Silva's statement and practice ("in this house the architect, the craftsman and the artist have worked together"[41]) can serve to deconstruct patriarchal histories of building and architecture. Time and again, she also challenges a modernist concept of master, aesthetic dominance, and hierarchical concepts of disciplines.
For De Silva, the village is not merely the backdrop against which an event takes place, but rather it is the stage itself, and its architecture the actor. Architecture, body, and movement thus encounter one another as actors. In Pierre Chenal's 1929 film *L'Architecture d'aujourd'hui*, which Le Corbusier helped create, a camera moves along one of Le Corbusier's houses. The main actors are the camera, the house, and their relation, while the inhabitants are more responsible for showing or demonstrating how to use the house. In describing Le Corbusier's houses, Beatriz Colomina explains that "the house is no more than a series of views choreographed by the visitor, the way a filmmaker effects the montage of a film."[42] However, the architect is granted the authority to direct the camera and decide which portion of the image will be shown. Though the movement that creates a view of the outside is ascribed to the subject within the space, we are still dealing with representative architecture in which possible bodily movements and perspectives have already been determined, meaning that the architect remains the most formative element in this context. By taking the moving body as a point of departure, De Silva's architectural concept adds an element to this always already predefined view.

Though there has been much speculation about the film, I find the perspective of movement to be a productive point from which to examine the relationship between architecture and film. Therein, one can find what can perhaps be seen as a critique of representation within De Silva's work, which is based on subjects who are endowed with movement and agency within spaces, and on building architecture to accommodate rather than dictate these movements.
– CUT –

39 bell hooks, "Black Vernacular: Architecture as Cultural Practice," in *Art on My Mind: Visual Politics* (New York: The New Press, 1995), 151.

40 For more extensive research on the topic, see Christian Kravagna, *Primitivism in Habitat*, http://www.transculturalmodernisms.org.

41 De Silva, *The Life & Work of an Asian Woman Architect*, 119.

42 Beatriz Colomina, "Häuslicher Voyeurismus," in *Privileg Blick. Kritik der visuellen Kultur*, ed. Christian Kravagna (Berlin: Edition ID-Archiv, 1997), 218.

Literature

Fahim Amir, Eva Egermann, Moira Hille, Johannes Köck, Jakob Krameritsch, Christian Kravagna, Christina Linortner, Marion von Osten, and Peter Spillmann. "Model House–Mapping Transcultural Modernisms." *Texte zur Kunst. Artistic Research*, vol. 82 (June 2011): 147.

Chowdhury, U.E. "High Cost Housing and Interiors." In *Marg*, vol. XV, no. 1, (1961/Reprint 1998): 26-28.

Colomina, Beatriz. *Privacy and Publicity. Modern Architecture as Mass Media*. Cambridge, MA: MIT Press, 1994.

Colomina, Beatriz. "Häuslicher Voyeurismus." In *Privileg Blick. Kritik der visuellen Kultur*. Edited by Christian Kravagna, 201–222. Berlin: Edition ID-Archiv, 1997.

De Mel, Neloufer. *Women & the Nation's Narrative. Gender and Nationalism in Twentieth Century Sri Lanka*. Colombo: Social Scientists' Association, 2001.

De Silva, Minnette. *The Life & Work of an Asian Woman Architect*. Colombo: Smart Media Productions, 1998.

De Silva, Minnette. "A House in Kandy." *Marg*, vol. VI, no. 3, (1953): 4–11.

Derrida, Jacques and Eric Prenowitz. "Archive Fever: A Freudian Impression." *Diacritics*, vol. 25, no. 2 (Summer, 1995): 9–63.

Eisenstein, Sergei. "The Cinematographic Principle and the Ideogram." In *Film Form*. Edited by Jay Leda, 28–44. New York: Harcourt, 1977.

Eisenstein, Sergei: *Das dynamische Quadrat. Schriften zum Film*. Leipzig: Reclam, 1988.

Fox Weber, Nicholas. *Le Corbusier: a life*. New York: Knopf, 2008.

Chris Gordon and Kilian Kist. *Chandigarh. Forty Years after Le Corbusier*. Amsterdam: Architectura and Natura Quarterly 40, 1993.

Hernández, Felipe, Mark Millington, and Iain Borden (eds.). *Transculturation. Cities, Spaces and Architecture in Latin America*. Amsterdam: Rodopi, 1998: xi.

Hille, Moira. Interview with Madhu Sarin, March 14, 2011. Chandigarh, http://www.transculturalmodernism.org. Accessed May 1, 2013.

Holert, Tom. "Artistic Research: Anatomy of an Ascent." *Texte zur Kunst. Artistic Research*, vol. 82 (June 2011): 56.

hooks, bell. "Black Vernacular: Architecture as Cultural Practice." In *Art on My Mind: Visual Politics*, 145-151. New York: New Press, 1995.

Kalia, Ravi. *Chandigarh. The Making of an Indian City*. New Delhi: Oxford University Press, 1987.

Mumford, Eric. *The CIAM Discourse on Urbanism 1928–1960*. Cambridge, MA: MIT Press, 2000.

Model House–Mapping Transcultural Modernisms. Accessed April 1, 2013. http://www.transculturalmodernism.org.

Pieris, Anoma. *Architecture and Nationalism in Sri Lanka. The trouser under the cloth*. London: Routledge, 2012.

Prakāsh, Vikramāditya. *Chandigarh's Le Corbusier. The Struggle for Modernity in Postcolonial India*. Seattle: University of Washington Press, 2002.

Reed, Susan. *Dance and the Nation. Performance, Ritual, and Politics in Sri Lanka*. Madison, Wisconsin: University of Wisconsin Press, 2010.

Sarin, Madhu. *Urban planning in the Third World: The Chandigarh Experience*. London: Mansell, 1982.

Sarin, Madhu. "Beyond the Margins of Planning." In *Chandigarh. Forty Years after Le Corbusier*, 67-69. Amsterdam: Architectura and Natura Quarterly 40, 1993.

Sharma, Kavita, Chitleen K. Sethi, Meeta, and Rajivlochan. *Chandigarh Lifescape. Brief Social History of a Planned City*. Chandigarh: Government Press, 1999.

Steyerl, Hito. *Die Farbe der Wahrheit. Dokumentarismen im Kunstfeld*. Vienna: Turia & Kant, 2008.

Varma, P.L. "Corbusier's Brave New World: Personal Impressions." *Architecture + Design*. Le Corbusier in India (September–December 1987): 47.

Von Moos, Stanislaus. *Chandigarh 1956*. Zurich: Scheidegger & Spiess, 2010.

Home/Nation/ Gender

Modern Architectural Practices in Sri Lanka

Anoma Pieris and Moira Hille in Conversation

Moira Hille: In the first chapter of your book, *Architecture and Nationalism in Sri Lanka: The Trouser Under the Cloth* (2012), you refer to the connection between domesticity and decolonization and a politicization of the private sphere through colonialism and nationalism. What history and role does the domestic space or home have as an actor in this phase? How did the emerging importance of the house and home as ideological space change the understanding, meaning, and aesthetic of architecture in Sri Lanka?

Anoma Pieris: The argument in my book is, firstly, that the architecture of the colonial public sphere was largely determined by colonial actors—architects, engineers, superintendents of public works—and that they used exogenous models, which were sometimes adapted to the local context. These spatial norms and forms dominated the urban and institutional landscape, offering few opportunities for self-determination. As a result, the home, as the private domain, became an intense site of experimentation and was rapidly transformed by new elites to meet social expectations and aspirations. Whereas public forms of social mobility were largely framed by colonial governmental structures, the home, as the primary site of self-fashioning, created opportunities for marginal castes, women, and ethnic others to explore new and more lucrative identities. The hybrid nature of these identities and the negotiation between Eastern and Western values in their creation and adaptation is implied in the metaphor, the "trouser under the cloth." The term, which is based on the name for a mode of dress worn by native gentlemen and prescribed for official regalia, embodies inherent tensions within colonial metropolitan values.

At this point I might observe that a number of scholars have challenged this public vs. private divide by illustrating how colonial and indigenous elites combined expertise and resources in the production of colonial cities. The most recent book to make this argument is Preeti Chopra's *A Joint Enterprise* (2011), but I might also mention that the work of Peter Scriver and Shanti Jayewardene is complicating this dialectic. This is also true in the shaping of Colombo during the early twentieth century, which, although typically attributed to colonial planners, was essentially a joint enterprise. However, it took form through the organization of private space followed by public amenities, rather than the reverse.

Once we move to the era of nation building, my second argument, the public sphere becomes available to the once-colonized subjects, and they produce a different model for public architecture. The first model, produced via the colonial Public Works Department, is of a monumental architecture derived from palatial and religious buildings. This becomes the architecture of official nationalism and is in many ways an extension of early twentieth century Victorian eclecticism. The forms are quite exclusive, majoritarian, and assume an authoritative presence. In short, the first generation of architecture post independence is brokered by colonial architects and represents their translation of both colonial and Eastern values. Indigenous architects and a range of actors, including the much-neglected craftsmen and laborers, are involved in their production.

The Sri Lankan case is remarkable for its resistance to this official nationalism in the private sphere. Educated in secular modernism overseas, the first generation of Sri Lankan (or at that time Ceylonese) architects rejected these monumental forms for a far more domestic aesthetic. They—and here I am referring, firstly, to Minnette De Silva and after her to Geoffrey Bawa, who is far better known internationally—invested their careers in the creation of an aesthetic derived from the local vernacular. Courtyard houses, roadside verandahs, village temples, grain storage structures, all became inspirations for a new architectural vocabulary. The appropriation of these forms was in terms of form, space, material, and technology and was prompted by a period of import substitution (when Sri Lanka was socialist), where architects were forced to look for local solutions. The end result was that many of the homes and institutions they built during the 1960s and 70s were derived from domestic architecture with no reference to monumental forms. So while Sri Lanka was becoming increasingly hegemonic along ethno-national lines, these architects resisted this process quite literally.

My argument shifts again towards the end of the book when I explore how economic liberalization changes this rather modest early approach in order to cater to the new programs of globalization. I look at the parliament, a key signifier of the national self and the desire for international visibility, and the resort hotel, which repackages culture for external consumption. Whereas discourses on vernacular architecture always had an anthropological slant, the late twentieth century discourse on regionalism identified monumental structures as signifying regional cultures. Bawa's parliament was produced and recognized, externally, through that discourse but sits very uncomfortably within it. My argument is that the parliament is an elaboration of the vernacular approach, where the simple pavilion structure is reproduced at a scale and for a program it cannot match. It presents a very convincing image of a resistant indigenization when compared to the eager embrace of modernist designs and architects in Chandigarh, Dhaka, and Islamabad, but contains various incongruities that deny site, local materials, and technologies so fundamental to the vernacular approach.

Shanti Jayewardene, the first critical historian of Sri Lankan architecture who wrote on Bawa in 1984, argues that the five-pavilion configuration of the parliament is derived from monastic complexes in the ancient Buddhist capital at Anuradhapura. While the aesthetic is a synthesis of modern and traditional vocabularies, her argument creates an opening for a different line of analysis on how and when Bawa referred to monumental traditions, which may well contradict my position on the vernacular derivative. I do hope she writes about it. The wonderful thing about Bawa is that since he was so reticent about his own approach, there is plenty to debate on. I believe we should not try to fix him as a modernist or regionalist, create a retroactive climatic manifesto, or even institutionalize and commodify him. But we (broadly generalizing of course) are guilty of doing all these things...

MH: How did the idealization of the home affect a feminist critique on domesticity? Is there an articulated feminist critique nowadays on this emergence of the affirmation of the home as it evolved during the struggles for independence?

AP: If we look closely at the Ceylonese context, we find that Christianization enabled the rapid transformation of the domestic sphere along anglophile lines, most evident in the adaptation of Portuguese, Dutch, and British modes of dress by local elite women, particularly for weddings. In some ways the home was an elaboration of this change, aided by a cast of butlers, tutors, and governesses who trained elite ladies in appropriate behaviors. Eurasian and Burgher women would have informed and influenced these practices. The feminist scholar Kumari Jayawardena has written extensively on this subject, for example in *The White Woman's Other Burden* (1995). These women and their denationalization was the target of early anti-colonial nationalism and saw a highly politicized movement in dress reform that strove to constrain them in an appropriate dress code derived, ironically, from Victorian ideas of morality. However, nationalist modes of dress were also adapted internally in imitation of Indian behaviors when local ladies began wearing saris instead of dresses. For the period following independence, I have reproduced an image from the first advertisement for the Ceylon Government Railway launched in 1956 where all three trains are given gendered identities and represented as coy damsels, the southern princess, the highland maiden, and the northern goddess. We can see how nationalist rhetoric continued to recast women as representatives of an uncontaminated tradition, even in this case when associated with modern technology.

The gendering of the home is more pertinent to current analyses of the Sri Lankan ethnic conflict, where the home has been violated at many levels. I have recently written about filmic representations of gender and the home around cultural anxieties related to female soldiers. The female suicide bomber is the antithesis of the traditional homemaker and there has been much feminist debate around her politics. Feminist scholarship is lacking in architecture particularly in scholarship in or on Asia. I might mention Swati Chattopadhyay's *Representing Calcutta* (2005) and Ananya Roy's *City Requiem* (2003) as examples of a feminist approach. A recent issue of *Gender, Place and Culture* (2012), edited by Gülsüm Baydar, combines a number of essays along these lines.

Yet, even at a more basic level, information on women architects is lacking, revealing perhaps how patriarchal the profession and professional practices still are. We have plenty of female students studying architecture but many female professionals struggle in isolation unless they are supported by male partnerships. This has a lot to do with how elite clientele are sought and won and the insidious politics of large commissions. This lacuna is also evident in publishing and pedagogy. The Aga Khan Trust, which produced the most significant design monographs on non-Western architects during the 1980s—and was a trailblazer in this regard, neglected to include women. *Women in Architecture* by the Hecar Foundation (2000) is a useful book to refer to. While there are several prominent young women architects, for example, India's Anupama Kundoo, Thailand's Kanika Rkul, and Sri Lanka's Hiranti Welandawe, whom I have written about, only the Japanese architects such as Itsuko Hasegawa and Kazuyo Sejima have reached international status.

MH: You name Minnette De Silva as a central actor who uses and combines vernacular construction methods, regional materials, and aesthetics with modern materials, designs, and construction methods. She is one of the first architects in Sri Lanka who has established a modern regional style of architecture. But there is also a certain bulkiness in De Silva's architecture, as you say, she "never framed a tropical landscape or subscribed to the picturesque gaze." Could one read this as resistance to a nationalist aesthetic of the home as a fundament of the nation? Also, Minnette De Silva was the CIAM (*Congrès International d'Architecture Moderne*) delegate for India and Ceylon for over ten years, at a time when there was a shift from the functionalist notion of the home as a machine for living towards a naturalized notion of habitat. Can you relate this shift in the CIAM discourses to a shift in architectural debates in Sri Lanka and vice versa?

AP: To respond to your first question, De Silva certainly wrote quite scathingly about the monumental Buddhist architecture of the independence era and produced the vernacular against it. I see certain Indian characteristics in her designs, a particular relationship of scale and materiality and a decorative quality that does not conform to the aesthetic norms that we are schooled in—the consequence, perhaps, of her formative years in India. But architectural aesthetics are based on exogenous frameworks imposed by Western curricula, and we make judgments about good or bad aesthetics via a Western gaze. Bawa, on the other hand, deftly synthesized a vernacular scale with picturesque vistas and spatial relationships derived from the European tradition. For this reason his approach is immediately attractive to Western visitors. For example, I doubt that De Silva would use a classical statue of a male nude or Roman pavilion in her work, but we are quite happy to absorb it as a feature of Bawa's work and label his architecture Sri Lankan.

With regard to the CIAM discourse, De Silva's essay in the 1965–66 journal would have been the avenue for translating CIAM ideals to local practitioners. *Marg* and its role were less well known, and by then its focus was shifting to fine art and craft. Also, due to her years away and lack of involvement in the local architectural school, these ideas were not developed in any substantial way. De Silva's contribution to vernacular architecture discourse was subsumed by Bawa's reputation for producing it as an aesthetic.

MH: In 1954, an exhibition on low-cost housing took place in Delhi initiated by the Indian Government and the UN. The concept of the exhibition was the village as an expression of a living environment. How do you see the interconnection of home, village, and nation at this time in Sri Lanka? What does the village mean on an aesthetic and political level, as an interface between home and nation?

AP: In my book I barely touched on the serial production of domestic space as a form of social engineering. I felt that was an entirely different discussion related to settlement ideology, and Sri Lanka has been a major player in this area dating from the early settlement schemes of the 1950s through to the Village Reawakening projects of President R. Premadasa (1980s–90s). More recently, neo-liberal scenarios of post-tsunami reconstruction and more hegemonic postwar resettlement revisit these highly politicized responses. The fact is that politicians consistently manipulated the village for their own ends. Ananda Coomaraswamy raised the model of an idealized village life against what he saw as the denationalization of the elite (1909). The Sinhala villager, alienated from his land by colonial plantations, was idealized against Tamil plantation workers during the 1930s when the Ceylonese sought constitutional reform. The rural poor were the subject of early reformist agendas and the object of socialist nationalism during the 1950s. Yet even following economic liberalization, politicians always idealized the village so as to ensure rural votes. We might argue that in some ways, despite the monumental forms expressed in official architectures, the politicization of the village paralleled the revival of vernacular architecture, creating an environment receptive to the idealization of rural values and imagery as fundamental to Sri Lankan identity.

De Silva held an exhibition on twelve villages at the Commonwealth Institute, which appears to continue the discussion on rural community values. It is something worth looking into.

MH: For many years architectural modernism was described as a singular phenomenon with Western origin. The focus in our project is on transcultural aspects focusing on the interconnections, political circumstances, and different actors which and who were involved in different modernist projects. How would you relate the term transculturality to the emergence of regional modern architecture as you researched it in Sri Lanka?

AP: Many in the first generation of architects, and by that I mean those educated during the 1950s and 1960s, passed through the Architectural Association School in London and were impacted by the program in tropical architecture run by Maxwell Fry and Jane Drew and later headed by Otto Koenigsberger. So we may argue that in Sri Lanka—as it was, say, in Singapore—tropical modernism was their first response. This is certainly evident in the work of De Silva, Bawa, and a third architect, Valentine Gunasekara. Bawa was clearly influenced by European modernism and the British picturesque tradition, although his time in Italy may be equally instrumental in informing his vernacular approach. David Robson is keen to trace strains of modernism within Bawa's approach in contrast with—perhaps—what might be seen as his eclecticism. De Silva's architecture is a hybrid of her Indian, Ceylonese, and European influences. Her greatest mentor was Le Corbusier, whose connection with her has been written on by Charles Jencks. Gunasekara toured the USA and met Richard Neutra, Louis Kahn, Paul Rudolph, the Eames, and worked in Eero Saarinen's office under Kevin Roche. This exposure informed his design orientation. His work is reminiscent of the Californian strain of modernist regionalism. But I am reluctant to call this architecture regionalist or even to use the term so liberally. Regionalism is a very political term with specific meanings for Asia. Kenneth Frampton's polemical repositioning of the modernist avant-garde has no direct relevance for Asia, although great pains have been made to rethink Asia in terms of his criteria. Can one, in all honesty, have a discussion of Asian architecture that leaves out social, cultural, and political issues and focuses on site, climate, light, and tectonic. I think not...This may be possible in a postindustrial environment where social security is guaranteed, but in Asia we must deal with environmental and social forces.

MH: Within this understanding of regionalism, craftsmen, for example, were assigned a new role. In *Dance and the Nation: Performance, Ritual, and Politics in Sri Lanka* (2010), Susan Reed described the changing role of the dancers in the era of decolonization and nation-building from an invisible part of Sri Lankan culture to a figure of expression of Sri Lankan nationalism through the development of tradition and folklore. How exactly did the role of the craftsman change? And in relation to this, what did this mean concerning the role and meaning of the construction workers?

AP: Political regionalism in Asia was based on Cold War alliances and non-alignment. The adoption of the term regionalism after the Western aesthetic discourse, in ignorance of this association, needs to be problematized. That said, I find it unconscionable that books on Asian architects fail to acknowledge other actors (village masons, craftsmen, manual laborers) employed in a project, transposing the invisibility of labor in colonial relations onto new postcolonial class hierarchies. The jarring reality is that the textured, visceral environments of Asia that so delight postindustrial Western sensibilities are achieved through abominable labor practices: poor wages, appalling living conditions, and reluctance to train or mechanize. If, like Ananya Roy, you examine female labor relations, the conditions are even worse. The Sri Lankan architectural profession has expended minimal energy in training laborers or craftsmen. A recent PhD thesis by Milinda Pathiraja (University of Melbourne 2010–2011) exposes these lacunas. What we see (across the nineteenth and twentieth centuries) is a remarkable shift in labor practices. Initially we have traditional medieval castes of craftsman largely of South Indian origin patronized by the royal court in Kandy and discussed in detail in Coomaraswamy's *Medieval Sinhalese Art* (1908). Following the fall of Kandy (the hill country capital that resisted colonial rule) in 1815, many of them came southward to coastal areas augmenting the craftsmen created by colonial industry—the fisher-carpenter caste of Moratuwa. An entire chapter in my book demonstrates how the carpenter caste rose in the colonial economy due to their ability to reproduce themselves in the colonial public sphere through architecture, whereas the indigenous farming elites found themselves unable to command this labor resource to the same extent. The Sinhala carpenters combined with Muslim masons on many urban projects. The introduction of concrete created opportunities for lime burners. Towards the late colonial period we see how government projects begin to employ and produce skilled and unskilled workers, changing these caste-based economies. The abstraction of labor occurred through metropolitan building projects of the Public Works Department. Today the equivalent process would be evident in an entire generation trained on worksites in the Middle East.

The vernacular revival in architecture undoubtedly saw a rejuvenation of (labor intensive) craft-based traditions, particularly in relation to timber-work, tiling, and roofing practices. Bawa was responsible for reintroducing long discarded materials and features into domestic spaces and known for recycling building elements. He worked with specific baas's (village masons), and they in turn learned on the job. At the beginning this was a recognizably sustainable approach. When the materials were applied to larger programs it became unsustainable. Vernacular aesthetics, sustainable practices, and craftsmanship go hand in hand when the architecture remains at a domestic scale, but this relationship is unviable in a large program (resort hotel or parliament), and the desired hand-crafted aesthetic effect can only be achieved by other means.

Literature

Baydar, Gülsüm. "Sexualised Productions of Space." *Gender, Place and Culture: A Journal of Feminist Geography*, vol. 19, no. 6 (2012): 699-706.

Chattopadhyay, Swati. *Representing Calcutta: Modernity, Nationalism, and the Colonial Uncanny*. London: Routledge, 2006.

Chopra, Preeti. *A Joint Enterprise: Indian Elites and the Making of British Bombay*. Minneapolis: University of Minnesota Press, 2011.

Coomaraswamy, Ananda K. *Essays in National Idealism*. Colombo: Colombo Apothecaries Co. Ltd., 1909.

Coomaraswamy, Ananda K. *Medieval Sinhalese art: being a monograph on medieval Sinhalese arts and crafts, mainly as surviving in the eighteenth century, with an account of the structure of society and the status of the craftsmen*. Broad Campden: Essex House Press, 1956.

De Silva, Minnette. "Experiments in Modern Regional Architecture in Ceylon, 1950–1960." *Journal of the Ceylon Institute of Architects* (1965-66): 13-17.

Frampton, Kenneth. "Toward a Critical Regionalism: Six Points of an Architecture of Resistance." In *The Anti-aesthetic: Essays on Postmodern Culture*. Edited by Hal Foster, 16-30. Port Townsend, WA: Bay Press, 1983.

Jayawardena, Kumari. *The White Woman's Other Burden: Western Women and South Asia During British Rule*. Routledge, 1995.

Jayewardene, I. S. (Shanti). "The Work of Geoffrey Bawa: Some Observations towards a Historical Understanding." MS dissertation, History of Modern Architecture, University College London, London University, 1984.

Jayewardene-Pillai, Shanti. *Imperial Conversations: Indo-Britons and the Architecture of South India*. New Delhi: Yoda Press, 2007.

Jencks, Charles. *Le Corbusier and the Continual Revolution in Architecture*. New York: The Monacelli Press, 2000.

Pathiraja, Milinda. "The Idea of 'Robust Technology' in the Definition of a 'Third-World' Practice: Architecture, Design and Labour Training." PhD Thesis, Faculty of Architecture, Building and Planning, University of Melbourne, 2010–2011.

Pieris, Anoma. *Architecture and Nationalism in Sri Lanka: the trouser under the cloth*. New York: Routledge, 2012.

Reed, Susan A. *Dance and the Nation. Performance, Ritual, and Politics in Sri Lanka*. Madison: The University of Wisconsin Press. 2010.

Roy, Ananya. *City Requiem, Calcutta: Gender and the Politics of Poverty*. University of Minnesota Press, 2003.

Scriver, Peter. *The Scaffolding of Empire*. CAMEA Conference Proceedings, University of Adelaide, 2007.

Somaya, Brinda, and Urvashi Mehta. *An Emancipated Place*. The proceedings of the conference and exhibition held in Mumbai. *Women in Architecture – 2000 Plus*. Mumbai: Hecar Foundation. February 2000.

"Twelve Villages: a study of habitat in India, Bangladesh, and Sri Lanka at the Commonwealth Institute, London, 7–31 July" (1987), exhibition catalogue.

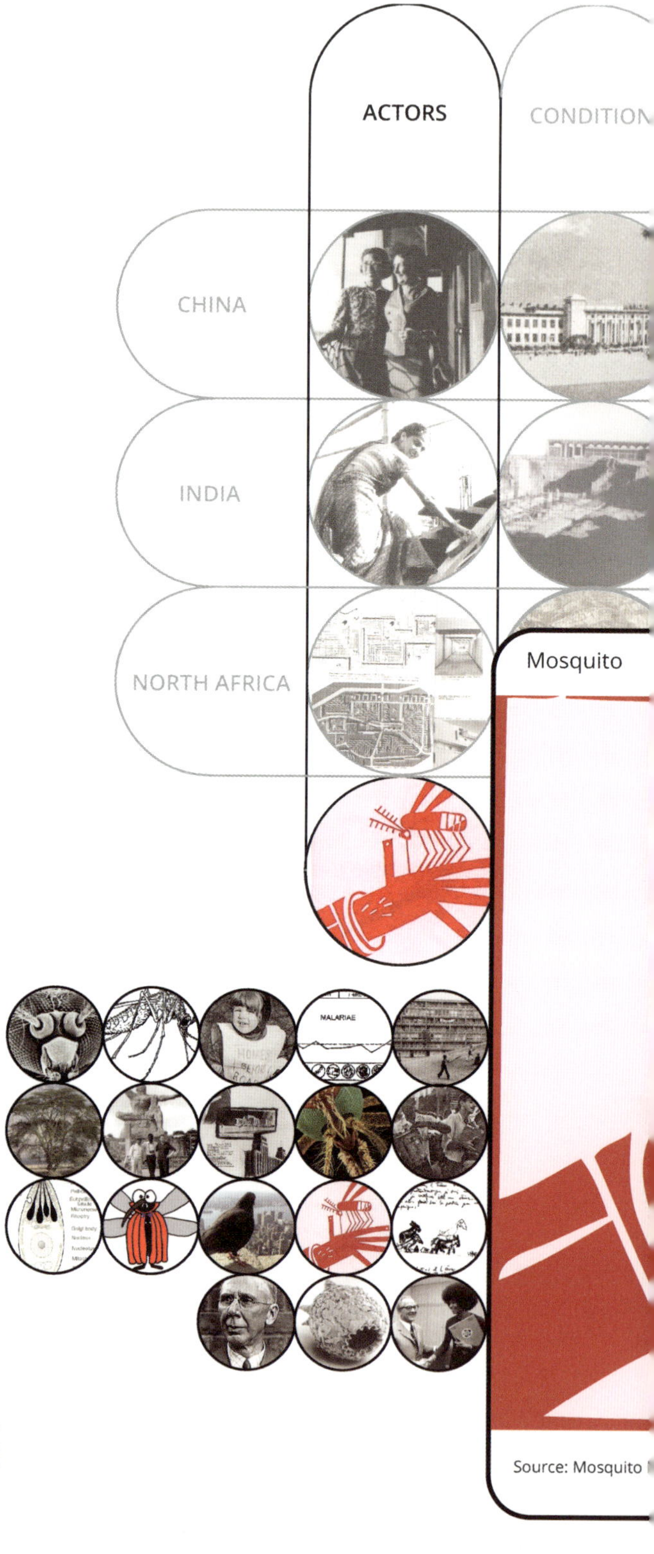

With Animals

VENTS | DEBATES & DISCOURSES | CONCEPTS | ART & RESEARCH | THEORIES

×

, 2005 ▼

Animals

Zone Sanitaire

Contact Zone

Urban Planning

Colonization

Dwellers and Strayers

Modernist Zoopolitics in Post/colonial Worlds

Fahim Amir

> **One dark night—when people were in bed,**
> **Old Mrs. O'Leary lit a lantern in her shed;**
> **The cow kicked it over, winked its eye and said,**
> **There'll be a hot time in the old town tonight.**
>
> **—Chicago Tribune**

As a modern myth goes, one of the greatest disasters of the United States in the nineteenth century, the great fire of 1871 that destroyed one third of the entire city of Chicago, was caused by "a hitherto unremarkable cow."[1] Mrs. O'Leary, her legal owner, had tried to milk the cow on an exceptionally hot Sunday evening when the unruly animal kicked over the lantern lighting the shed and sparked a hellish inferno that ate humans, animals, and architecture alike.[2]

The reconstruction of Chicago in the following years helped modernize the city and prepared it for its unparalleled rise to become the "hog butcher for the world" by the end of the century. The rebuilding also attracted architects who saw it as a laboratory for urban innovation, constructing, for example, the Reliance Building in 1895 as a harbinger of the "international style" that would dominate the twentieth century. Skyrocketing land prices and new regulations concerning fire safety had led to the erection of the first skyscraper in the world in 1884, the Home Insurance Building, housing the office of legendary meatpacking industrialist and robber baron Philip Armour, whose company motto was the famous "we feed the world." More than simply a marketing slogan, the Union Stock Yards of Chicago indeed processed the majority of US meat until the 1920s—more than any other place in the world. Connecting producers with their markets, revolutionizing work organization and efficiency while inventing cooling technologies to transport the precarious substance of mammal flesh, Chicago indeed became "nature's metropolis,"[3] the world capital of animal death and the nexus of "a new animal landscape that was governed as much by economics as by ecology."[4]

It was probably Chicago that inspired critical theorist Max Horkheimer to publish his 1934 aphorism, "Skyscraper," which employed an architectural image to describe late capitalist society: The skyscraper would have at its top the "feuding tycoons" and reach down to the "poor, the aged, and the sick."[5] Below

1 Hannah Higgins, *The Grid Book* (Cambridge, MA: MIT Press, 2009), 1.
2 Richard F. Bales, *The Great Chicago Fire and the Myth of Mrs. O'Leary's Cow* (Jefferson: McFarland, 2002).
3 William Cronon, *Nature's Metropolis: Chicago and the Great West* (New York: W. W. Norton, 1991).
4 Ibid., 224.
5 Max Horkheimer, "Skyscraper," in *Dawn and Decline: Notes 1926–1931 and 1950–1969*, trans. Michael Shaw (New York: Seabury Press, 1978), 66.

these were the floors reserved for the exploited colonies, but even lower, deep inside the intestines of the architectural leviathan, the animals were incarcerated in the basement of society:

> Below the spaces where the coolies of the earth perish by the millions, the indescribable, unimaginable suffering of the animals, the animal hell in human society, would have to be depicted, the sweat, blood, despair of the animals. [...] The basement of that house is a slaughterhouse, its roof a cathedral, but from the windows of the upper floors, it affords a really beautiful view of the starry heavens.[6]

As a refugee fleeing from Nazi terror in Europe, Horkheimer would later spend time in the United States where his opinions about the relationship between the functioning of modern society, animals and animality would be further elaborated.[7] But while Horkheimer's animals were mostly conceptualized as passive recipients of capitalism's atrocities during the formation of bourgeois subjectivity and painted as the total victims of history, another refugee fleeing war-torn Europe, Sigfried Giedion, took an apparently similar but in fact entirely different approach concerning the relations between space, animals, and social philosophy.

Giedion, the long time secretary-general of CIAM, had been invited by Walter Gropius to hold the Charles Eliot Norton Lectures at Harvard University from 1938–39 that would culminate in his work *Space, Time and Architecture*, (1941). While the latter would become the theoretical groundwork for generations of architecture students who wanted to educate themselves about modernist architecture, it was his time in the United States that allowed him to gather the documents and materials that would form the basis of his *Mechanization Takes Command* (1948). In this book, which included more then 700 images, Giedion ascribed the crisis of modern subjectivity, the feeling of being lost in and irritated by modern times and mass society, to the emergence and diffusion of machines. The central chapter, titled "Mechanization of Death: Meat," deals with the relationship of the modern city to its slaughterhouses and draws on diverse materials to document the (mostly unsuccessful) attempts to mechanize killing and meat packing in Chicago. This chapter was the center of his project at that time, because if Giedion's thesis was the resistance of living matter to mechanization and the problems it posed, the resistance of living and dead animals against the mechanized slaughterhouse was its logical culmination point.

In Giedion's account, all attempts of the celebrated heroes of progress—the engineers—failed in Chicago because of the "subjectivity" of the animals, who were not so easily deceived to willingly run to their death, and the "bodily constitution" of the animals that (economically) forbid too careless handling in life or death. Until this day, a slaughtered animal cannot be disassembled by machines; it still is a bloody monopoly of human manual labor. Giedion's compelling argument: because most machines failed to integrate the living or dead animal into mechanized production, the social organization of human labor itself had to be mechanized. Before the rapid transformation of small-scale butchery into the world's biggest integrated industry, a handful of skilled workers would kill and disassemble an animal. Now over 160 workers were involved, each assigned with a special task and clocked to the rhythm of the moving conveyor belt. The invention of the disassembly line soon inspired Henry Ford, who had visited Armour's plant, to construct the assembly lines for automobile production (soon displacing horses with cars in public life). Giedion's account of the relationship between animals, technology, and architecture now appears in sharp contrast to Horkheimer's approach: While the latter saw only vulnerability in animals as capitalism continued its course of reificating all social relations, the former understood the resistance of animals both as obstacles to and catalysts of capitalist modernization.[8]

On a formal level, Giedion's approach throughout his book resembles more contemporary forms of art-based research than seemingly sober variations of a history of technological development. Throughout the book, artworks seem to have the same heuristic value to Giedion as calculations and patent drawings. Artistic methods such as montage appear to transport his arguments, and his selection of images range from stills of surrealist films to historical commercial advertisements. Giedion is more interested here in "other actors" such as the anonymous engineers of the industrial age whose story Giedion wants to tell in re-enacting the plots of traditional historiographies that need a genius of some sort in its center.

In the spirit of Giedion's work I want to portray exemplary animals as active parts of urban planning and the production of space, as co-producers of city life, and unruly dwellers, and strayers whose actions and interrelations determined the course of history and the shape of cities along with human activity. I will focus on the first half of the twentieth century and concentrate on mosquitoes and cows in post/colonial constellations as real living beings.

6 Ibid.

7 Famous are the passages on animals and animality in the Dialectic of Enlightenment, written with Theodor W. Adorno and originally published in 1947. For the animal issue in the work of the Frankfurt School, see John Sanbonmatsu, *Critical Theory and Animal Liberation* (Lanham: Rowman & Littlefield Publishers, 2011).

8 In taking living animal agency and the bodily resistance of animals as primary and assigning capitalism a secondary role of re- and counteracting, Giedion's analysis interestingly resembles Operaist theory, an Italian Marxist discourse that argues for the conceptual and political autonomy of living labor against the over-accentuation of allegedly objective developments of capitalism in economic theory and political practice. For the methodology of Operaism, see Steve Wright, *Storming Heaven: Class Composition and Struggle in Italian Autonomist Marxism* (London: Pluto Press, 2002).

Warm Wars and Tiny Architects

The period in which Europeans conquered most of tropical Africa between 1880 and the First World War was also a time of rapid advance in tropical medicine. Before these advances, malaria had been known for centuries but associated with swampy, humid, and often heated geographies and its supposedly hazardous, bad air— Italian "mal aria."[9] Until the nineteenth century, malaria was successfully fought in most parts of Europe with drainage and large-scale geo-engineering. So, by the end of the nineteenth century, the often fatal fever was no longer significantly present in most parts of Western Europe "and thus already acquired some of its modern associations with distant lands and hot climates."[10] Malaria was considered to be by far the most serious health threat to Europeans living in the African tropics (especially imperial bureaucrats) and a key obstacle to the further colonization of areas beyond the coasts of Africa, South America, and Asia.

While Louis Pasteur had proven that microscopic organisms were responsible for some diseases, it was a trans-imperial medico-military network involving actors from and in China, India, Great Britain, France, and Algeria that enabled Ronald Ross to combine scattered theories and material evidence to prove his "mosquito theory."[11] Philosopher and sociologist Bruno Latour argues about the far fetching consequences of the Pasteurians: "If it had been necessary to make colonial society only with masters and slaves, there would never have been any colonial society. It had to be made with microbes, together with the swarming of insects and parasites that they transported."[12]

At the beginning of the twentieth century the discovery of mosquitoes as carriers and vectors of the pathogen agent facilitated small and large-scale architectural, terra-forming, and urban planning projects.[13] Indeed it had been a multitude of tiny flying females looking for a drop of blood for their offspring that changed the course of history once again.[14]

Ross visited the capital of Sierra Leone, supposedly the most malaria-infected spot in the British Empire, Free Town, in 1899 and recommended four measures: the destruction of breeding pools, the destruction of larvae by kerosene or humans, the shutting off of houses against mosquitoes, and the construction of European houses on elevated sites.[15] The Colonial Office sent its own expedition to study the situation and soon identified the "real" problem—the African child. While African adults had only mild attacks, African children very often became seriously ill: "It is universally the practice in Tropical Africa to allow and even encourage native huts to be built close to European houses. These huts always contain numerous children with parasites and Anopheles with sporozoites ready for injection."[16]

After the African child was understood by colonial medicine as the main reservoir of pathogens, the segregation of the white settlers from the African children seemed to be the proper solution. The question remained, how far should the Europeans be removed from African children and the African population in general. In short: how far could a mosquito fly? It was agreed "that the residential quarters of Europeans should be completely divided from the native towns or communities by at least a quarter of a mile."[17] The important aspect here is that the supposed size of the habitat of the mosquito became the measurement by which to separate the habitats of colonizers and colonized.

Since mosquitoes were thought to be nocturnal creatures, the segregation had to be most severe at night. So while the officials could fulfill their responsibilities during the day in the city, during the dangerous African nights they would be safeguarded in gated communities. But since the European officials did not want to forgo the luxuries that made the colonies so attractive, e.g., servants, keeping two servants in special separate rooms at the backside of the houses was permitted, undermining the whole segregationist health effort.[18]

9 Robert Sallares, *Malaria and Rome: A History of Malaria in Ancient Italy* (New York: Oxford University Press, 2002).
10 Jennifer Yee, "Malaria and the Femme Fatale: Sex and Death in French Colonial Africa," *Literature and Medicine* 21, no. 2 (2002): 201.
11 Jeanne Guillemin, "Choosing Scientific Patrimony: Sir Ronald Ross, Alphonse Laveran, and the Mosquito-Vector Hypothesis for Malaria," *Journal of the History of Medicine and Allied Sciences* 57, no. 4 (October 2002): 385–409.
12 Bruno Latour, *The Pasteurization of France*, trans. Alan Sheridan and John Law (Cambridge: Harvard University Press, 1988), 144.
13 Timothy Mitchell, *Rule of Experts: Egypt, Techno-politics*, Modernity (Berkeley: University of California Press, 2002), 19–53; Maria Kaika, "Dams as Symbols of Modernization: The Urbanization of Nature Between Geographical Imagination and Materiality," *Annals of the Association of American Geographers* 96, no. 2 (2006): 276–301; Paul S. Sutter, "Nature's Agents or Agents of Empire? Entomological Workers and Environmental Change During the Construction of the Panama Canal," *Isis* 98, no. 4 (December 2007): 724–54.
14 Humans exposed to malaria and yellow fever in childhood and having survived had much better chances to survive these diseases again than those exposed to it in adulthood. Considering the role of this acquired differential immunity for anticolonial struggles, environmental historian John Robert McNeill argues: "Historians for generations have brilliantly illuminated this age of revolution. One thing that has escaped their spotlight is the role of mosquitoes in making the revolutionaries victorious." John Robert McNeill, *Mosquito Empires: Ecology and War in the Greater Caribbean, 1620–1914* (Cambridge: Cambridge University Press, 2010), 193.
15 Leo Spitzer, "The Mosquito and Segregation in Sierra Leone," *Canadian Journal of African Studies* 2, no. 1 (Spring 1968): 52–54.
16 Stephen Frenkel and John Western, "Pretext or Prophylaxis? Racial Segregation and Malarial Mosquitos in a British Tropical Colony: Sierra Leone," *Annals of the Association of American Geographers* 78, no. 2 (June 1988): 216.
17 Ibid.
18 This later proved to be a vast underestimation, since female mosquitoes can fly up to three kilometers in search of human blood, as the US military would later find out while researching possible attacks on Cuba through weaponized mosquitoes. Jeffrey A. Lockwood, *Six-Legged Soldiers: Using Insects as Weapons of War* (New York: Oxford University Press, 2009).

Some officials opposed these sanitary-spatial politics because it was feared that segregation would not allow white people to act as "teachers and friends" to Africans—a popular legitimization of colonialism at that time. But at various points in the French and British Empire, the segregationist option was chosen for health and social reasons. In 1902 and 1919, meetings of all principal medical officers for all British West African colonies were organized by the Colonial Office. There the decision was made and a plan was prepared "to complete the segregation of the European population in all African towns within ten years, but the plan was easier to apply in designing new towns than in rebuilding old ones."[19]

The segregationist mosquito doctrine was handled differently all over Africa, from the strictest form, practiced in the Belgian Congo, where the cordon sanitaire encompassed a golf course, a botanical garden, and a zoo, to West Africa, occupied by the French, where in the new city of Dakar all thatch-roof houses were burned in the European residential areas after the plague of 1914, or even the German colony of Cameroon, where the medical authorities had published a city plan in 1904 favoring a six-part subdivision of the city based on "race" and "race mixture."[20]

Hill stations, formerly keeping the Europeans above the swampy areas and originating in the Indian context, were now expanded to other areas to protect them from the supposedly infected local population.[21] In South Africa, hill stations even became part of the "clean air circuit" that attracted many sick and weakened Europeans from the crowded European cities to regain their health and strength in the colonies before traveling back to attend to their duties at home.[22] At the same time, hill stations and European "healthy quarters" allowed civil servants to bring their families along, a process that helped end decades of racial intermingling and personal relationships on various levels.

In 1915, the year after the completion of the Panama Canal, the newly founded Rockefeller Foundation took over the mosquito campaign and launched a worldwide program to study and control mosquitoes all over the planet—transnational corporate philanthropy with a militaristic twist: "Disease was to be defeated not by improved social conditions or medical intervention but by the physical elimination of the enemy species."[23]

Bee Modern in Donkey Urbanism

While the mosquito stood for all the dangers and unpleasantness of life that colonialists feared, another insect can rightly count as the mosquito's counterpart in the Western imaginary landscapes and especially in the works of Le Corbusier: the honeybee.

The supposed subjectivity of bees as hard-working social animals, living as "bee colonies" in orderly organized sociality within self-built architectural city-habitat structures has inspired much visual production and moral reflection since antiquity. As a state-like, condensed vertical structure in an open garden-like space, the beehive was also regularly depicted by Le Corbusier and employed as part of his visual and conceptual vocabulary. The beehive appears in Le Corbusier's *Urbanisme* from 1925 on a two-page montage of six images on page 166. The left page shows three pictures: the patio of the royal palace, one of park scenery, and one of the Tuileries. Three city maps are found on the right page: the area around the Tuileries, a section of Le Corbusier's "city of today," and a part of the Champs-Élysées. The picture of the garden on the left and the map of Le Corbusier's plan are both bigger in size and centrally placed between the two other pictures below and above them.

The visual rhetoric of arrangement gives these two pictures an eminent and elevated position: the ideal city and its map. The picture of the garden shows a slightly wild park in Paris—the Park Monceau. The only non-organic structure in the park is a little white box in the left part of the picture that is slightly elevated above the grass by stilts. The only architectural structure on Le Corbusier's picture of the ideal city fit for today's needs is—a modern beehive: "Le Corbusier's suggestions for town planning, in brief, can be summed up as an intention to concentrate the population in compact dwelling blocks, off the ground and separated from each other by space and natural vegetation. Is it any surprise then that this type of ideal city was conceived with the apiary as the model?"[24]

But Le Corbusier had his own mosquito: the donkey. The first pages of Le Corbusier's *Urbanisme* start with the Manichean enemy of Le Corbusier and his Modulor: the pack donkey, whose monstrous agency supposedly produced

19 Spitzer, "The Mosquito and Segregation in Sierra Leone," 52–54.
20 Philip D. Curtin, "Medical Knowledge and Urban Planning in Tropical Africa," *The American Historical Review* 90, no. 3 (June 1985): 602.
21 Ibid., 608.
22 Sheldon Watts, "British Development Policies and Malaria in India 1897–1929," *Past & Present*, no. 165 (November 1999): 141–81.
23 Harriet Deacon, "Racial Segregation and Medical Discourse in Nineteenth-Century Cape Town," *Journal of Southern African Studies* 22, no. 2 (June 1996): 287–308.
24 Mitchell, *Rule of Experts: Egypt, Techno-politics, Modernity*, 26.

paths en passant that laid the original maps for the topology of all great European cities. According to the architectural mastermind, London, Paris, and Rome are all haunted by the spirits of the lazy beast of burden. Le Corbusier argues that the pack donkey's non-linear paths are the reason for their congestion and inefficient temporalities of movement.

In her reflections on *The Burdens of Linearity*, architectural theorist Catherine Ingraham asks why animals, beasts of burden to be precise, played such an important role at crucial points in both Claude Lévi-Strauss's and Le Corbusier's writing. In both cases, real and imaginary animals suddenly came up when questions of controlled spatiality and its transgression were topical. Her assumption is that the contrast of urbanist or architectural lines and animal paths "offered a certain resistance to the various tactics of ideality. [...] In this scheme, linearity—an ideal system based on the same 'passage to the limit' that pure geometry is based on—must be perpetually won away, through philosophical means (Cartesian intellectualism, for example), from animality, irrationality, impropriety, disease, and death."[25]

Le Corbusier may have made his peace with the donkey at the end of his life in Chandigarh. According to a local worker, Le Corbusier was so thankful for the labor of the working animal, without which the city never could have been built, that he even thought about erecting a donkey monument as a symbol of his gratitude.[26] Be that as it may, the contradiction that industrial aesthetics could only be built with pre-industrial means was solved if not in theory, at least in practice. Le Corbusier and his partners had to find out while building Chandigarh.

A Happily Conscienceless Horde of Parasites

Chandigarh is not just any city. Impressive proof of the power of a young republic with an entire city as a picture of its future, Chandigarh was visited by representatives of other postcolonial states such as Pakistan or Burma, allowing them to draw lessons for their own urban design projects.[27] But the Chandigarh Master Plan had many masters and was by no means the concise plan of a coherent architectural subject, as dominant modes of architectural history still tell the story: "various modernities were involved in the planning of Chandigarh and these were questioned, contested, deconstructed, and reconstructed many times during the planning process."[28]

I would like to pursue a hitherto completely neglected aspect of the planning and architectural history of the City Beautiful: the role of nonhuman actors, mainly cows, in the postindependence process. The Indian independence movement was able to celebrate the liberation from the yoke of colonial power in 1947. Shortly after, the birth of the republican successor states of Pakistan and India led to massive shifts in the social, political, cultural, and economic tectonics within and between the two sibling states. The new border suddenly ran across the state of Punjab; Lahore, the capital—and the cultural center of India since the Mughal period—fell to Pakistan, and the rest of the economically important state was divided between the two countries. In the midst of riots and violence, twelve and a half million people had to flee—the Muslims towards Pakistan, the Hindus in the opposite direction. In the Chandigarh City Museum, which provides information about the planning and building process of the city in a permanent exhibition, the story of Chandigarh starts with large-scale photography of the expulsion and flight of Hindus from Pakistan. Many hundreds of thousands of refugees rejected state trains that were protected by the Indian security forces and chose the difficult and dangerous trek on foot. Otherwise they would have had to leave their dairy cows behind. The depiction of the immediate history of the founding of the city shows the small-scale farmers with their cows as a "companion species," their relationships being torn apart and remade in the postcolonial dynamics.[29]

The attractiveness of Chandigarh clearly lies in its greenness. City Beautiful, the official municipal name for Chandigarh, not only refers to the topology of spacious and well-maintained roads, but also to the vegetation that was planted along the highways and within sectors. But apart from very general statements by Le Corbusier concerning the color and size of the plantings, the local landscape designers had a free hand.[30] Probably the most important actor in this context was the Indian official, M. S. Randhawa, the chairman of the Landscaping Committee during the construction of Chandigarh and later in the country's capital, New Delhi. Randhawa's contribution to the aesthetics of Chandigarh is considered as important as those of the European architects.

A problem plagued Randhawa and the Landscaping Committee since the first plantings, according to meetings that Le Corbusier and his brother attended with regularity: stray cattle, mainly cows, who feasted on the imported exotic plants and often rested on the roadside or directly on the street. The Landscaping Committee meeting minutes show ongoing problems concerning

25 Juan Antonio Ramírez, *The Beehive Metaphor: From Gaudí to Le Corbusier* (London: Reaction, 2000), 123.

26 Catherine Ingraham, *Architecture and the Burdens of Linearity* (New Haven: Yale University Press, 1998), 85.

27 Vibhor Mohan, "Corbusier Wanted a Donkey Monument," *The Times of India*, September 11, 2010.

28 Madhu Sarin, *Urban Planning in the Third World: The Chandigarh Experience* (London: Mansell Publishing, 1982); Ravi Kalia, *Chandigarh: The Making of an Indian City* (New York: Oxford University Press, 1999).

29 Nihal Perera, "Contesting Visions: Hybridity, Liminality and Authorship of the Chandigarh Plan," *Planning Perspectives* 19, no. 2 (2004): 75–199.

30 Donna Haraway, *When Species Meet* (Minneapolis: University of Minnesota Press, 2006).

stray cows, often in connection with their local owners, and they employed different analyses of the problem, seeking different solutions in order to handle this problem during construction and afterward.[31]

As was typical of modernist city planning, agricultural use of animals was forbidden in the city; an exception was the 500-acre residential buildings in the far north. Residents of these prestigious estates had permission to own a dairy cow; containers for the collection and disposal of cow dung were built in modernist aesthetics. Before long this exemption was eliminated.

Because the city was mainly used for bureaucrats who lived there and worked for three territorial administrative units in the early years, the Indian technocrats were not pleased by stinking dung—neither from the stray cattle nor the modernist containers in front of the villas. Stray cows were also an obstacle to governmental automobile traffic.

The idea of a garden city that should soften or resolve the contradictions between country and city in the form of integrated landscape design was never intended in Chandigarh, where a zone of several kilometers around the city was free of settlements and commercial activities were prohibited. In the course of various phases, refugees and immigrants built settlements in and around Chandigarh, many allowing space for dairy cows.

Given the fact that Chandigarh had been built against the opposition of the local rural population, it may be not surprising that the Landscaping Committee resorted to state violence to solve the problem of stray cows. Point sixteen, the last item on the agenda of the Landscaping Committee meeting on April 24, 1954, proposed the "destruction of all remaining villages" as the final solution to the "stray cattle" problem. As a result of the rapidly growing success of peasant militants who joined forces in socialist collectives, this vision proved to be unrealistic. In addition, newcomers quickly founded new village-like settlements around Chandigarh with their cows never too far away.

In the following years, the Landscaping Committee considered fencing in the city as a whole, but this urbanist anti-cow approach proved futile; the construction of the fence would have consumed the Landscaping Committee's entire budget. The plants would have been saved, but no money for the planting itself would have remained. The fence was not an issue anymore, but the Landscaping Committee under the directorship of Randhawa succeeded in reassigning one school building to function as a "cattle pond." Captured stray cattle were held temporarily in the former school and only handed over to the rightful owners after they paid a fine. Since the penalty was quite low, this measure had limited success. Moreover, the unclaimed animals had to be provided with food, which also created unexpected costs.

Having the animals killed by state officials was never really an option, even less so in postcolonial India. In 1955, the local government had passed the Punjab Prohibition of Cow Slaughter Act, which punished the intentional killing of cows with two years of prison. In an ethnically and religiously heated political climate, the cow was rediscovered as a "national animal." The idea was to protect the sacred cow from the marauding Muslims, even though it was never clear if any of the few remaining Muslims in Punjab had ever really killed a cow. Until the partition of India, a complex system of division of labor along caste and religious affiliation had existed; this social fabric was torn by the secession and the riots and flights after the partition. Until 1947, Muslim butchers had taken the male calves and older cows and handed the remains over to leather production companies, which were mainly in Hindu hands.[32] Now the Muslims were missing in Punjab to do the job, but hordes of stray cattle were flocking to the city that could not be killed.

At the Landscaping Committee meeting on February 15, 1955, the decision was made to transport unclaimed animals to the distant Kalesar forest. This plan did not work, as the animals were returning to their villages on their own. In the following years, the Landscaping Committee tried to make the city cow-free through different measures. For example, a second "cattle pond" was built, and a separate municipal entity was formed whose job it was to capture the animals wherever they could. At one point, the Landscaping Committee even considered officially rededicating the entire capital area as a forest reserve, because higher penalties could then be imposed on the owners of stray cattle. Finally, the establishment of a Gaoshala, a religiously motivated sanctuary for cows, was established, paid for by private donations. This way cows could be permanently concentrated in one place and the urban area was freed from the unwanted dwellers, strays, and eaters who did not seem to fit into the modernist aesthetics of the City Beautiful.

A comment in the daily newspaper *The Tribune* from July 4, 1959, entitled "COWS – THE GARDEN VARIETY," summarized the stray cattle situation of Chandigarh:

> It would be nice to be a cow. In Chandigarh it certainly would. We have a large population of stray cows who live off the fat of the land without a thought as to whose land it is or whether they have the right. A happily

31 Surindera Singh Bhatti, *Chandigarh and the context of Le Corbusier's "Statute of the Land." A Study of Plan, Action and Reality* (Chandigarh: Panjab University, 1990), 1134.

32 For an analysis of biopower and criminal cows in India, see Anand Pandian, "Pastoral Power in the Postcolony: On the Biopolitics of the Criminal Animal in South India," *Cultural Anthropology* 23, no. 1 (2008): 85–117.

> conscienceless horde of parasites, they have become a part of our way of life. And since nothing whatever is done about them by the authorities, I presume they are also part of the town plan—a kind of primitive charm, to ward off the evil eye from this most modern and perfect of cities.

It was not until the early sixties of the twentieth century that it was possible to tackle the problem of stray cattle in Chandigarh. Up to 900 cows were loaded onto trucks monthly and driven several thousand miles to the south of India. This strategy was ultimately effective; the number of cows in the city dropped (to rise again twenty years later and produce even more noise, but that is another story). By this time, Randhawa had become the top landscaper in New Delhi. In this position he combined efforts to free the public spaces of Chandigarh and New Delhi from cows.

The fact that the cows felt attracted to the cityscape and resisted removal is certainly due to the availability of food sources and its diversity in the city, especially the buffet of exotic vegetation provided by the Landscaping Committee. Local farmers and the authorities responsible for stray cattle control agreed, however, that the cows stayed in the city because they were plagued by mosquitoes, especially in the morning and evening hours. Few mosquitoes were found at the roadsides and on the streets, and the movement of cars produced pleasant artificial ventilation.

But the cow dung and the mosquitoes accompanying the dung not only caused aesthetic concerns in the city; they seemed to produce medical hazards. Manure provided the ideal breeding conditions for mosquitoes as a cause of fatal malaria. The cow is and was part of a whole culture; only a few kilometers away from the city, diametrically opposed convictions were found. Once a year in the rural villages around Chandigarh the ground floor of the dwellings were and still are treated with a mixture of cow products, including manure. This is supposed to guarantee happiness for a year and protect against mosquitoes. The concrete and bricks of Chandigarh are not suitable for this treatment nor was it wished that the materials of a new area should be chronopolitically polluted with these remnants of a pre-modern era. The villages were called "*cucha* villages," referring to their building practice using unburned bricks. But the subjects and their webs of cultural production of meaning and social interconnectivity did not conform to the purity of plans and ideas. A report from the beginnings of Chandigarh illustrates this point:

> At the time when the first housing designs were developed, the architects tried to interview the government employees and their wives to seek their opinion about the house plan for their category. A government official's wife objected to the designs because there was no provision for a wall-

> surface on which cow dung cakes could be plastered. When she was told that in Chandigarh she would not be allowed to keep a cow in her house, she was outraged. What was the point in becoming a government official if you could not have the prestige of keeping a cow?[33]

The stray cattle of Chandigarh still enter and leave the City Beautiful every day at dusk and dawn through the area of the new IT park that functions as the cows' entryway into the city. They were in the city before there was a city; they have struggled with planners and their agencies, and still are here to make the city what every city is—a multi-species habitat consisting of many multi-species habitats, neither innocent nor wholly holy, but part of human living since the beginning of cities and settlements.

33 S. P. Gupta, *The Chandigarh* (Chandigarh: ESS PEE Publication, 2010).

Literature

Adams, David P. "Malaria, Labor, and Population Distribution in Costa Rica: A Biohistorical Perspective." *Journal of Interdisciplinary History*, vol. 27, no. 1 (Summer 1996). Cambridge, MA: MIT Press: 75–85.

Bales, Richard F. *The Great Chicago Fire and the Myth of Mrs. O'Leary's Cow*. Jefferson: McFarland, 2002.

Bhatti, Surindera Singh. *Chandigarh and the context of Le Corbusier's "Statute of the Land." A Study of Plan, Action and Reality*. Chandigarh: Panjab University, 1990.

Bruchhausen, Walter. *Medizin zwischen den Welten: Geschichte und Gegenwart des medizinischen Pluralismus im südöstlichen Tansania*. Göttingen: V&R Unipress, 2006.

Bunge, Eric and Juan Antonio Ramirez. "Bee Modern: An Interview with Juan Antonio Ramirez." *Cabinet: A Quarterly of Art and Culture, Animals*, no. 4 (2001). http://www.cabinetmagazine.org/issues/4/bunge.php.

Carter, Eric D. "'God Bless General Perón': DDT and the Endgame of Malaria Eradication in Argentina in the 1940s." *Journal of the History of Medicine and Allied Sciences*, vol. 64, no. 1 (2008): 78–122.

Chandra, Bipan, Mridula Mukherjee, and Aditya Mukherjee. *India After Independence*. New Delhi: Penguin Books, 1999.

Cronon, William. *Nature's Metropolis: Chicago and the Great West*. New York: W. W. Norton, 1991.

Curtin, Philip D. "Medical Knowledge and Urban Planning in Tropical Africa." *The American Historical Review*, vol. 90, no. 3 (June 1985): 594–613.

Deacon, Harriet. "Racial Segregation and Medical Discourse in Nineteenth-Century Cape Town." *Journal of Southern African Studies*, vol. 22, no. 2 (June 1996): 287–308.

Evenson, Norma. *Chandigarh*. Berkeley: University of California Press, 1966.

Frenkel, Stephen and John Western. "Pretext or Prophylaxis? Racial Segregation and Malarial Mosquitos in a British Tropical Colony: Sierra Leone." *Annals of the Association of American Geographers*, vol. 78, no. 2 (June 1988): 211–228.

Giedion, Sigfried. *Mechanization Takes Command: A Contribution to Anonymous History*. New York: Oxford University Press, 1948.

Guillemin, Jeanne. "Choosing Scientific Patrimony: Sir Ronald Ross, Alphonse Laveran, and the Mosquito-Vector Hypothesis for Malaria." *Journal of the History of Medicine and Allied Sciences*, vol. 57, no. 4 (October 2002): 385–409.

Gupta, S.P. *The Punjab*. Chandigarh: ESS PEE Publication, 2004.

Gupta, S.P. *The Chandigarh*. Chandigarh: ESS PEE Publication, 2010.

Gerhardt, Christina. "The Ethics of Animals in Adorno and Kafka." *New German Critique*, vol. 33, no. 1 (Winter 2006): 159–168.

Haraway, Donna. *When Species Meet*. Minneapolis: University of Minnesota Press, 2006.

Higgins, Hannah. *The Grid Book*. Cambridge, MA: MIT Press, 2009.

Horkheimer, Max. "Skyscraper." In *Dawn and Decline: Notes 1926–1931 and 1950–1969*. Translated by Michael Shaw, 66ff. New York: Seabury Press, 1978.

Ingraham, Catherine. *Architecture and the Burdens of Linearity*. New Haven: Yale University Press, 1998.

Jha, D. N. *The Myth of the Holy Cow*. London: Verso, 2002.

Kaika, Maria. "Dams as Symbols of Modernization: The Urbanization of Nature Between Geographical Imagination and Materiality." *Annals of the Association of American Geographers*, vol. 96, no. 2 (2006): 276–301.

Kalia, Ravi. *Chandigarh: The Making of an Indian City*. New York: Oxford University Press, 1999.

Latour, Bruno. *The Pasteurization of France*. Translated by Alan Sheridan and John Law. Cambridge: Harvard University Press, 1988.

Le Corbusier. *The City of Tomorrow and Its Planning*. New York: Dover Publications, 1987.

Lockwood, Jeffrey A. *Six-Legged Soldiers: Using Insects as Weapons of War*. New York: Oxford University Press, 2009.

Mavhunga, Clapperton Chakanetsa. "The Mobile Workshop: Mobility, Technology, and Human-Animal Interaction in Gonarezhou (National Park), 1850–present." Dissertation submitted in partial fulfillment of the requirements for the degree of Doctor of Philosophy (History), University of Michigan, 2008.

McLeod, Marc. "'We Cubans are Obligated Like Cats to Have a Clean Face': Malaria, Quarantine, and Race in Neocolonial Cuba, 1898–1940." *The Americas*, vol. 67, no. 1 (July 2010): 57–81.

McNeill, John Robert. *Mosquito Empires: Ecology and War in the Greater Caribbean, 1620–1914*. Cambridge: Cambridge University Press, 2010.

Mitchell, Timothy. *Rule of Experts: Egypt, Techno-politics, Modernity*. Berkeley: University of California Press, 2002.

Mohan, Vibhor. "Corbusier Wanted a Donkey Monument." *The Times of India* (September 11, 2010).

Oldstone, Michael. *Viruses, Plagues, and History: Past, Present, and Future*. New York: Oxford University Press, 1998.

Pandian, Anand. "Pastoral Power in the Postcolony: On the Biopolitics of the Criminal Animal in South India." *Cultural Anthropology*, vol. 23, no. 1 (2008): 85–117.

Perera, Nihal. "Contesting Visions: Hybridity, Liminality and Authorship of the Chandigarh Plan." *Planning Perspectives*, vol. 19, no. 2 (2004): 75–199.

Protocols of the Landscaping Committee of Chandigarh, Union Territory, 1952–1967.

Ramírez, Juan Antonio. *The Beehive Metaphor: From Gaudí to Le Corbusier*. London: Reaction, 2000.

Sallares, Robert. *Malaria and Rome: A History of Malaria in Ancient Italy*. New York: Oxford University Press, 2002.

Sarin, Madhu. *Urban planning in the Third World: the Chandigarh experience*. London: Mansell Publishing, 1982.

Slater, Leo Barney. "Malarial Birds: Modeling Infectious Human Disease in Animals." *Bulletin of the History of Medicine*, vol. 79, no. 2 (Summer 2005): 261–294.

Sanbonmatsu, John. *Critical Theory and Animal Liberation*. Lanham: Rowman & Littlefield Publishers, 2011.

Spitzer, Leo. "The Mosquito and Segregation in Sierra Leone." *Canadian Journal of African Studies*, vol. 2, no. 1 (Spring 1968): 49–61.

Sutter, Paul S. "Nature's Agents or Agents of Empire? Entomological Workers and Environmental Change During the Construction of the Panama Canal." *Isis*, vol. 98, no. 4 (December 2007): 724–754.

Watts, Sheldon. "British Development Policies and Malaria in India 1897–1929." *Past & Present*, no. 165 (November 1999): 141–181.

Wright, Steve. *Storming Heaven: Class Composition and Struggle in Italian Autonomist Marxism*. London: Pluto Press, 2002.

Yee, Jennifer. "Malaria and the Femme Fatale: Sex and Death in French Colonial Africa." *Literature and Medicine*, vol. 21, no. 2 (Fall 2002): 201–215.

The Tribune. Chandigarh. All issues from 1959.

Interviews (September 2011):
Interview with cattle owners on the outskirts of Chandigarh who preferred to stay anonymous.

Interview with Mr. Surender Kumar Sharma, Municipal Corporation Chandigarh.

Interview with Mr. M.N. Sharma, first chief architect of Chandigarh and associate of Le Corbusier.

Interview with Dr. P.C. Sharma, Government Museum & Art Gallery, Chandigarh.

No Collar, No Master

Workers and Animals in the Modernization of Rio de Janeiro 1903–04*

Nádia Farage

At the beginning of January 1904, a note in the Rio de Janeiro newspaper *A Nação* reported that there had been gunfire at a city slaughterhouse and a circus.[1] A laconic note that might have passed unnoticed were it not for the intriguing connection it establishes, at first sight, between disparate locations. The link between the two is the presence of animals and, from this perspective, the note is an invitation, which I take up here, to reflect upon the codification of the presence of animals in town and the consequent political conflicts during the urban reform of the Brazilian federal capital, Rio de Janeiro, in the first decade of the twentieth century.

Epidemic outbreaks of yellow fever and smallpox throughout the nineteenth century and the bubonic plague at the start of the twentieth, ravaged the port of Rio de Janeiro, resulting in heavy losses to commerce, most notably to coffee exports. In addition to this, in the eyes of the intellectual elite, Rio de Janeiro—with its narrow streets, colonial houses and ridden with epidemics—epitomized the backwardness of the country.
Reacting to this, the newly established republic aimed to reform the capital—following the model of Paris and, more closely, that of Buenos Aires—in order to make it attractive for foreign investment. To further this goal, the federal government designated engineer Francisco Pereira Passos as the mayor of the city and physician Oswaldo Cruz as Director of Hygiene, who had recently arrived from Paris, enthused with Pasteurian theory. Under the direction of both, the rebuilding of the central and port areas of the city was accompanied by sanitary measures to prevent epidemics. While the mayor ordered the old colonial town to be destroyed—an authoritarian process which the local population, the *cariocas*, captured in the expression *bota-abaixo* or "take it down"—hygiene officials entered the slums and fumigated or burned the few belongings of the poor. The whole set of measures—very problematic in terms of constitutional rights—was contemporaneously described as "sanitary despotism."

In the last few decades, this process has been a topic of interest to historiography, which has emphasized the sanitization of society.[2] However, this historiography tells very little about the impact of the sanitization process on the animal population, which was also gravely affected. As microbes or bacteria entered the popular imaginary, so, conversely, cows, pigs, dogs and other

1 *A Nação*, January 10, 1904.
2 Jaime L. Benchimol, *Pereira Passos, um Haussmann tropical: a renovação urbana da cidade do Rio de Janeiro no inicio do seculo XX* (Rio de Janeiro: Departamento Geral de Documentação e Informação Cultural, 1992); Sidney Chalhoub, *Cidade Febril: cortiços e epidemias no Rio de Janeiro Imperial* (São Paulo: Cia das Letras, 1999); Myriam Bahia Lopes, *O Rio em movimento: quadros médicos e(m) história, 1890–1920* (Rio de Janeiro: Fiocruz, 2000); Nicolau Sevcenko, *A revolta da vacina: mentes insanas em corpos rebeldes* (São Paulo: Cosac Naify, 2010).

species were, from that moment, expelled from urban space and rendered invisible to urban dwellers. The sanitary model, which came into being at the start of the twentieth century, would persist thereafter and, in its most aggressive form, would regulate the lives of animals, conceiving of them as commodities the surfeit of which would be disposable in the modern city. Intruders they would be, co-dwellers never more.

The rebuilding of Rio de Janeiro was thus a crucial moment in the establishment of a bio-politics and, for this reason, it constitutes a strategic locus by which the political and ontological disputes around the correlate definitions of animal and human in Brazilian modernity can be envisaged.

Animal Co-Dwellers: A Sketch

Keith Thomas's classic study delineates the gradual movement in England, from the end of the nineteenth to the first decades of the twentieth century, which created the conditions for the subsequent industrial production of animals.[3] Notably, it was due to the expulsion of stock-rearing farms and slaughterhouses to the outskirts of the cities, which veiled the suffering and death of animals from urban sensibilities.[4] As Claude Lévi-Strauss[5] pointed out some time ago, social distance constitutes the symbolic operator by which the animal is transformed into an anonymous multiplicity, exactly describing the condition of animals in modern industrial societies, in sharp contrast to the domestic rearing of animals, which is based upon dense social relations between human and animal.

Such a transition can be detected in the context of the Rio de Janeiro of the beginning of the century. A brief examination of the press of those years presents a picture of a town populated by varied species of animals, mostly domestic ones: advertisements in the newspapers reveal houses with pastures in residential areas, coach houses, barns and widespread urban trade in milking cows and their calves, pigs, chicken, ducks or birds. This can be seen, for example, in the advertisements of the daily *Correio da Manhã* in the beginning of the year 1903:

> For sale—a heifer, first pregnancy two months ago, very cheap. Contact at Catumby St, 5.
> For sale—a small donkey, young, and very tame. It is perfect. Price 140$000. Frei Caneca St, 200.[6]

Or,

> For sale—excellent cows, Cerqueira Lima St, 24, Riachuelo station.
> For sale—a beautiful dapple-grey horse, a young pacer. Contact at Dias da

> Cruz St, 35, Meyer.
> For sale—a Zebu ox, to see and contact at Botafogo Beach, 170, hotel.[7]

It is also necessary to mention that dogs and donkeys, especially the latter, worked to complete exhaustion in public transport systems and were constantly replaced.[8] In addition, there were worn out cattle that crossed the town to die in the urban slaughterhouses, the cirques and even sporadic bullfighting in the residential area of Laranjeiras:[9]

> Tauromachy: It will be the last of the season, the bullfighting announced for tomorrow, in the bull ring at Larangeiras. The funds will be for the charity benefit of the Asylum of N. S. Auxiliadora. The public, for sure, will not leave an empty seat in the bull arena.[10]

Large houses in residential areas were often advertised as including pasture for grazing, for example:

> For sale [...] 22$000 a house with many rooms in the center of an expansive property, just two minutes from the Engenho Novo station [...] On the property there are many fruit trees and pasture for three or four animals.[11]

And, in order to get a plausible image of the presence of animals in town the sight of the "continuous flight of insects" on the meat exhibited for sale at the streets must also be mentioned.[12]

When raising so-called farm animals in town was forbidden in January 1903, a significant number of accusations and complaints were presented to the municipality targeting piggeries, barnyards, and coach houses in residential areas of the town.[13] Although the complaints may have veiled existing quarrels between neighbors, they are still telling of the conspicuous presence of animals in town.

3 Keith Thomas, *O homem e o mundo natural: mudanças de atitude em relação às plantas e os animais, 1500–1800* (São Paulo: Companhia das Letras, 1988).

4 See also Coral Lansbury, *The Old Brown Dog: Women, Workers and Vivisection in Edwardian England* (Madison: University of Wisconsin Press, 1985).

5 Claude Lévi-Strauss, *O Pensamento Selvagem* (São Paulo: Cia Ed.Nacional, 1976); see also, Elisabeth de Fontenay, *Le silence de bêtes: la philosophie à l'epreuve de l'animalité* (Paris: Fayard, 1998).

6 *Correio da manhã*, January 3, 1903.

7 *Correio da manhã*, January 4, 1903.

8 Francisco Pereira Passos, *Mensagens do Prefeito lidas na Sessão do Conselho Municipal* (Rio de Janeiro: Typographia da Gazeta de Notícias, 1903–1907).

9 Bullfighting and other animal fights for public entertainment were forbidden in Brazil by Federal Decree n.16.590 in 1924.

10 *Correio da manhã*, January 3–4, 1903.

11 *Correio da manhã*, January 8, 1903.

12 Pereira Passos, *Mensagens do Prefeito lidas na Sessão do Conselho Municipal*, 7.

13 *Livro de Queixas e Reclamações da Municipalidade do Rio de Janeiro*, Arquivo Geral da Cidade do Rio de Janeiro, 1903.

Indeed, besides the obvious exploitation of animal labor, which fed and moved the town, we can assume that the co-residence and social proximity of animals made it difficult to reduce them, in their condition and being, solely to commodities. This is manifest in the touching description of the suburbs of Rio de Janeiro by the Brazilian writer Lima Barreto in early 1900:

> The most distant streets from the line of the Central Railway are full of patches of grass and weed, on which families place clothes to bleach under the sun. From morning to evening, the terrain is populated by all kinds of small domestic animals: hens, ducks, teals, goats, sheep, and pigs, not to mention dogs which fraternize with all of them.
>
> In the evening, from every gate sounds a "gathering call": "Mimoso! An owner calls her goat. Sereia! It is a sow that a child beckons home, and so on. Sheep, goats, teals, hens, turkeys—all enter through the front door, cross the length of the house and retire to the backyard.[14]

Lima Barreto witnessed precisely the multifold process that initiated the forced decline of domestic animal rearing, expelling animals from Rio's urban space, as well as the state-sponsored systematic extermination of undesirable animals. Following Foucault,[15] it would be a truism to point out that the definition of undesirable was informed by linkages of the modern medical-sanitary project and the architectural plans for the city: as a necessary correlate, the new aesthetics had a new ethical codification, which aimed to create a "clean" social space.

The Pest and the Stray

At the outset was the battle against flies, which had been targeted as transmitters of yellow fever. In a chronicle of 1903, Lima Barreto[16] satirized the campaign, by investing the fly with a narrative voice to describe its fatal encounter with a young dandy physician with thick black hair—a caricature of Oswaldo Cruz—who, tormented by a fly for one night, had sworn eternal revenge against the species. Indeed, the campaign against yellow fever was understood as a war, which was mirrored in the vocabulary used to refer to it: as mentioned before, anti-fly squads were organized to fumigate all the slums, pensions and dwellings of the poor in central areas of the city.

At the same time, due to the bubonic plague, a program aimed at exterminating rats and mice was put in place. Oswaldo Cruz had previously tested his techniques to combat the plague in the port of Santos between 1899 and 1900. According to his own report, he adopted the same technique deployed by the Americans in Philippines, which encouraged the population to hunt rats and mice.[17] The Hygiene Directory offered a small sum of money as an incentive for each animal delivered. The purchase of rats and mice by the State, although viewed with suspicion by the population,[18] actively engaged the poor quarters of the city. However, this trade in rodents left space for private rearing and brokers: a broker from the nearby town of Niterói became sadly famous for charging the municipality the then significant sum of 8,000 Réis for the delivery of a consignment of mice.[19] As early as February 1903, critical references to the bio-medical combat against mice, and the corresponding experimental bacteriological research on the plague, appear in the carnival parade: in a masquerade ball hosted by Lucinda Theatre, a guinea pig and two rats were mixed in among the clowns and Adonis and Venus callipygia.[20] The carnival of 1904 took up the topic again with its polka "Rato-Rato" (Rat-Rat), which was a big hit that year. A rough translation of the lyrics is as follows:

> Rat, rat, rat
> For what reason did you gnaw my kist?
> You, insolent and malevolent rascal
> Rat, rat, rat
> I shall see your last day
> Will the trap haunt you
> And satisfy my want
> Who conceived of you?
> No other than the devil, you'd better believe it!
> Who gave you life?
> It was a mother-in-law at death's door
> Who created you?
> It was revenge, I guess
> Rat, rat, rat
> Messenger of the Jew
> When the trap is sprung
> You, cowardly monster,
> Do not come with your kikiki, please

14 A. H. Lima Barreto, *Clara dos Anjos, Prosa Seleta* (1904) (Rio de Janeiro: Nova Aguilar, 2001), 691–92.

15 Michel Foucault, *Vigiar e Punir: nascimento da prisão* (Petrópolis: Vozes, 1987).

16 Lima Barreto, "Memórias de um stegomya fasciata. (1903)," in *Toda Crônica*, vol. 1, eds. Beatriz Resende and Rachel Valença (Rio de Janeiro: Agir, 2004), 64–65.

17 Oswaldo G. Cruz, "Relatorio acerca da Molestia Reinante em Santos, apresentado pelo Dr Oswaldo Gonçalves Cruz a S.Ex. o Sr Ministro da Justiça e Negócios Interiores," *Opera Omnia* (Rio de Janeiro: Imp. Brasileira, 1972), 323–72.

18 Nádia Farage, "De ratos e outros homens: resistência biopolítica no Brasil moderno," in *Manuela Carneiro da Cunha: o lugar da cultura e o papel da antropologia*, eds. Claude Lépine et al. (Rio de Janeiro: Ed. Beco do Azougue, 2011), 279–309.

19 Edigar de Alencar, *O carnaval carioca através da música* (Rio de Janeiro: Livraria Freitas Bastos, 1965), 77.

20 *Rio Nu*, February 25, 1903.

Old, impudent gnawing rat
Old rat, you horrify me
I will show you I am wicked
My pence is guaranteed
I will never release you, no matter what.

The polka was apparently inspired by the *jota de las ratas* movement of the famous satiric zarzuela *La Gran Via* (1886, by the Spanish maestros Villaverde and Chuenca), which referred to the opening of an avenue in Madrid, displacing thieves, sailors and rats. Irreverent, with an offensive anti-Semitic reference, the polka "Rato-Rato" simultaneously mocked both the rats and the government. The pipe and chorus parodied the peculiar sound of the animals as well as the call of the mice brokers in the streets. One may note that the polka does not make any reference to the disease brought by the rats, but only to the losses caused by mice as co-dwellers—"For what reason do you gnaw my *kist*?" The mice hunt is an act of counter-revenge, but the animal—the child of revenge, the malevolence of the mother-in-law and of the devil—turns to be, at the same time, a commodity: "My pence is guaranteed, I will never release you, no matter what."

No debate on the matter is allowed; useless would be the protest, the "kikiki" of the rat. Indeed, a pragmatic agreement appears to be established between the scientific and popular conceptions of the rat, settling upon a common meaning, although based on different motives, for the notion of a pest animal.

Furthermore, the state's battle against flies or rats was triggered by a demographic calculus, as the priority target for sanitary control was the quantity of animals—further mediated by invisible legions of microbes or bacteria. The war waged against animals was constantly mocked in the press, as can be seen in the satirical newspaper *Rio Nu*:

> Public Health, with the new regulations, will comprise a division consisting of three brigades: killing flies, killing mice and killing dogs, all of them commanded by Dr. O. Cruz in the post of general. The Ministry of War is astonished.[21]

This scornful note makes a point, however, about the alignment of the animals targeted for elimination—it highlights the link established by demography. Indeed, it seems that it is the countless number of animals that equalizes different species—and different inter-species relationships—in the same classificatory position of "pest." This is the route through which the elimination or expulsion process reached the domestic animals, those socially closer species that Donna Haraway has rather optimistically designated as "companion species."[22] The reality is that from 1903 on, the demographic control of animal populations in the streets—be they rats, dogs or cows—was, significantly, the responsibility of the Public Cleansing Department.

The regulation of the presence of animals in urban space was not a unique initiative of the Republican period. Indeed, a municipal by-law of September 11, 1838, had already set up detailed laws on the movement of cattle, their slaughter and commerce in fresh meat, as well as the movement of horses and donkeys.[23] The same by-law forbade the rearing of pigs and goats in yards, and dogs from wandering the streets. In 1892, the Municipality of Rio de Janeiro addressed the issue of dogs once more making their registration obligatory: unaccompanied dogs should be collected by the Municipality and sent to scientific laboratories for experiments.[24] The very notion of the "stray," as one can see, emerged from these rules and political practices. The law was never enforced, however, during the nineteenth century. It was the project of urban renewal, which consolidated the modern ethical project that created the conditions that led to the fulfillment of the legislation's attempt.

New Customs, Old Laughter

Nicknamed "The Perfect"—a good-humored corruption of the Portuguese *prefeito* ("prefect," or more correctly, mayor)—Pereira Passos passed legislation governing animals as one of his first acts of governance on January 6, 1903. There's nothing like a Kings' Day to start a career of a vice-king, opined a "lettre d'un missiu" to the mayor in intentionally broken French.[25]

The decree of January 6, 1903 included amendments to the Code of 1838 that prescribed the rearing, the transit and the commercialization of animals, dead or alive, in town. Thus, the movement of cows in urban areas, and door-to-door milking, which was a customary practice of the time, were forbidden: "I also abolished the rustic practice of milking cows in public streets, as the cows were covering the paths with their dejecta, scenes that certainly no one will judge proper to a civilized city."[26]

Furthermore, the new regulations controversially prescribed that hygiene officers inoculate cattle against tuberculosis and the inspection of livestock, be it for milk or slaughter.

21 *Rio Nu*, January 9, 1904.
22 Donna Haraway, *The Companion Species Manifesto: Dogs, People and Significant Otherness* (Chicago: Prickly Paradigm Press, 2003).
23 In *Código de Posturas, Leis, Decretos e Editaes da Intendência Municipal do Districto Federal*, 1894 (Rio de Janeiro: Papelaria e Typographia Mont'Alverne).
24 *Jornal do Commercio*, August 25, 1892.
25 *Rio Nu*, January 7, 1903.
26 Pereira Passos, *Mensagens do Prefeito lidas na Sessão do Conselho Municipal*, 7.

In the case of milk, the regulations aimed to avoid its adulteration with water—a practice that the newspaper *Rio Nu* playfully said to be "homeopathic dynamisation." This was also done to prevent commerce in milk from cows affected by tuberculosis, of which there were a considerable number at the time. The obligatory sanitary inspection of slaughterhouses aimed to both control cattle diseases and to prevent the deterioration of meat sold by street vendors. The regulations that prescribed the inspection of live animals on government premises gave rise to long judicial disputes with private slaughterhouses. Nevertheless, the official statistics demonstrate that cattle failed to pass the inspections not so much due to transmissible diseases,[27] but due to malnutrition or traumas from long trips on foot or in closed train wagons with no food or water for days, as they often came from distant estates or even neighboring Uruguay. Many were dead on arrival.[28]

The same regulations stipulated that the slaughter of cattle could only take place in public butcheries which were then slowly moving to the periphery of the city, in order, it was maintained, to avoid the stampede of cattle in the streets, then a common occurrence, causing the city dwellers great alarm and perhaps some concern for the terrified animals, which often sought refuge in nearby houses and even churches.[29]

In this regard, referring to municipal prohibitions on the slaughter of cattle and meat commerce in Rio, the libertarian periodical *Gazeta Operaria* was the only voice to boldly state: "As a matter of ideas and sentiments, we are against those who eat corpses..."[30]

This strong stance is detailed further below. Yet, the banishment of dairy cows from urban spaces caused perplexed, if not indignant reactions in the press. On January 7, 1903, the *Rio Nu* newspaper commented that the "Supreme Intendant" had forbidden "the cow men to deliver milk door to door, claiming that some of the tamed cows they lead might be bitten by a wild one." The comic aspect of the comment relied upon double entendres, as in the pornographic patois of the time, "unruly cows"—or in general, "cattle"—were coquettes or prostitutes. In the same vein, johns and pimps were *marchands*, the cattle merchants; brothels were the "slaughterhouses" and, in the continued metaphor, sexual intercourse was referred to as "slaughter." Betrayed husbands were referred to as the "oxen."[31]

Sparse notes in the press reveal that the population contested the prohibition. An article in *Rio Nu* reports:[32]

> A few days ago a young man led his aunt's cow to pasture [...] when a Municipal Officer decided to imprison him and take the animal to the pound, despite the fact that the young man swore that he was not a milk dealer.

> The zealous municipal authority would have had his way, if, while many curious assistants debated the fact, the smart boy had not run, pulling the cow along with him, to take refuge in his grandmother's pasture, few steps from the scene of the event.

Popular reaction targeted not only cows. The use of horses and donkeys for transportation, on which public and cargo transporters depended, was then taxed at three thousand Réis per head. This was undoubtedly the main reason for a coachmen and carriers' strike in January 1904, which made waves in the city's political waters. I shall return to this point further below. For now, it is sufficient to note that the carriers claimed that the tax made their labor more vulnerable to exploitation, as most of them were employees. It did not pass unnoticed, as stated in the press, that the tax also led to a hyper-exploitation of animals, whose owners, in order to evade the tax and protect their interests, cut back on the number of animals used to carry out their operations and even reduced their feed—whips were the only abundance these animals knew, as the owners sought to extract more work from the fewer animals available.

Finally, it is necessary to mention the rabid—excuse the unavoidable pun—campaign Pereira Passos launched against dogs in the city. Municipal regulations required all dogs in the city to be registered, upon payment of a prescribed fee. In addition, a fine was levied on owners who allowed dogs to roam freely. Sheep dogs were the only exception, which, if properly registered could wander the streets by themselves. Thus, the rules imposed yet another tax on the population; and those who could not afford the tax ran the risk of having their dogs taken from them. The data shows that the tax on dog registrations culminated in revenue of 96,701 Réis in 1903, and declined in the subsequent years, indicating that the population either refused or simply could not afford to pay.[33] Abandoned dogs—classified in official documentation as vagrant dogs—were hunted down and exterminated. According to the press, 13,000 dogs were exterminated between 1903 and 1904.[34] Pereira Passos reported the following for the year 1904: "I ordered the urgent capture and elimination of thousands of dogs that strayed near the city, giving to it the repugnant aspect of certain eastern cities and with grave loss to public security and morality."[35]

27 Pereira Passos, *Mensagens do Prefeito lidas na Sessão do Conselho Municipal*.
28 For an analysis of cattle slaughter, see J. V. Gomes Dias, "O rigor da morte: abate humanitário e produção industrial de animais no Brasil contemporâneo," Dissertação de mestrado inédita, IFCH UNICAMP, 2009.
29 For the analogous case of London, in the same period, see Coral Lansbury, *The Old Brown Dog: Women, Workers and Vivisection in Edwardian England* (Madison: University of Wisconsin Press, 1985).
30 *Gazeta Operária*, February 8, 1903.
31 *Rio Nu*, February 25 and 28, 1903.
32 *Rio Nu*, January 17, 1903.
33 Pereira Passos, *Mensagens do Prefeito lidas na Sessão do Conselho Municipal*, 21.
34 *A Nação*, February 14, 1904.
35 Jaime L. Benchimol, "Questões Municipais," [1905] in *Pereira Passos, um Haussmann tropical: a renovação urbana da cidade do Rio de Janeiro no inicio do seculo XX* (Rio de Janeiro: Departamento Geral de Documentação e Informação Cultural, 1992).

As one can well imagine, this moral argument for the elimination of dogs on account of their mating in public provided an endless source of pornographic satire. In a chronicle published by *Rio Nu* on February 14, 1903, the author, pretending to hold a political office, declared in his manifesto that: "No dog may play seesaw in the middle of the streets, without previous knowledge of the municipality officer."

The same newspaper sarcastically reported on January 13, 1904: "Yesterday, the police arrested a couple of dogs for being united in wedlock without license of the Municipality."

The tensions created by the bio-political practices of the state began to culminate and led to a riot against obligatory smallpox vaccination in November 1904, but that will not be pursued here. Let us stick to the mordacious, Rabelaisian laugh of the population during Carnival, which continued beyond the period of the ritual.

In 1904, the Carnival—the acme of cultural critique of the carioca population—would once more, and with renewed vigor, take regulating animal presence in urban areas as its theme: indeed, cows and dogs were not left out of the street parades and carnival balls. It is quite amusing that the masques, incorporating animals in the ritual event, challenged the municipal prohibition and allowed them to circulate at will during the nights of Carnival. In a malicious reference to the town council, the *Fenians*, a carnival association, paraded an allegory under the name "Rats of the Council" with an array of masked dogs, mice and mosquitoes representing "the three chased species."[36] Another association, the Democrats, opened the parade with nothing less than a clarion band of masked *Stegomya fasciata*, the feared mosquitoes; another allegory the Democrats presented under the title "The Hunting Down of Dogs" showed a parade "defending the liberty of dogs."[37] This was probably the parade of "dogs" referred to by R.de Athayde (n.d:214), which, divided between those "registered" and "unregistered," sang this good-humored protest:

> This beautiful cage
> Which comes with no obstacles
> Is the nicest invention
> Of the genial Dr. Passos
> From one extreme to the other of the streets
> Climbing and descending mountains
> Wherever it passes it gathers
> Vagrant dogs
> Always frenetic land
> Unmatched in the whole world
> Wonderful city

> Long live Rio de Janeiro!

It is worth remembering the perfect symmetry between the municipal regulations that targeted animals and those targeting unemployed people or informal workers, as beggars, prostitutes, ruffians, gamblers, street vendors and slum dwellers were also arrested or removed from the central areas of the city. Therefore, it is no coincidence that the Head of Police when reporting on the street riots in November 1904, referred to "vagrants and ragged women" as coming out of "burrows" to set the city awry. This symmetry, along with the political process of animalization it reveals, was the object of a rather Swiftian irony in the pages of *Rio Nu*: "Following what the Prefect has been doing to vagrant dogs, the Head of Police will order the caging of all minors without owners who wander the streets of the city. Well done."[38]

The extreme image of "bare lives," as Giorgio Agamben acutely describes it, are animal lives. Thus conceived, within the bio-political calculus that is under consideration here, "bare life" is also "excess life"— the crowd in its uncontrollable numbers, whether they are human or animal.[39]

However, from a popular point of view, bio-political symmetry seems to have produced solidarity as a counterpart: the banishment and elimination of animals invoked a range of responses, from cultural comment to popular reaction.

Freedom for Piety

Indeed, not only cultural critics challenged the "sanitary despotism" of the time. Official documentation from the period reveals evidence of workers who took direct action to free captured animals. The complaints register of the municipality for the year 1903 includes this entry:

> Yesterday at about eleven o'clock, the dog collection cart arrived here, accompanied by a squad of Municipal Officers, who seized a large number of dogs, some belonging to workers in the textile factory. As they were leaving and passing the gates of the factory, the cart was attacked by the workers, who liberated all the encaged dogs. As a result of these events, the fiscal officer arrived at the place, looking for soldiers to arrest the workers, who already had returned to their work in the factory [...]
> At the gate of the factory, the officer insisted that the soldiers invade the factory to arrest the workers who had released the dogs and who were

36 *Correio da Manhã*, February 18, 1904.
37 Ibid.
38 *Rio Nu*, January 6, 1904.
39 Giorgio Agamben, *The Open: Man and Animal* (Stanford: Stanford University Press, 2004).

back at their work, which the soldiers refused to do, alleging they could not be ordered by a civilian authority.[40]
(Casern of the Sixth Policial Post in the 4th of October of 1903.
[signed] Pedro Manoel de Souza, Commander)

The coachmen and carriers' strike in January 1904, mentioned above, is undoubtedly another exemplary instance of worker solidarity with animals. "*Vira a joça*" ("dump the trash") was the call of the strikers and the picketers as they proceeded to overturn and immobilize carts and trolleys around the city. However, it is quite significant that when the strike erupted, the first target was a dog collection cart, which was broken into to free the animals.[41] It seems that the action was supported by the population, as the press also reported another dog collection cart being dumped and the dogs released in a different sector of the town on the same day.[42]

Based on the documentary evidence of the time, the practice of releasing dogs was indeed a recurrent event in those turbulent years. Even the prefect acknowledged this, reporting that he had to order a police escort "in order to prevent the populace from destroying the carts collecting vagrant dogs."[43] This case is diametrically opposed to those of the classical studies of E. P. Thompson and Robert Darnton,[44] where animals appear as a sign of bourgeois power in class struggle. British historiography, from the 1980s on, had already formed strong counter examples to Darnton's bourgeois cats, pointing out that the first actions against bull-baiting came from workers in the manufacturing city of Birmingham, and that during the nineteenth century the British humanitarian movement's multifold struggle against cruelty to animals was deeply rooted in workers' associations. Regrettably, British historians tended to read the humanitarian movement as a surrogate for class struggle rather than an ideology in its own right.[45]

In the first years of the twentieth century in Rio de Janeiro, as elsewhere, workers may have seen their own destitute lives mirrored in the persecution of animals. However, I suggest that the acknowledgment of similitude was not confined to this, but overflowed and brought about active resistance in defense of the existence of animals *tout court*. In other words, if bio-power symbolically equated animals with poor men, the workers' reaction was not to negate the equation, but to creatively turn it into a struggle for life. I argue that to a certain extent the intelligibility of such resistance relied on naturist ideas present in the workers' circles of Brazil at the time.

Naturism had its origins in French anarchism at the end of the nineteenth century and spread via international anarchist links to South America, mainly through periodicals published in Catalunya. So the very idea of interspecies solidarity was not alien to Brazilian libertarianism, as it was a pervasive assumption in all currents that, between the end of the nineteenth to the first decades of the twentieth centuries, claimed human freedom would only be attained by putting an end to production and returning to nature.

In broad terms, libertarian naturism affirmed that capitalism had corrupted the human condition by taking it so far from nature. Hence the struggle against capitalism demanded the eschewal of all technologies, generally speaking, of the artificial. Human beings, it was asserted, should go back to nature, to live side by side with other living beings. This general principle became a primary mark of difference, separating naturists from communists and even anarchists, because the concept of revolution of the latter two still retained the line of production, raising the objection from the naturists that production would always produce slaves. Returning to nature was apparent in a variety of practices such as vegetarianism (or a kind of veganism *avant la lettre*, refusing the consumption of all animal by-products), crudivorism, nudism, and in gathering fruits instead of agriculture.

Two periodicals in Rio de Janeiro spread libertarian naturist ideas: *Gazeta Operária*, published in the years 1900 through 1903 and 1906, and *A Vida*, published in the years 1914 through 1915. They appeared alongside the pamphleteering work of anarchist Eugenio George and writer Lima Barreto, the latter of whom was strongly influenced by Tolstoi and Kropotkin.

Peter Kropotkin's *Mutual Aid*, published in London in 1902, provided a sound theoretical basis for the idea of solidarity among species, for solidarity was a factor of evolution in his argument. Far from Darwin's idea of the predator as the most fit, Kropotkin argued that the most fit were bands of beings who helped each other against a hostile environment, an argument he held to be valid in relation to humans (be they primitive or peasant communities, or anarchist collectivities) as well as animals. The concept of solidarity in Kropotkin, as the author acknowledges, is equivalent to the notion of piety in Rousseau—a natural feeling which is present in all living and sentient beings. Inverting the poles of social Darwinism, which extends nature to social categories, Kropotkin reads the relationship among species as a field of intense sociality, a solidarity network against nature, a concept he confined to climatic or geological

40 *Livro de Queixas e Reclamações da Municipalidade do Rio de Janeiro*, 89–90.
41 *A Nação*, January 10, 1904.
42 *Correio da Manhã*, January 10, 1904.
43 Jaime L. Benchimol, "Questões Municipais."
44 E. P. Thompson, *Senhores e Caçadores: a origem da Lei Negra* (Rio de Janeiro: Paz e Terra, 1997); Robert Darnton, *O grande massacre de gatos e outros episódios da história cultural francesa* (Rio de Janeiro: Graal, 1986).
45 James C. Turner, *Reckoning with the Beast: Animals, Pain and Humanity in Victorian Mind* (Baltimore: Johns Hopkins University Press, 1980); David Perkins, *Romanticism and Animal Rights* (Cambridge: Cambridge University Press, 2007).

phenomena. In this line, the author praised the small, anonymous lives based on solidarity, of animals or workers who give their lives for the sake of others.

It seems that the Kropotkian idea of a solidary network of sentient life, when transposed to the industrial and urban ambiance, found its crucial anchorage in domestic species, the ones man "encages for fun, kills for pleasure and subdues to forced labor and torture.[46] In this vein we can understand one of Lima Barreto's melancholic passages in defense of animals: "it is over their suffering, it is over their own lives that we erect ours."[47]

From a naturist point of view, the hyper-exploitation of animal work and life was the ultimate form of slavery that still needed to be abolished. Animal slavery was also human slavery: only in the company of men, "reduced to misery, undernourished, compelled to agglomeration and dirt" do animals live a degraded existence, because human life is degraded by capitalism.[48] On the eve of the war in 1914, the periodical *La Vie Anarchiste* reiterated that human slavery sprang from animal slavery, with the advice: "if you understand that [...] your children will not be prison-fodder."[49] The expression "prison-fodder" eloquently manifests naturist reasoning of a homologous fate of animals and workers in the context of capitalist production.

In this frame, workers' resistance to the expulsion and killing of animals in Rio de Janeiro gains full meaning as a struggle against the commoditization of life. Alas, "piety was held prisoner in the dungeons of repression," as the *Gazeta Operária* remonstrates in 1906, protesting against indifference to the brutal violence towards animals and entreating: "may all living beings emancipate themselves."[50]

It is true that "sanitary despotism" persisted in the control of animal lives in urban space, in the imposition of more miserable conditions on their lives and the strict regulation of their death. It is also true that dogs have not freed themselves of collars, nor have workers freed themselves of masters.

Nevertheless, the struggle for solidarity at the beginning of the twentieth century would endure in popular memory, as we can see in the samba by Alberto Ribeiro, a hit sung by Carmen Miranda during the Vargas dictatorship in 1937:

> I like very much a vagrant dog
> Which walks alone in the world
> With no collar and no master.

The samba points out the burden of class even for animals; while some have lunch and dinner, others have not a bone to chew. But, together with a shared class condition, an echo of past struggles can be heard: a human voice expresses affection and empathy with a vagrant dog, and the vagrant dog in the song—the dog with "no collar and no master"— pays a canine homage to the anarchist slogan "no country and no master."*

46 Eugênio George, *Loucuras da Medicina* (Rio de Janeiro: Pap. Moderna, 1927), 11.

47 A. H. Lima Barreto, *Prosa Seleta: Contos e histórias de animais* [1919], *Coisas do reino do Jambon* [1953] (Rio de Janeiro: Nova Aguilar, 2001), 1020.

48 Eugênio George, *O perigo das vacinas* (Rio de Janeiro: Pap. Moderna, 1927).

49 In *Viva la naturaleza! Escritos libertarios contra la civilización, el progreso y la ciencia (1894–1930)*, ed. J. Rosseló (Barcelona: Virus Editorial, 2008), 68–71.

50 *Gazeta Operária*, December 12, 1906.

* This paper is part of a work in progress on libertarian naturism and anti-vivisection ideas in modern Brazil, granted by FAPESP, the Research Foundation of the State of São Paulo. I thank my students and my colleagues, Sidney Chalhoub and Mauro Almeida, for their useful comments. My special thanks to Derek Matyszak for assistance in the English version.

Literature

Agamben, Giorgio. *The Open: Man and Animal*. Translated by Kevin Attell. Stanford: Stanford University Press, 2004.

Alencar, Edigar de. *O carnaval carioca através da música*. Rio de Janeiro: Livraria Freitas Bastos, 1965.

A Nação, January 10 1904; February 14, 1904.

Athayde, Raimundo de. *Pereira Passos, o reformador do Rio de Janeiro*. Ed. A Noite. Rio de Janeiro, n.d.

Bahia Lopes, Myriam. *O Rio em movimento: quadros médicos e(m) história, 1890–1920*. Rio de Janeiro: Fiocruz, 2000.

Benchimol, Jaime L. *Pereira Passos, um Haussmann tropical: a renovação urbana da cidade do Rio de Janeiro no inicio do seculo XX*. Rio de Janeiro: Departamento Geral de Documentação e Informação Cultural, 1992.

Chalhoub, Sidney. *Cidade Febril: cortiços e epidemias no Rio de Janeiro Imperial*. São Paulo: Cia das Letras, 1999.

Código de Posturas, Leis, Decretos e Editaes da Intendência Municipal do Distrito Federal. Rio de Janeiro: Papelaria e Typographia Mont'Alverne, 1894.

Correio da Manhã, January 3-4, 1903; January 8, 1903; February 18, 1904.

Cruz, Oswaldo G. "Relatorio acerca da Molestia Reinante em Santos, apresentado pelo Dr Oswaldo Gonçalves Cruz a S.Ex. o Sr Ministro da Justiça e Negócios Interiores." *Opera Omnia*, 323-372. Rio de Janeiro: Imp. Brasileira, 1972.

Darnton, Robert. *O grande massacre de gatos e outros episódios da história cultural francesa*. Rio de Janeiro: Graal, 1986.

Farage, Nádia. "De ratos e outros homens: resistência biopolítica no Brasil moderno." In *Manuela Carneiro da Cunha: o lugar da cultura e o papel da antropologia*. Edited by Claude Lépine, et al., 279-309. Rio de Janeiro: Ed. Beco do Azougue, 2011.

Fontenay, Elisabeth, de. *Le silence de bêtes: la philosophie à l'epreuve de l'animalité*. Paris: Fayard, 1998.

Foucault, Michel. *Vigiar e Punir: nascimento da prisão*. Petrópolis: Vozes, 1987.

Gazeta Operária, February 8, 1903; December 12, 1906.

George, Eugênio. *Loucuras da Medicina*. Rio de Janeiro: Pap. Moderna, 1927 a.

George, Eugênio. *O perigo das vacinas*. Rio de Janeiro, Pap. Moderna, 1927 b.

Gomes Dias, J. V. "O rigor da morte: abate humanitário e produção industrial de animais no Brasil contemporâneo." Dissertação de mestrado inédita, IFCH-UNICAMP, 2009.

Haraway, Donna. *The companion species manifesto: dogs, people and significant otherness*. Chicago: Prickly Paradigm Press, 2003.

Jornal do Commercio, August 25, 1892.

Kropotkin, Peter. *Mutual Aid: A Factor of Evolution*. London: William Heineman, 1902.

Lansbury, Coral. *The old brown dog: women, workers and vivisection in Edwardian England*. Madison: University of Wisconsin Press, 1985.

Lévi-Strauss, Claude. *O Pensamento Selvagem*. São Paulo: Cia Ed.Nacional, 1976.

Lima Barreto, A. H. "Memórias de um stegomya fasciata. (1903)" In *Toda Crônica*. Edited by Beatriz Resende & Rachel Valença, vol. I, 64-65. Rio de Janeiro: Agir, 2004.

Lima Barreto, A.H. *Clara dos Anjos, Prosa Seleta*. (1904) Rio de Janeiro: Nova Aguilar, 2001.

Lima Barreto, A.H. *Contos e histórias de animais*. (1919) *Coisas do Reino do Jambom*. Prosa Seleta. Rio de Janeiro: Nova Aguilar, 2001.

Livro de Queixas e Reclamações da Municipalidade do Rio de Janeiro. ms. Arquivo da Cidade do Rio de Janeiro, 1903.

Pereira Passos, Francisco. *Mensagens do Prefeito lidas na Sessão do Conselho Municipal*. Rio de Janeiro: Typographia da Gazeta de Notícias, 1903–1907.

Perkins, David. *Romanticism and Animal Rights*. Cambridge: Cambridge University Press, 2007.

Rio Nu, January 7, 17 and 25, 1903; February 14, 1903; January 6, 9 and 13, 1904.

Rosseló, Josep M. (ed.) *Viva la naturaleza! Escritos libertarios contra la civilización, el progreso y la ciencia, 1894–1930*. Barcelona: Virus Editorial, 2008.

Sevcenko, Nicolau. *A revolta da vacina: mentes insanas em corpos rebeldes*. São Paulo: Cosac Naify, 2010.

Thomas, Keith. *O homem e o mundo natural: mudanças de atitude em relação às plantas e os animais, 1500–1800*. São Paulo: Companhia das Letras, 1988.

Thompson, Edward Paul. *Senhores e Caçadores: a origem da Lei Negra*. Rio de Janeiro: Paz e Terra, 1997.

Turner, James. *Reckoning with the beast: Animals, Pain and Humanity in Victorian Mind*. Baltimore: John Hopkins University Press, 1980.

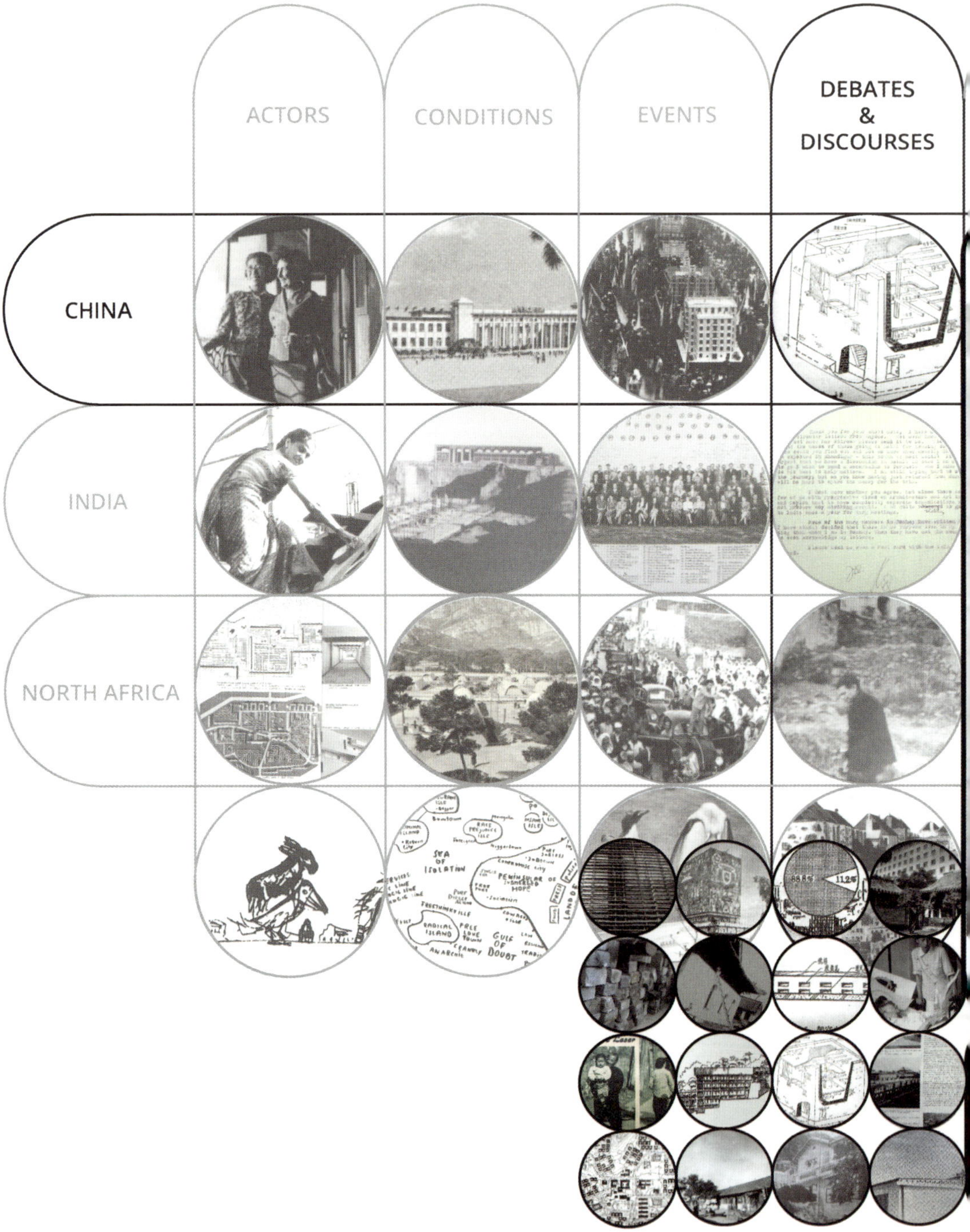
ACTORS
CONDITIONS
EVENTS
DEBATES & DISCOURSES
CHINA
INDIA
NORTH AFRICA

In China

metric projection of a Tibetan house

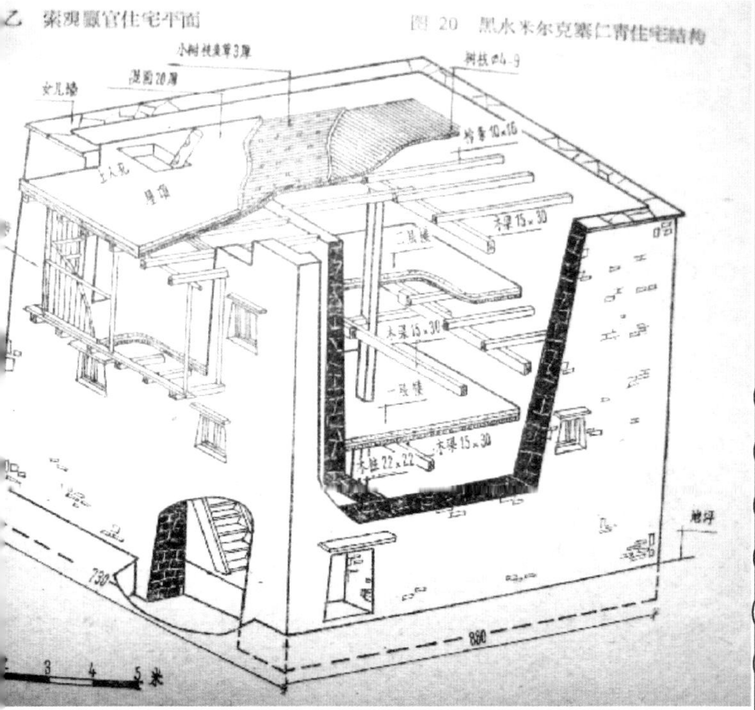

nometric projection of a vernacular Tibetan house as pub-
in the official Chinese architecture magazine Jianzhu Xuebao
early 1960s. The drawing accompanying an article about
onal Tibetan architecture is part of a wider interest and
in regional vernacular architecture among Chinese archi-
n the early 1960s.

In China

Communism

Walking on Two Legs

Vernacular Modernism

Jianzhu Xuebao

Regionalism

Mythopoeic[1] Affairs
The Role of Vernacular Architecture in Maoist China

Christina Linortner

The Role of the Vernacular

In the 1930s architects Lin Huiyin and Liang Sicheng conducted a survey on ancient Chinese temple architecture on behalf of the Society for Research in Chinese Architecture. Both had been educated at Penn School in Philadelphia under a strict Beaux Arts curriculum and spent their honeymoon visiting Italy. The quest to find the oldest and most authentic structures possible led the young upper class architects to the most remote parts of China, and these architectural surveys culminated in Liang Sicheng's publication *Chinese Architecture: A Pictorial History*, which can be regarded as the foundation of Chinese architectural historiography on which basis young architects created a national architectural style in the 1950s.

Traveling had become an integral part of architectural education from the nineteenth century onwards, and when young architecture graduates in Europe and the United States left their academies and their cities and set out on a voyage to the South to experience the Grand Tour, apart from the obligatory itinerary of the classical monuments, inevitably many of the "ordinary" dwellings caught their eye and ended up in sketchbooks.[2] As Paul Overy has stated, the encounter with—and subsequent adoption of—vernacular architecture of the Mediterranean and North Africa into the formal vocabulary by architects not only reflected that "admiration for Middle Eastern vernacular architecture was common among 'progressive' architectural circles in the early years of the twentieth century," but that these "evoked otherness [...] implicit in architectural tours to North Africa and the Middle East."[3] Hence, vernacular architecture has never opposed modern architecture but was a strong sub-current from the beginning.

During their travels in the various provinces, rural vernacular dwellings also drew the attention of the architects Liang and Lin, as is evident from the abundance of archived photographs. Initially, none of these found their way into publication or were studied like the sacred architecture. These images

1 The term mythopoeic is taken from a recent dissertation by Karin Jaschke and understood as she describes it: "as part of an intellectual lineage concerned with nonrational modes of thought and practice explored at different times and in different disciplinary contexts in relation to traditional mythologies, the worldviews and epistemologies of early and small-scale societies, artistic creation, psychological dispositions, and broader philosophical societal constellations, including modern ones." Karin Jaschke, "Mythical Journeys: Ethnography, Archeology, and the Attraction of Tribal Cultures in the Work of Aldo van Eyck and Herman Haan," (PhD Thesis, Princeton University, 2012), 7.

2 Paola Tosolini, "Other Itineraries: Modern Architects on Countryside Roads," *The Journal of Architecture* 13, no. 4 (2008): 427–51.

3 Paul Overy, "White Walls, White Skins: Cosmopolitanism and Colonialism in Inter-War Modernist Architecture," in *Cosmopolitan Modernisms*, ed. Kobena Mercer (Cambridge, MA: MIT Press, 2005), 59.

were published posthumously many years later, after research on vernacular architecture had been institutionalized.[4]

In this article I want to focus on the role of vernacular architecture in China and the different roles it was assigned to in relation to modernist architecture and modernization processes in China in the early communist period after 1949. First, I want to examine how non-Western vernacular architecture became a significant component in Western postwar architectural discourse. Against this backdrop I am going to trace how architects Margarete Schütte-Lihotzky and Werner Hebebrand synchronically developed their own ideas about the role of traditional housing in modernized China on separate visits in 1956 and 1957 with the objective of getting a first-hand picture of the progress of the young socialist country. Secondly, I am going to show what roles were given to vernacular architecture in China at times of economic crisis and fundamental social, political, and cultural transformations. The ambiguity between vernacular building knowledge and the ideas of development in times of Maoist socialism are reflected in the work of architect Hsia Changshi, who utilized a body of research on vernacular architecture in South China's Guangdong Province as a background to build within a formal language derived from European modernism. I also want to give a brief account of a shift towards a new interest in vernacular architecture in China's architecture discourse expressed by one of its main official voices, the architectural magazine *Jianzhu Xuebao*.

Architecture and Traveling

In his seminal essay "Traveling Cultures," James Clifford examined the work of the "normative or ideal-type" ethnographic scope of work by looking at it as a culture of its very own. Shifting the focus and attention from the ethnographer's object of examination towards the underlying conditions and (omitted) context of the "fieldwork"—that in general had been regarded as the essential part of the discipline—has profoundly changed the discipline. Clifford claims that the prioritized standing of fieldwork in anthropology leads to a series of blanks and omissions neglecting, e.g., national contexts, the university home, travel itself, discursive aspects of the work, translations, altogether what Georges Condominas called the "'préterrain', all those places you have to go through and be in relation with just to get to your village or that place of work you will call your field."[5]

As Clifford considered the practical and discursive field of the discipline of anthropology a culture, in the following case study I would like to consider and investigate (the discipline of) modernist architecture not only as a culture but argue that modernist architecture of the twentieth century was also a traveling culture. Forming international networks to push forward the enterprise of modernist architecture, traveling long distances to promote one's individual work to colleagues, attending universities in other countries, undertaking study trips, taking on commissions abroad, etc., had made traveling a significant and vital component of the disciplinary practice.[6] However, this tendency was multiplied through the diverse experiences of forced migration and amplified mobilities during and after the Second World War.

Préterrain I: Charta of Habitat and the Ethnographic Turn

As much as China's architecture production and radical spatial transformation is a topic in today's debates in Western architecture circles, it was just as absent throughout the debates in the 1950s when what has recently been coined an "ethnographic turn" took place in Western postwar modernist architectural discourses.[7] This turn resulted from an increasing discontent with the latest developments in modernist large-scale urban projects and concerns about what direction to take in the future. In particular, the younger generation integrated their interest and research about far away architecture into their professional practice. Aldo van Eyck wrote an editorial for *Forum* magazine about a voyage he had undertaken with his fellow architect Herman Haan to Mali to explore the ancient Dogon settlements in 1951 and 1952. Another instance is a new urban housing typology based on an Indonesian long house and explorations of collective living in Morocco, introduced by Peter and Alison Smithson in 1952 for their Golden Lane Estate competition entry. This tendency towards an increasing interest in non-Western architecture became noticeable at the ninth CIAM (*Congrès International d'Architecture Moderne*) in Aix-en-Provence in 1953 to the older members as well. Sigfried Giedion stated that one of the specific characteristics of this CIAM congress was the "cultural influx of far-flung continents." The three major themes discussed in Aix were first, the shift from a focus on urbanism as manifested in the Charta of Athens towards a concentration of questions of dwelling in the form of a Charta of the Habitat. Second was the role of aesthetics and art, and third, the role of the younger generation of architects within CIAM. In addition, an exhibition by students from a recent "expedition to explore native cultures in Cameroon" showed local architecture, leading Giedion to postulate, "primitive architecture is the direct

4 Wu Liangyong, *Collected Works of Liang Sicheng*, vol. 8 (Beijing: China Architecture & Building Press, 2001).

5 James Clifford, "Traveling Cultures," in *Cultural Studies*, eds. Lawrence Grossberg, Cary Nelson, and Paula Treichler (New York: Routledge, 1992), 100.

6 This might be true for a limited number of the ideal-type architects, as they are represented in specialist literature, monographs, and autobiographies of the protagonists.

7 Jaschke, "Mythical Journeys: Ethnography, Archeology, and the Attraction of Tribal Cultures in the Work of Aldo van Eyck and Herman Haan," 14.

expression of life forms that have been preserved through the course of time deeply rooted in human and cosmological conditions."[8]

CIAM was smitten with their new discovery of this natural dignity of the primitive hut, contrasting with the soulless prefabricated house. Contemporary architecture could regain its humbleness. While Giedion called his essay "Universalismus und Regionalismus" (Universalism and Regionalism), it conveys the idea of the vernacular based in romanticism as "a timeless realm beyond the reach of social tensions or commercial ambitions," emphasizing "indigenous traditions," "authenticity," "folk virtues," and "an idyllic harmony between humans and nature."[9] It is a space opposed to the modern, evoking "the informal, spontaneous use of space unsanctioned by official laws and rules."[10]

Préterrain: And China? Socialist Developmentalism

Despite the novel interest among CIAM protagonists in non-Western culture and although a great number of Chinese architects had studied and worked in Europe, throughout CIAM's existence China does not appear on its map. Entering "China" as a keyword into the CIAM archives does not result in a single hit.[11] After the 1949 communist shift, China's modernization mostly took place outside the scope of the Western architectural focus.

The time of the *Jianshe* (reconstruction), the umbrella term for all phenomena of political, social, and economical nature that emerged during the years of transformation into a socialist state economy signaled a rational realignment of the relationships between state, society, man, and nature and mobilized the individual to participate in this collective project of modernization. [...] In this context a special role was assigned to urban development, urban planning, and the building industry in general; these spheres of activity function as discursive points of intersection where material and metaphoric contexts of meaning of the term Jianshe converge.[12]

After the 1949 revolution and the establishment of the People's Republic of China, architectural modernism was discontinued as a specific architectural form and instead expressed through the broad implementation of centralized and standardized housing and design necessary for the bio-political organization of a socialist life, the adoption of intrinsically modernist concepts such as the American neighborhood unit, the transfer of educational models, and an emphasis on industrial buildings.

The transition of the old China to the new socialist state order was supported by consecutive official political campaigns, each containing countless principles and guidelines. Many of them were directly targeted at issues of housing, construction, and urban planning and reflected the current state of affairs. "Serving production as well as people's livelihoods,"[13] was a slogan of the First Five-Year Plan; during a later period of the same plan it changed to "production first, livelihood second."[14] Towards the end of the Second Five-Year Plan, known as the "three difficult years" (1959, 1960, 1961), the lowering of housing standards was promoted with the slogan "thrifty is revolutionary."

Chinese scholarship and architectural discourse inside China has only very recently taken this period into account, and it is still hardly considered more than a mere reproduction of Soviet planning models in the West. During the first years of building the new China, when the Soviet Union served as a role model for general development, "Learning from the Soviet Union" was promoted not only for urban planning and housing schemes but was also partly implemented on a university level, encouraging the fast training of professional experts. Even though this period is commonly regarded as block-internal colonization, Susanne Stein has shown that transfers of knowledge were neither one nor two directional, but a manifold network of interconnections.

These two discursive sets, including the heated debates about the Charta of Habitat, the crisis of first generation modernism, and the turn towards issues located in and in relation to the non-West is what I would like to call the discursive *préterrain* of Margarete Schütte-Lihotzky and Werner Hebebrand's trip to China in 1956 and 1957.

Traveling to China

In 1956 Margarete Schütte-Lihotzky was invited to China as part of an official Austrian delegation of professionals to learn about the progress of the young

8 Sigfried Giedion, "Habitat," 9. CIAM Kongress, gta Zürich, 1953.

9 Gwendolyn Wright, "On Modern Vernaculars and J.B. Jackson," in *Everyday America: Cultural Landscape Studies After J.B. Jackson*, eds. Chris Wilson and Paul Groth (Berkeley: University of California Press, 2003), 166.

10 Mark Fiege, "Private Property and the Ecological Commons in the American West," in *Everyday America: Cultural Landscape Studies After J.B. Jackson*, eds. Chris Wilson and Paul Groth (Berkeley: University of California Press, 2003), 223.

11 A search in the CIAM archive for China, Chine, Chinese, Chinois and Peking, Shanghai, Nanking neither renders any results in the CIAM collection nor in Sigfried Giedion's correspondence (information from Daniel Weiss, archivist at gta Archiv, ETH Zürich, March 2, 2013).

12 Susanne Stein, "Von der Konsumentenstadt zur Produktionsstadt: Visionen von 'Aufbau' und Urbanisierung im Neuen China, 1949–1957," (PhD Thesis, University of Tübingen, 2008), 5.

13 Junhua Lue, Peter G. Rowe, and Jie Zhang, eds., *Modern Urban Housing in China: 1840–2000*, (New York: Prestel, 2001), 105.

14 Ibid., 106.

communist country.[15] The group traveled to five cities in five weeks in September and October 1956.[16] The itinerary consisted of joint trips and individual arrangements according to the individual professions. The sites of interest—most likely selected by the host, the Chinese People's Association for Cultural Relations with Foreign Countries—consisted mainly of places displaying the country's recent developmental progress such as factories, universities, and a cultural program including a huge political rally on Tiananmen Square.

As a result of this trip, Schütte-Lihotzky adapted the newly gained insights and impressions of China's progress in regard to urban planning and architecture in the manuscript *China's Megacities. A Visual Travel Diary*.[17] The small book gives an impression of the on-going debates and conflicts that arose in urban planning during the first decade of the newly established nation-state and, having been part of designing and building the socialist culture of the Soviet Union almost two decades earlier, Schütte-Lihotzky enthusiastically recognized the social improvements that had taken place since her first visit to China in 1934. But the manuscript is also a firm testament of how Schütte-Lihotzky adored the urban structure of old Beijing and its courtyard houses by referring to it as "one of the most beautiful cities in the world—and as the biggest garden city of the world."[18] Although Schütte-Lihotzky's task was to gain an understanding of the current state of architecture and urban planning during the journey, she was taken with the traditional courtyard house, the *Siheyuan*, and spent a considerable amount of time and effort studying its features in depth. The inherent logic and coherence of traditional Chinese architecture and towns affected Schütte-Lihotzky—otherwise a strict rationalist—in such a way that she spoke almost romantically of its advantages. Addressing the question of how to rebuild China's old cities, Schütte-Lihotzky pleaded for a preservation of "this giant garden city with its wonderful silhouettes of walls, doors, and rolling rooftops." In general, the new regime had not used the old courtyard houses for urban housing schemes. Even though a number of low-rise settlements had been erected after 1949 in Shanghai in the first phase, this typology was later considered a waste of space and subsequently replaced by multi-story buildings. In 1956, in light of the anti-waste campaign, a shift from Soviet row housing schemes to local, economical low-rise courtyard typologies took place, as can be seen in the entries of the 1958 national housing competition. Some of the proposed layouts were based on the *Lilong* typology.[19] Nevertheless, Schütte-Lihotzky proposed to categorically maintain the low-rise principle of the existing garden city. The deficient infrastructure and poor condition of the courtyard houses would not allow renovation, but instead a new modern version of the courtyard house was to be developed, carefully introduced with necessary taller buildings that would not destroy the harmony and elegance of the existing settlements and would not alter the proportion of the area covered by buildings and open space. She cited a design by an old friend of hers as an exemplary approach. This low-rise housing project for an unknown location in Beijing had been published in the 1957 edition of the magazine *Werk und Zeit* from the German Werkbund by one of its members, architect Werner Hebebrand. Hebebrand and Schütte-Lihotzky had worked together in Frankfurt under Ernst May and later both followed him to Moscow. Hebebrand traveled to China shortly after Schütte-Lihotzky, and his design was intended as gift to his Chinese hosts.

In 1952 he had become the head of the city planning department in Hamburg, leading its re-construction, and professor of urban planning at the University of Fine Arts in Hamburg. He also led the rebuilding of a German CIAM group after the war. In 1957 Hebebrand was selected to take part in an official study trip to China. The Association of Chinese Architects, which was also a member of the UIA (International Union of Architects), had invited delegates from their German counterpart associations from both parts of the recently divided country, consisting of four architects from West Germany and eight GDR delegates. The group traveled via Moscow to Changchun, Beijing, Shanghai, Nanking, and Mukden during a five-week trip, participating in a formal reception with China's prime minister Zhou Enlai, shaking hands with Mao, meeting local urban planners and architects, giving lectures, and visiting sites of contemporary and ancient China. The tour was not only covered by Chinese media, but also after their return several articles were published in German newspapers reflecting the architects' experiences and the progress and problems of the young country. During the voyage Hebebrand started to design a prototype for a settlement based on the Chinese courtyard typology mixed with multi-story dwellings.

15 Mostly known for her design of the "Frankfurt kitchen," Schütte-Lihotzky was not only an avid traveler but had worked abroad before the war, first in Frankfurt in the 1920s, then in the Soviet Union. After leaving the Soviet Union in 1937 she went to Istanbul, where she became part of an exile Austrian resistance group. In 1941 she eventually returned to Austria where her clandestine work was uncovered, and she was imprisoned until 1945. After the war Schütte-Lihotzky, a member of the Communist Party, was part of the CIAM Austria group. She took part in CIAM 7 and was engaged in ongoing debates about the Charta of Habitat.

16 A geographer and his wife, a national economist, an artist, an art historian/sinologist, and two zoologists.

17 The manuscript was published post mortem in 2007. Karin Zogmayer and Margarete Schütte-Lihotzky, eds., *Millionenstädte Chinas: Bilder- und Reisetagebuch einer Architektin* (Vienna: Springer, 2007).

18 Ibid., 37.

19 From 1860 on, a transcultural typology, the Shikumen or Lilong houses, developed in the British concession in Shanghai with elements taken from the Chinese courtyard house as well as the British workers' housing. The combination of industrial pre-fab construction methods, imported materials such as cement, plaster, or US pine wood, and the integration of sanitary facilities with an inner courtyard, south-facing doors, and vernacular motifs resulted in a distinctive form of two- to three story dwellings and neighborhoods; Chunlan Zhao, "Socio/Spatial Transformation in Mao's China: Settlement Planning and Dwelling Architecture Revisited (1950s–1970s)," (PhD Thesis, Katholieke Universiteit Leuven, 2007), 161.

> The original merging of modern knowledge of town planning with traditional elements of Chinese dwelling culture mark this plan as an impressive document of cosmopolitan attitude, as it should exist within the relations between foreign peoples, so that a mutual understanding can emerge. During the talk Werner Hebebrand pointed out that the Chinese themselves are still searching for the architectural form that best expresses their new will of life. At first the political situation gave way to a representational architecture of a strong Soviet influence, and partly these notions are still present today. For some time however, a heated controversy has ensued over independent forms of expression, giving hope for substantial progress in this area. Possibly Hebebrand's design could contribute to this matter, precisely because it is far away from trying to convince Chinese architecture of a characterless modernity.[20]

Hebebrand sent a copy of the article to Schütte-Lihotzky, who used his design as a potential future model for housing schemes in the New China in her own manuscript. The design did not go unnoticed in China either. In the April 1958 issue of China's architecture magazine, *Jianzhu Xuebao*, Hebebrand's design was published on the very last page, and Chinese architects were asked to submit their opinion on the subject.

Four years later Hebebrand developed a housing scheme on the basis of single-story courtyard dwellings for a new development area in Hamburg, calling them "Atrium houses." The urban layout of this development strongly resembled the one he had completed four years earlier for his fellow Chinese architects. He argues:

> The well-proven single-story type, propagated more than 30 years ago by Ludwig Hilberseimer in his manuscripts on town planning, attains final perfection through the addition of the garage. In Scandinavian countries this form of living is more popular for practical reasons, but also in regards to quality of planning and realization—considerably superseding our method of construction. In Southern countries, but also the Far East, Ancient China, and in Japan the courtyard house typology is not only the highest developed dwelling culture, but undertakes the task to protect against sun, wind, and dust. At our latitudes special attention has to be paid to the exact opposite—to catch the sun for the apartment—not only in summer time, but especially in winter.[21]

Vernacular Constraints

In 1958, one year after Hebebrand's visit to China, Mao announced the Great Leap Forward, the Second Five-Year Plan, and a mass campaign for steel production that would have one of the most severe impacts on China's recent history. Resulting in immense scarcity, almost all building activity came to a halt. Many architects were sent out to rural areas to support the transformation of rural settlements into people's communes, and a lot of them encountered the rural parts of China for the first time. According to Zhang Jie, their rural circumstances, isolated from any access to research resources in their field, made them turn to what was there, and many of them started to study local vernacular architecture.[22]

Officially the "Walking on Two Legs" campaign that "revised earlier versions that over-emphasized industry over agriculture and the urban over the rural in both economic and construction perspectives" came into effect.[23] Besides industrial modernization and technological progress, a special focus was also put on small-scale production and on the recourse of local modes of production. For architecture this meant a combination of both modern and traditional methods. Architects and planners were called on to consider efficient and resource-friendly construction and recollect old techniques. The government continued to increase its focus on vernacular and local building practices as the budgetary constraints and general economic circumstances tightened. The 1958 national design competition constituted a "clear return to the local context. [...] A nation-wide standard design approach, which required the considerable support of a modernized building industry, was no longer stressed. Instead, local dwelling traditions were encouraged, including their spatial organization, building technique, and materials."[24] In the same year a conference on local design was held and turned into a national exhibition later focusing on buildings "including houses made with bamboo-woven walls in the Sichuan Province and buildings constructed with materials other than steel, iron, cement, wood, or brick in Harbin."[25]

The extensive use of bamboo was promoted, bringing about experiments with "'bamboo-concrete' in floor panels, attempts to make door and window frames with a special type of clay,"[26] a gymnasium with a bamboo structure, or the implementation of traditional hearth heating from North China in multistory buildings in a few cases, but most exemplary was the housing construction in the case of the Daqing oil field in Heilongjiang province.

20 Justus Bueckschmitt, "Vorschlag für ein Wohnviertel in China," *Werk und Zeit*, no. 10 (1957): 1.
21 Werner Hebebrand, *Zur Neuen Stadt* (Berlin: Gebrüder Mann, 1969), 37–38.
22 Christina Linortner, unpublished interview with Professor Zhang Jie, Tsinghua University, October 20, 2011.
23 Zhao, "Socio/Spatial Transformation in Mao's China," 148.
24 Ibid., 161.
25 Lue et al., *Modern Urban Housing in China*, 153.
26 Zhao, "Socio/Spatial Transformation in Mao's China," 146–47.

Other conferences followed in Zhangjiang in 1961 and in Wuxi in 1963 where, "based on the investigation of local geographical conditions and climate, some designs with local features also appeared. Research on traditional construction skills also brought some changes to the practice of copying the Soviet experience."[27] In December 1962 a Rural Housing Design Symposium was held, and vernacular dwelling types were published in China's Architectural Journal together with examples of regionalist adaptations of architecture in other Third World countries.[28] While the Western visitors and CIAM members looked at ancient building traditions, these depictions focused on modern developments in these nations.

The interest in local materials and their manufacturing methods triggered by the rise of thriftiness was furthered through the decentralization of a major sector of construction work: "Starting from 1959, each province, city, or autonomous region took over the responsibility of organizing standard housing designs from the State Construction Commission."[29] Accordingly, research groups on local housing were installed throughout the provinces and sparked a much greater understanding of Chinese architecture, which is reflected in the *Jianzhu Xuebao* issues from the years 1960–63. They feature a series of surveys of folk dwellings of minorities throughout China's provinces.

Climate Responsive Architecture in South China

Economic constraints and the ruling paradigm of thriftiness put limitations on and challenged architects and planners' professionalism. In some cases this created opportunities to bypass the strict framework of official guidelines restricting architectural expression. In the 1950s in Guangdong Province, South China, a specific regional architectural modernism evolved, promoted by a group of architects affiliated with the South China University of Technology. One of the main protagonists was the architect Hsia Changshi who, like many of his fellow architects in that generation, had studied abroad and adapted ideas he had encountered during his education to specific local conditions he found in South China. While the official line for architecture and construction was geared to the Soviet model under the slogan "Learning from the Soviet Union" and simultaneously a Neo-Sino-Classicism, a climate-adaptive approach in South China allowed for the otherwise discredited modernist architectural language using horizontal lines in its design that was associated with the Western capitalist class enemy. The consequences of the Great Leap Forward had not only caused a rigid austerity program, but matters related exclusively to architectural questions with no relevance for the re-construction of economy or general welfare were commonly considered rightist. However, the study of vernacular architecture and the use of local building methods and material had been promoted by the officials.

In order to expand his professional practice beyond this, Hsia Changshi developed a number of techniques utilizing economic, vernacular, and rational elements, climatic matters, and the study of spatial qualities in garden architecture to create a distinct regional adaptive architecture. The use of modernist principles such as functionality, "sincerity" of material, and structure can be seen as passive resistance encouraging the growth of an architectural thinking that was unconventional and controversial at that time and place. Architectural practice in Guangzhou among Hsia Changshi and his colleagues was oriented around building, teaching, and research. A research center for vernacular architecture with a special focus on Lingnan gardens was established. Hsia and his colleague Mo Bozhi conducted site surveys with their students; archival photographs show students measuring vernacular architecture.

The way vernacular architecture was appropriated by the cases described above is an example of "how a shared history of art and ideas was experienced differently around the globe."[30] On their trips to China, Western visitors Schütte-Lihotzky and Hebebrand were inspired by the traditional courtyard house and strongly pleaded for a modernist remake of the typology to use for future housing in China. "The more collectivist our life becomes," Lihotzky argues, the faster "architects and urban planners should be agonizing about where and how spaces of quiet and concentration could be created within big cities, as well as individually in the context of housing, as well as collectively within public buildings like libraries, museums, pools, etc." Otherwise "the accelerated pace of work and traffic" could lead to "a nervous breakdown and an intellectual scantiness sealing the fate of the peoples."[31] Their praise of the low-rise housing as a peaceful antipode to the busy modern collectivist life can be viewed in the context of the discussion around the CIAM Charta of Habitat that aimed at a revision of the urban visions of the first generation modernists focusing on the immediate surrounding of the dwelling, rather than the "cell" and models of zoning. At the same time, the debates in China were dominated by a constant aggravation of economic constraints and politically motivated requirements. Duanfang Lu has claimed that this factor is one of the signifying characteristics of what she coined "Third World Modernism." While Schütte-Lihotzy and Hebebrand focused on the spatial qualities of the old Chinese housing typology, in China the vernacular was used in multiple fashions. These ranged from a vehicle for the grander nation-building project to an adequate formal and technological language of modesty and inherent rationality in times of

27 Lue et al., *Modern Urban Housing in China*, 159.
28 Duanfang Lu, *Remaking Chinese Urban Form: Modernity, Scarcity and Space, 1949–2005* (London: Routledge, 2006), 122.
29 Lue et al., *Modern Urban Housing in China*, 348.
30 Kobena Mercer, ed., *Cosmopolitan Modernisms* (Cambridge, MA: MIT Press, 2005), 7.
31 Zogmayer et al., *Millionenstädte Chinas: Bilder- und Reisetagebuch einer Architektin*, 52.

heightened scarcity to the utilization of this modesty to develop an individual architectural language opposing the political demands, as in the case of Hsia Changshi.

Literature

Bueckschmitt, Justus. "Vorschlag für ein Wohnviertel in China." *Werk und Zeit*, no. 10 (1957): 1.

Clifford, James. "Traveling Cultures." In *Cultural Studies*. Edited by Lawrence Grossberg, Cary Nelson, and Paula Treichler, 96–116. New York: Routledge, 1992.

Fairbank, Wilma. *Liang and Lin: Partners in Exploring China's Architectural Past*. Philadelphia: University of Pennsylvania Press, 1994.

Fiege, Mark. "Private Property and the Ecological Commons in the American West." In *Everyday America: Cultural Landscape Studies After J.B. Jackson*. Edited by Chris Wilson and Paul Groth, 219– 232. Berkeley: University of California Press, 2003.

Giedion, Sigfried. (1953). "Habitat" zum 9. CIAM Kongress Giedion, P.1, GTA Zürich: 43-T-15-1953-9.

Hebebrand, Werner. *Zur Neuen Stadt*. Berlin: Gebrüder Mann, 1969.

Hoa, Léon. *Reconstruire la Chine: trente ans d'urbanisme 1949–1979*. Paris: Moniteur, 1981.

Hsia, Changshi. "Problems of Lowering the Temperature of Buildings in the Subtropical Zone." *Jianzhu Xuebao*, 10 (1958): 36–39.

Hsia, Changshi and Bozhi Mo. "Lingnan Gardens." *Jianzhu Xuebao*, 03 (1963): 11–14.

Jaschke, Karin. "Mythical Journeys: Ethnography, Archeology, and the Attraction of Tribal Cultures in the Work of Aldo van Eyck and Herman Haan." PhD Thesis, Princeton University, 2012.

Liangyong, Wu. *Collected Works of Liang Sicheng*. vol. 8. Beijing: China Architecture & Building Press, 2001.

Linortner, Christina. Unpublished Interview with Professor Zhang Jie, Tsinghua University, October 20, 2011.

Lu, Duanfang. *Remaking Chinese Urban Form. Modernity, Scarcity and Space, 1949–2005*. London: Routledge, 2006.

Lu, Duanfang. *Third World Modernism: Architecture, Development and Identity*. London: Routledge, 2010.

Lue, Junhua, Peter G. Rowe, and Jie Zhang (eds.). *Modern Urban Housing in China: 1840–2000*. New York: Prestel, 2001.

Mercer, Kobena (ed.). *Cosmopolitan Modernisms*. Cambridge, MA: MIT Press, 2005.

Overy, Paul. "White Walls, White Skins: Cosmopolitanism and Colonialism in Inter-War Modernist Architecture." In *Cosmopolitan Modernisms*. Edited by Kobena Mercer, 50–67. Cambridge, MA: MIT Press, 2005.

Peng, Changxin. "Regionalism and Realism: Hsia Changshi's Ideas on Modern Architecture in China." *South Architecture*, vol. 2 (2010): 36–41.

Stein, Susanne. "Von der Konsumentenstadt zur Produktionsstadt: Visionen von "Aufbau" und Urbanisierung im Neuen China, 1949–1957." PhD Thesis, University of Tübingen, 2008.

Tosolini, Paola. "Other Itineraries: Modern Architects on Countryside Roads." *The Journal of Architecture*, vol. 13, no. 4 (2008): 427-451.

Wright, Gwendolyn. "On Modern Vernaculars and J.B. Jackson." In *Everyday America: Cultural Landscape Studies After J. B. Jackson*. Edited by Chris Wilson and Paul Groth, 163–177. Berkeley: University of California Press, 2003.

Zhao, Chunlan. "*Socio/Spatial Transformation in Mao's China: Settlement Planning and Dwelling Architecture Revisited (1950s–1970s)*." PhD Thesis, Katholieke Universiteit Leuven, 2007.

Zogmayer, Karin and Margarete Schütte-Lihotzky (eds.). *Millionenstädte Chinas: Bilder- und Reisetagebuch einer Architektin*. Vienna: Springer, 2007.

Walking on Many Legs

Spatial Productions between State Socialism and Third World Modernism in Maoist China

Duanfang Lu and Christina Linortner in Conversation

Christina Linortner: Architectural modernism is still widely perceived (within the field) as originating in the West (Europe and the United States) from where it spread to the rest of the world, rather than as a product of an ongoing transcultural process. However, in recent years with the rise of postcolonial thought this one-directional perspective has been revised by a number of scholars both in the Western and non-Western world. Still, most of the best-known examples (with a few exceptions of course) of (late) modernist architecture in Latin American, African, and Asian countries were built by Western architects. I am referring to prominent examples such as Le Corbusier's Chandigarh, Kahn's design in Bangladesh and India, Drew's and Fry's plans for the University of Ibadan in Nigeria, Gropius's work for Baghdad University, etc. There are a few other examples of well-known non-Western architects, such as Kenzō Tange, Oscar Niemeyer, and Hassan Fathy, but the enormous spatial transformations in the Chinese context have largely been ignored in (Western) postwar architecture discourse and hardly appear on the map. In recent years you have published two books, *Remaking Chinese Urban Form* (2006) and *Third World Modernism* (2011), that open up a new perspective on the neglect of China's spatial production in and beyond the context of (architectural) modernism. How would you describe the modernism/modernity and its conditions/constraints of postwar Chinese space production? (And why has it been so neglected in and outside of China?)

Duanfang Lu: While modernity has constantly wrestled with the differences of histories, cultures, nationalities, and ethnicities, dominant discourses tend to focus on the universality, rationality, and homogeneity of the modern. Under the assumption that only Western society is truly modern, Western Cold War scholarship, for example, depicted state socialism as a type of "unmodernity" when measured with normative standards of capitalist modernity. Meanwhile, conventional architectural historiography is marked by its ordering of heterogeneous design practices into progressive movements and codification of aesthetically exemplary buildings into stylistic categories. Things that mess up the neat categories are excluded. As a result, up until the last three decades, the official history of modern architecture had focused on its development in the West, and academic inquiry with the built environment in China and other "developing societies" concentrated on traditional forms. Little attention was devoted to their modern architecture, which was considered merely lesser forms of Western modernism, apart from a very small number of architects such as those you mentioned who fit the categories. Inside China, under the catch-up complex—the urgent desire to keep up with the most developed countries—researchers had concentrated their energy on learning what others were doing and deciding on what was to be done next, rather than reflecting on what had been done and what was happening.

As Pierre Bourdieu points out, one often knows what one does, but does not know what one doesn't do. Reflecting on the actual effects on what one does in a broad context is a daunting task, not to mention that China has been a particularly huge and complicated entity embedded in a long history and a tangled world system. I struggled painfully with the task of grasping and describing the essence of Chinese modernity for a few years. Eventually, starting with "the beginning of a new time" seemed appropriate. Let us not forget that for at least one millennium much of Asia was a loosely integrated ensemble of regions, countries, and cities held together by a tribute-trade system centered on China. This is simultaneously a political-economic framework and an epistemological system. To peripheral components, China was modern culturally, politically, economically, and epistemologically. Financially, for instance, while the history of money in China dates back four millennia, money did not become the dominant medium of exchange in Japan until the twelfth century (by using currency imported from China), Korea until the fifteenth century, and Vietnam until the eighteenth century. The phrase *tianxia*, literally "under the heavens," was used to denote the entire geographical world under the rule of the emperor since at least the first millennium BC. The latter was positioned at the center of this celestial/temporal/spatial structure. When an emperor ascended the throne, the year would be changed to Year One under the title of his reign. If one knows this history well, one can see how radical it was to adopt the Greenwich Mean Time system as the nation's official time system. This not only represented a ruthless break with a self-referential, Sinocentric historical and spatial framework, but also positioned the nation in a relationship of synchronic temporality with other nations of the world. China found itself not only as one of the many, but also lagging behind. Seeking the fastest track to "wealth and power" (*fuqiang*) became the nation's most urgent task during the late Qing and Republican periods, but the efforts were disrupted by wars. After the 1949 revolution, the catch-up complex was further complicated by revolutionary drives: a perpetual search for an alternative future by constantly transcending the independent revolution, the socialist revolution, industrial modernity and more, "one after another." This forceful temporality to which the nation subscribed itself constitutes a fundamental aspect of Chinese modernity.

Spatial production in socialist China needs to be examined against this context. To keep up with advanced capitalist countries, China, like other socialist countries, decided to focus on the development of capital-intensive heavy industry, but the attempt was constrained by limited resources. The national austerity policy was adopted; the state privileged production over consumption to accumulate maximum capital for industrialization. This policy was quickly translated into new conceptualizations of urban space and construction. There were major efforts to convert the "cities of consumption" into the "cities of production" during the 1950s. Urban functions in commerce, finance, and services were suppressed; most of the city's manpower and resources were transferred to industrial development. State investment in urban development was tilted heavily towards productive construction—the erection of structures that were directly related to production—and biased against non-productive construction—the erection of structures that rendered services for people. The challenges China was facing were similar to those faced by other "developing countries" at the time. I have, therefore, characterized Chinese modernity as socialist and Third World.

CL: What is your particular interest when looking at Chinese urban form of the 1950s and its dominant element, the "work unit" (*danwei*)? What is there to see and learn beyond its physical appearance?

DL: I am interested in seeing the built environment not as an autonomous arena but rather a social field with important political implications. The development of the work unit as the dominant urban form under Chinese socialism is a significant example here. The work unit—the socialist enterprise or institute—functioned not only as workplace but also as a social institution in China. It was also a territorial unit that possessed a distinct spatial form that integrates work, housing, and a variety of social facilities such as nurseries, canteens, clinics, and shops in close proximity within its walled compound(s). Residents might conduct most daily affairs without leaving their unit. The characteristic form of the work unit had profound effects on urbanism under Mao. The work unit as the focus of urban life resulted in a small community atmosphere lacking anonymity, a peculiar urban experience not found in other modern cities. The design of the work unit created an institutionally non-sexist environment that supported the activities of employed women and their families. In contemporary China, urban women were expected to have paid employment, while homebound women were the exception. The work unit's integration of production, residence, and social services on a manageable scale greatly facilitated the functioning of two-worker families. Public kitchens and canteens offered alternatives to cooking at home, and nurseries within the unit compound reduced the time spent commuting.

The distinct mixed land-use pattern of the work unit also had important environmental significance. The close association of workplace, residence, and social facilities greatly reduced the need for urban residents to travel beyond their unit compound. Such an urban form depended little on the provision of an extensive and expensive public transport system. As Clifton Pannell observed in the late 1970s, major Chinese cities such as Shanghai and Beijing had a very small number of buses and other public transport vehicles: the number for both cities was around 2,200 in 1977, much less than other Western cities of similar sizes. Without any private cars, the principal modes of travel at the time were bicycling and walking. Energy consumption was also reduced through shared facilities such as canteens and public bathhouses. It is indeed an incredible environmental achievement to have an urban system based on minimum energy costs without creating serious dysfunctions in economic and social organization.

Despite these positive features, there were negative implications at the urban level. The enclosed character of the work unit resulted in less choice, social interaction, and heterogeneity. Georg Simmel, in his analysis of the modern city, contrasts urban space, where density and diversity constantly put the individual in touch with a myriad of possibilities, to rural space, where individual movement and opportunities are restricted. In the Maoist city, one's social life was largely confined within one's own work unit, which was separated from other parts of the city physically and socially. As there was little done to facilitate interactions in society at large, the urbanite in the Maoist city was restricted to the concentric social pattern centered on the work unit. The streets had fewer shops, restaurants, ads, recreational centers, and other urban facilities. The social environment of the work unit encouraged socialist collectivism while discouraging social heterogeneity, which is central to Wirth's notion of "urbanism as a way of life." As a result, there was a high level of homogeneity in terms of life styles, and fewer chances for urban interactions leading to innovations.

CL: As a communist country, architecture in China after 1949 and before the Sino-Soviet split in 1960 was widely regarded as derivative of the Soviet model of space, and by identifying the work unit as one of the crucial principles of urban and social organization in China you understand the idea of the neighborhood unit (by Clarence Perry) as a traveling typology that is entangled in a global web of manifold capitalist, socialist, or postcolonial histories and contexts. Simultaneously, you show how the work unit became a distinct and unique feature of Chinese Socialist space making. Can you elaborate on this apparent ambiguity?

DL: The first stage of construction (1949–52) bore the mark of the previous era; Chinese architects were free to make their own stylistic decisions. But you are right; very soon, as the Chinese Communist Party aligned the nation with the socialist camp and considered China a "junior member" of the Soviet-led alliance of communist countries, the Soviet influence began to permeate every aspect of Chinese rebuilding. During the 1950s, more than 10,000 advisors from the Soviet Union were invited to assist various modernization programs in China, and their opinions often outweighed local objections to key decisions. In the sphere of architectural production, Soviet advisors sought to transplant "Socialist Realism" to China, the national style which had been established in Russia since the 1930s as a reaction to the adoption of "decadent bourgeois styles," including constructivism, which had flourished in the USSR earlier, and the International style, which developed in capitalist society. The slogan for this style was: "Socialist in content, national in form." Under this notion, the Revivalist style, first developed by Western architects in Republican China, was re-fashioned as the revolutionary style of the socialist state.

In the field of residential planning, the idea of the neighborhood unit was introduced to China in the 1930s. It was employed by Japanese colonial planners in the planning of cities such as Changchun and Datong, and used by Chinese planners in planning proposals for several major cities immediately after World War II. Socialist planners experimented with several competing residential planning ideas during the 1950s. The microdistrict (*xiaoqu* in Chinese and *mikrorayon* in Russian), an idea from the Soviet Union and essentially similar to the neighborhood unit schema, gradually gained favor. With the exception of a few built examples of the microdistrict, however, planners failed to realize the model to any great extent under Mao (1949–76). Instead, the work unit gradually became the de facto dominant form to organize the Chinese city.

Chinese urban form, as it exists today, bears little resemblance to what Chinese socialist planners had in mind. Yet by looking into the production process of space, I consider that urban form and function under Mao were nonetheless "socialist" in nature, as they were produced as part of socialist production and accumulation strategies. My study shows that the integral spatial form of the work unit was the unique outcome generated by the conflicts between the needs of capital accumulation and the necessity of labor reproduction within a peculiar socialist/ Third World context. Industrial expansion caused a dramatic growth in the urban population in the 1950s. As mentioned earlier, under the national austerity policy, little state investment was allocated to non-productive construction. Rapid urban growth and biased investment policies created an immense scarcity of crucial consumption facilities; there was a constant shortage of housing and facilities. Much conflict was generated between the needs of accumulation and the necessity of labor reproduction.

My archival research reveals that the building of living facilities within work units was often accomplished through construction outside the state approved plan, resource hoarding, and exchanges via informal channels. This certainly did not happen automatically. Instead, it was a result of the conflicted relationship between the state, work units, and planners in the construction of essential consumption facilities. Although the Chinese state was depicted as a totalitarian regime in Cold War-era research, the control of the socialist state over enterprises and labor was structurally weak. Under socialism enterprises operate within soft budget constraints—that is, if a production unit suffers financial losses, the state will cover it sooner or later. Hence, the socialist economic system does not possess the kind of disciplinary control of enterprises characteristic of capitalism. Meanwhile, due to the lack of labor markets, layoffs, bankruptcies, and so on, the means for disciplining labor under socialism are less efficient than those under capitalism. The strong bargaining power of the work unit over the local government and the planning department, and workers over their work unit, played a key role in redirecting capital from production to consumption construction.

With the immense scarcity of consumption facilities causing severe political tension and strife during the 1950s, the state responded by imposing the responsibility of urban provision upon the work unit. Faced with political pressure from employees below and administrators above, unit leaders strived to meet the needs of their workers. The ideal model for residential development for planners was a combination of the principle of functional zoning and unitary neighborhood planning. Due to limited resources and weak planning power, however, planners failed to realize the model to any great extent before 1978. In theory, public ownership and the centrally planned system should provide favorable conditions for the realization of planning ideas. In practice, construction investment was channeled through all-powerful vertical sectoral lines, over which the planning department had little control. In theory, all construction projects should be put under the supervision of planners. In practice, planners operated in the lower echelon of the power system and did not possess adequate means for regulation. The Chinese state was sufficiently pragmatic not to follow planning orthodoxies blindly, but to adapt to the changing urban reality. Eventually Chinese socialism produced a unique urban form, which was an alternative to both capitalist and Soviet urbanism.

CL: At the beginning of *Remaking Chinese Urban Form* you used a quote by Mao claiming the potential that lies within poverty. What role does scarcity play in China's spatial production and the development of the built environment at that time and how did this affect the self-image of the country?

DL: I consider it a pity that recent postcolonial debates largely concentrate on modernity as a "cultural" dilemma, seeking ways to confront the problems of the Third World in terms of the issue of cultural identity alone. While the issue of identity politics is important, there remain, however, many social and spatial choices made in "developing societies" that cannot be well explained without including the dimension of scarcity. In fact, much of urban transformation in contemporary China can only be explained when scarcity, as a historically constituted condition, is taken into account. By using scarcity as an epistemic starting point for the understanding of Third World modernism, I hope to bring together political economy and the analysis of the postcolonial, the two spheres that have largely remained separated in current cultural debates.

Scarcity has profound effects on human agency. This is especially true when even a subsistence level of existence cannot be maintained. With a strong desire for survival, scarcity becomes a powerful magic wand, transforming individuals into collective human movements, with the virtues required to bring about revolutions—sacrifice, self-discipline, and fearlessness in the face of death, to name just a few. I believe this can partially explain why movements against capitalist domination, contradictory to what Marx had predicted, were de-radicalized in the "overripe" core but succeeded in the underdeveloped periphery. Therefore, in that well-known quote, Mao celebrated the fact that the Chinese were "poor and blank" and proclaimed that it was precisely because of such conditions that the desire for "change," "action," and "revolution" would be incited. For better or for worse, Mao was a real life Faust who aspired to build a brave new world by eliminating anything that stood in the way of modernization. With a characteristically Maoist thinking, scarcity was ironically turned into a favored condition—"a blank sheet of paper free of any mark"—in the push for modernization, so that scarcity and modernity were conceptually reconciled. Yet this synthesis was nonetheless a fragile one, constantly in danger of disintegrating into new contradictions in practice.

Facing tremendous difficulties to achieve industrialization in a poor country, the Chinese state adopted two basic strategies to achieve maximum accumulation of capital and surplus value: privileging production over consumption, and extracting surplus value from agriculture. China's accumulation rates were even higher than the Soviet Union's in comparable phases. An "anti-waste" (*fan langfei*) discourse arose soon after 1949. The rhetoric received a new impetus in 1955 when a resolution was made in the Soviet Union, which denounced the tendency of impractical extravagances in construction. In architectural practice, nationalistic structures with big roofs and traditional ornamentation were condemned as wasteful in 1955. Liang Sicheng, the Vice Chairman of the Beijing Urban Planning Committee, became the object of severe political attacks for being the main proponent of the national style. Under the austerity policy, construction was reduced to pragmatic designs; structures were built according to an ultra-economical standard and showed little aesthetic concern.

CL: Within the *Model House* project we developed an understanding of transculturality that considers the relationships and networks among the manifold actors that are involved in processes of building. In this perspective, can you describe the utopian people's commune movement with its aim to level the differences between the rural and the urban realms and is it possible to call it a transcultural project?

DL: The people's commune movement assembled knowledge, ideas, and people from different directions. In that sense, you may characterize it as "transcultural." Ideas for the purpose of the "education of desire" were cited from different sources: from Karl Marx's *The German Ideology*, the Paris Commune of 1871, to the peasant communes in the Soviet Union in the 1930s. Similarly, commune planning proposals were based on concepts such as functional zoning, communal housing, and microdistricts that were initially developed in other societies. Planners, architects, and students in spatial disciplines were sent to the countryside to help with commune planning. Peasants were mobilized to produce artwork to depict desired changes. Poetry competitions were held in villages, new folk songs were performed, and *dazibao*, the "big character poster," were employed to publicize poems and proposals. It was a period of fervent mass movement.

CL: The limited access to material and financial resources and concurrent processes of modernization including a constant pushing towards industrial development characterizes what you coined "Third World Modernism." Can you describe what exactly this "Third World Modernism" means for China (and in general)?

DL: In fact, the sense of being lacking was so powerful that the Chinese state quickly conceptualized the nation as one of scarcity. This new orientation allows a transposition of Chinese national identity from the state of "being less" to the state of "being lacking." A number of important conceptual shifts are made possible through this transposition, which can be briefly summarized as follows. First, the failure of desire is externalized by considering that the failure is due to scarcity—being lacking in means to achieve the goals—instead of due to its being "less than one" or "less civilized." Second, as the failure becomes an exterior condition, the distance between the nation's current state and its projected identity is justified as a relational term that exists only during a certain period and can be shortened via specific strategies. Third, as the possibility to learn from the failure is opened up, there arises a new need for self-knowledge and other knowledge besides Western knowledge. These constituted a unique Chinese sense of "Third World Modernism."

CL: The term immediately established an international network beyond the socialist brother states. What points of view are revealed, and what conflicts are negotiated within that context?

DL: China had consistently identified itself with the Third World and considered strengthening solidarity with other "developing countries" to be its basic foreign policy since the founding of the Third World coalition at the Bandung conference in 1955. The recognition of the importance of learning from other "developing countries" mentioned above conflated the South/North confrontation newly formulated by the CCP after the formal Sino-Soviet split in 1960. With China's increasing alienation from the USSR, the CCP attempted to lead a Third World challenge to superpower control. Mao's famous theory of the three worlds saw global space differently from the normal division of the three worlds. It considered the First World consisting of the two superpowers, the United States and the USSR, the Second World including the developed countries of Europe and Japan, and the Third World made up of both socialist and underdeveloped capitalist countries. As the Second World was "controlled and bullied by the superpowers," the contradiction between the two could be exploited by the Third World to unite the Second "in the common struggle for self-determination." Meanwhile, Jawaharlal Nehru's conceptualization of the "third way" for Asian nations provided a different conceptual framework to cope with the two superpowers in the Cold War. There were not only competitions for the leadership role between China and India, but also among other developing nations such as Indonesia and Sri Lanka.

The export of architecture to Third World countries as part of China's foreign aid programs has played an important role in this power negotiation process. Extensive Chinese architectural export began in 1956 as part of overseas aid programs within the Cold War context. In the decades that followed, Chinese architects built construction projects ranging from major national buildings to factories in Asia, Africa, and the Middle East. Among others, the Bandaranaike Memorial International Conference Hall (BMICH) in Colombo, Sri Lanka, represents one of the most significant examples. Designed by Dai Nianci, a prominent figure in the history of modern Chinese architecture, BMICH echoes both postwar tropical architecture and the iconography of Maoist utopianism. Due to its striking aesthetic appeal, BMICH has become a symbol of national identity and a premier tourist attraction in Sri Lanka. Notably, BMICH successfully hosted the Fifth Non-Aligned Summit Conference in August 1976, which in turn helped Sri Lanka to project its own global influence among Third World nations.

CL: Following the Sino-Soviet split in China there is a strong two-directional shift noticeable in architecture discourse. A great number of published articles in the official architecture magazines turn away from developmental topics such as hospital, factory, or school building and towards traditional vernacular modes of building that I understood as an attempt at nation building. On the other hand, as you mentioned in your book, in the very same magazines, examples of modern architecture outside of China emerge. So there is a simultaneous opening to the inside and the outside. What were the intentions behind that and what happened in both cases?

DL: In the early 1960s, the rethinking of Chinese modern architecture was fuelled by newly acquired lessons from the people's commune movement. The failure of the commune plan forced Chinese architects to re-examine the issue of architectural modernism. Although architects were eager to apply modernist design to rural development, the country was short of steel and concrete. By 1962, with a new focus on agriculture in economic development, the state mobilized architects to design new rural houses emphasizing the idea of "walking on two legs," a combination of both modern and traditional methods. In the December 1962 "Rural Housing Design" symposium, designers discussed the applicability of concrete structures in the countryside and recognized the necessity of adapting design to the realities of existing materials, technology, and skills. 1963 saw a sudden expansion of knowledge of vernacular forms in different parts of the country.

At the same time, when the reports of vernacular dwelling types were published in *Architectural Journal*, the same journal also began to extensively introduce architecture in Third World countries. The 1963 issues covered architecture in Indonesia, Cambodia, Burma, Cuba, North Korea, Vietnam, and Albania, while the 1964 issues added Egypt, Mexico, Ghana, Guinea, and Syria to the list. Unlike typical Western representations, these articles focused on the newly developed modernist architecture of Third World countries rather than their traditional structures. Authors paid particular attention to how architects in these countries adapted modernist buildings to local geographical, climatic, and cultural conditions. The narratives were filled with praise for the progress made in architectural modernization in these nations. Occasionally, a "sameness" was drawn between building traditions in China and those in other "developing countries." Sotto porticos (*qilou*) in Cambodia, for example, were associated with similar arrangements in the city of Guangzhou, which was followed by comments on the advantages of such arrangements in hot and humid weather.

Through these discursive parameters, the architectural practices of other "developing countries" were conceptually linked with those of China, creating a world of synchronic temporality and shared spatiality. The diverse interpretations of modernist architecture by these nations, along with the various local traditions of China's own, fuelled new imaginings of modern Chinese architecture. With regional characteristics emphasized in this new orientation, the early 1960s saw a flourish of design projects with a strong local flavor. The regional solidarity between China and the Third World countries destabilized the previous discursive framing of "Western modernist architecture," which once again became a subject of intellectual contention.

Key to this reassessment was a new cognitive distinction made between the modernism of the West and that of the Third World. While Chinese and Western modernist architecture were previously synthesized into a universal knowledge, the sameness was inevitably disrupted by the problems surrounding Chinese modernism against the backdrop of conflicting relations involving nationalistic concerns and the problem of underdevelopment. If scarcity was an inherited wound of Third World modernity, further modernization only made it deeper: millions of people lost their lives to starvation during the commune movement. The crisis gave rise to a new need for a modernism based on self-knowledge and other spatial rationalities besides that of the West.

A Modernist Project in China

Gan-da-lei Mudhouses in Early Daqing*

Chunlan Zhao

Unlike most Chinese cities featured in a rather long urban history of complicated socio-cultural development, Daqing is one of the few "new" cities that has emerged since the second half of the twentieth century. Initially developed as a dispersed network of numerous small settlements clustered around a large oil field in northeast China, Daqing became a brand new industrial town that transformed a vast territory of wild land into a fast growing area with both urban and rural features.[1] One of the main built forms in the early formation of Daqing, *gan-da-lei* housing was derived from a local vernacular housing typology with a double metaphorical meaning. It refers to not only the basic living unit in its material status but also to the fundamental working method and spirit of the first generation of residents who built them. The Daqing project can be seen as a proto-developmental enterprise, and, for a number of reasons explained in this article, became a model representing Mao's call to "build the country through thrift and hard work."

However, in contrast with substantial "propaganda" material in the form of small booklets, posters, newspapers, and magazines produced during the 1960s and 70s, there was a lack of academic interest in Daqing and *gan-da-lei* housing in the decades that followed.[2] While most of these earlier works were published anonymously or semi-anonymously, a more recent publication by Song Liansheng seems to be the first individual research done on this subject inside China.[3] In terms of more specific discussions on its settlement planning and architecture, only a few anonymous articles can be found in two issues of the domestic architectural journal *Jian Zhu Xue Bao* (JZXB) in 1966. Some more serious research on Daqing's planning appeared outside China in the

1 Daqing was selected by CCTV as one of the ten most glamorous cities in China of the year 2006: "The city has the largest oil field in China, which has created enormous material and spiritual wealth that deeply influenced the country. It is not only an energy city, but also an environmentally friendly city with development balanced between taking from and giving to nature, where the red-crowned crane likes to live. It is a place full of great energy!" From the organizing committee's comment, it is interesting to see the impact Daqing's earlier balanced urban-rural development had upon its later development.

2 Among materials published before the end of the 1970s, three pieces are considered most informative for this research, including: *Daqing jiashu geminghua de biaobing: Xue Guifang* (The Model of Daqing's Revolutionaries Family Dependents: Xue Guifang), compiled and published by Worker's Press in 1966; *Shiyou gungun jian taiyang: daqing gongren jiashi xuan* (Rolling Petroleum Towards the Sun: Collections of Daqing Worker's Family History), compiled and published by Shanghai People's Press in 1977; and *Dui Daqing jingyan de zhengzhi jingjixue kaocha* (A Political and Economical Research on Daqing's Experience), written by a special research group under the same name and published by People's Press in 1979. These anonymous works will be referred to as XGF, 1966; JTS, 1977; and DQZJ, 1979 respectively later in the text. Literature published after the 1970s includes *Daqing shizhi* (Daqing City Record) in 1988 and *Daqing jianshi* (Brief History of Daqing) in 1991.

3 Liansheng Song, *Gongye xue Daqing shimo* (The Beginning and End of the Campaign of Learning from Daqing in Industry) (Hubei: People's Press, 2005).

late 1970s and early 1980s;[4] an important book, *Reconstruire la Chine: Trente ans d'urbanisme, 1949–1979*, was published by Hua Lanhong under his French name Léon Hoa in Paris in 1981. Here, the renowned Chinese architect and planner gives us a clear, comprehensive picture of the modernization and urbanization process in China between the 1950s and 1970s, in which Daqing served as an important example to demonstrate the unique Chinese approach to building a self-reliant settlement by mixing urban and rural, heavy industry, and agriculture.[5] This paper intends to explore the historic trajectory of this modernist project in greater detail within the context of modern China.

1. Initial Programming and Preparation for Daqing

In order to catch up with the pace of national economic development after the First Five-Year Plan (1953–57), top leaders agreed that it was important to locate and build new petroleum fields in China to increase its production and transportation capacities. After two years of careful investigations in its northeast region, a vast oil field was detected under the Song-Liao Basin, and on September 26, 1959, the first petroleum was taken from the ground. The field was soon named Daqing, meaning great celebration, a double metaphor celebrating the discovery of the oil field and the upcoming tenth anniversary of the new People's Republic. But guaranteeing a quick oil output meant not only setting up working posts but also building settlements to meet the demands of basic living and logistics supplies for workers and their families. The leadership envisioned a "great combat" against the harsh environment to achieve acceptable living and working conditions.

The first difficulty in organizing such a campaign was the lack of labor, which was quickly solved when the central government approved the mobilization of 30,000 veterans and another 3,000 retired officers to join the force, many of whom were party members and youth league members. Some of them had participated in the Korean War. At the same time, professional personnel and equipment were also organized from different posts within the petroleum sector. On March 15, 1960, some 17,000 people had arrived in Daqing, including 11,000 veterans, 5,000 petroleum workers based in Daqing, and 1,000 workers from other posts. By early April the total personnel in Daqing had reached 40,000, including more than 1,000 technical cadres (experts, university professors, engineers, etc.).[6]

As revealed in Song Liansheng's study, relations between the locals and the newcomers were complicated. On one hand, the former group was very supportive towards the latter at the beginning. It was the local herdsmen who vacated their houses and stables to temporarily accommodate the "petroleum troop" and helped dig up the oil pond during the great combat period. But as the new petroleum equipment began filling more and more of the grassland, conflict and tension also grew between the two. It was reported that some herdsmen even dismantled a newly built refinery with written complaints from both sides that reached all related administrative levels and finally Premier Zhou Enlai.[7]

Locals were also supportive during the initial preparation for the Daqing project. Aside from large numbers of veterans, soldiers, and petroleum workers transferred from other locations, more than a thousand local technicians and builders were gathered from nearby cities and counties like Qiqiha'er, Jiamusi, Zhaoyuan, and Anqing. In addition to persuading local residents to vacate some of their houses, the local government arranged for a timber factory in the provincial capital Ha'erbin to provide mobile wooden houses as temporary shelters.

2. Construction of *Gan-da-lei* Housing

It wasn't long before the leadership agreed to prioritize oil production in order to meet the requirements of the national strategic plan, but pragmatic solutions also had to be found to provide basic housing. Given the difficult situation in the overall national economy caused by the Great Leap Forward and the Sino-Soviet split in the early 1960s, it was impossible for the state to further assist Daqing beyond what was mentioned above. As Vice Minister Sun argued, it was impossible to build even conventional one-floor brick and tile houses due to the lack of transportation and professional construction teams.[8] This meant that another unique "combat" was needed to provide mass housing as quickly and economically as possible.

4 In a special issue of the French journal *L'Architecture d'Aujourd'hui* in 1979, several authors contributed their studies on "architecture et urbanisme en Chine 1949–1979," including a three-page introduction to Daqing. In addition to academic publications, Dutch film producer Joris Ivens and his French partner Marceline Loridan also produced an interesting documentary film, *A Petroleum Field: Daqing*, which provides a vivid record of the daily life and working scenes in Daqing in the early 1970s.

5 Leon Hoa, *Reconstruire la Chine: Trente ans d'urbanisme, 1949–1979* (Paris: Moniteur, 1981). Due to a language barrier, this book was kept from many Chinese readers and researchers. Eventually it was translated by Li Yin, a Chinese journalist in Paris, and the Chinese version was published in China in 2006.

6 According to Song's research, due to the Cold War in general and the new Sino-Soviet tension in particular, the development of the Daqing oil field was kept secret with extra precautions in the early years. Later on, the public was told it was the Anda Agricultural Cultivation Farm. It was only when Daqing's steady increase in production ensured that China would reach ist goal of a self-sufficient petroleum supply that its real name was announced to the public at the end of 1963. Song, *Gongye xue Daqing shimo*, 163.

7 Ibid., 143–44.

8 Song, *Gongye xue Daqing shimo*, 97.

So how were they to build houses without bricks, cement, tiles, or even professional construction teams? The suggestion offered by the provincial government was adopted by the Daqing leadership, which was to learn from a dwelling architecture widely adopted in the northeast region of China: a simple mud house called *gan-da-lei*. It is built mainly with fine soil, a conventional building material available in northern China. Except for a small amount of wood for doors and window frames and some local plants as an insulation layer for the roof, the walls and the roof are both built with soil. The name *gan-da-lei*—literally drying-tamping-laying—refers to a basic local building technique to make the fifty-centimeter thick wall. These vernacular houses are said to have at least four advantages: 1) they can be built with local materials at no cost; 2) the building technique is easy to learn so that everyone could participate; 3) a lot of wood can be saved; 4) its thick mud wall and the use of a firewall ensures good insulation—warm in the winter and cool in the summer.[9]

Based on investigations conducted by in-house designers and construction technicians in nearby towns and villages, another mass campaign was initiated to build *gan-da-lei* houses. Under the direct guidance of some local builders, at the end of April 1960, a sample project with a total area of 512 m^2 was completed and another 2,500 m^2 finished with only their load-bearing structures. In addition, basic procedures and building code were also summarized to ensure the quality. Suggestions were made to improve the molding boards for making the mud wall, and the invention of an electronic tamper machine helped to more than double construction efficiency. From June 1960, all working units were requested to organize their own construction teams to build their houses.

Many difficulties arose throughout the process; for example, there was no transportation to ship the much needed timber from forests hundreds of miles away, some oil workers not only had to work on the oil fields but also to build houses, all technician cadres participated in construction in their spare time, and local builders were also organized to give on-site guidance. After working day and night for three months, a total of almost 1,000,000 m^2 of floor space was completed for *gan-da-lei* houses by the end of September 1960, which ensured that everyone could move in the newly built houses before the harsh winter.[10]

According to a rough calculation made at the time, the average cost per square meter was no more than thirty RMB, because the main building material was free, labor was free, some volunteered during their spare time, and others were on salary during working hours. If it were to be built with conventional methods, the average cost for a standard multi-floored public building and houses that could resist the extreme winter climate was no less than 200 RMB per square meter.[11] However, due to the lack of experience, there were serious problems with leakage in these early houses, and the follow-up maintenance cost seemed to be rather high. While some people started to question such an unprofessional approach, most people remained confident. By then, a few concentrated living quarters had been built, where four basic building types could be found—houses for people, warehouses for equipment, garages for automobiles, and cellars for vegetables. Such a mixed spatial juxtaposition of urban and rural, living and working, is in fact the defining feature of those early Daqing settlements, which reflects the vision and attitude of its planners and builders at the time.

After more thoroughly researching conventional construction methods and consulting more experienced local builders, the design team finally found solutions to solve the leakage and humidity problems. Moreover, a more standard building technique and procedure was developed after many experiments, which improved both the housing quality and construction speed. Different from the two common techniques—to build with pre-made clay blocks or to build with damp clay—designers invented a third method: to build the wall with a mixture of clay, straw, and mineral wastes poured into the molds made of wooden slabs. Because of its simple structure, mass participation in both construction and repairs was possible. Of the thirty-six construction procedures, regular oil workers and their families could complete twenty-two of them. During the quieter agricultural season in the subsequent years, workers and their families were organized to join the better-trained construction teams to build new homes or repair old ones. Such new houses had proved to be very successful in providing better insulation with their thick, tamped dry-earth walls and roof, and small openings for windows and doors.

As D. J. Dwyer later commented, "it is worth remembering that during the 1960s the Daqing oil field in Heilongjiang was opened up by laborers whose activities included not only building the oil installations and growing their own food but also erecting their own housing out of stamp earth."[12] Indeed, as Hua Lanhong has commented, the benefit of looking for a particular solution by considering local conditions and materials not only included such practical factors as low cost; it was also the start of searching for new methods, potentially leading to more appropriate solutions than the so-called modern ones, or finding a better combination with the latter.[13] This approach of building with local materials, knowledge, and manpower became an important component of the Daqing model.

9 Lanhong Hua, *Chongjian Zhongguo: Chengshi guihua sanshi nian, 1949–1979* (Reconstructing China: Urban Planning in Thirty Years, 1949–1979) (Beijing: SDX Joint Publishing Company, 2006), 113.

10 Song, *Gongye xue Daqing shimo*, 98–99.

11 Ibid.

12 D. J. Dwyer, "Urban Housing and Planning in China," *Transactions of the Institute of British Geographers* 11, no. 4 (1986): 489.

13 Hua, *Chongjian Zhongguo*, 114.

3. Self-Construction and the Role of Women

Residents not only built houses, but they also built public buildings in Daqing. The construction of schools can be seen as a representative case. During the early period of settlement construction, Daqing had adopted a strategy of "enrolling students first, constructing school buildings second." The first class for new students on the opening day of school was to build their school with their own hands. During the period when no school buildings were available at the beginning, teaching was done in various locations wherever possible. Canteens, warehouses, cattle barns, and corridors were frequently used. Basic furniture such as desks made of clay blocks and small benches made of remaining small pieces of wood were all handmade. Following the *gan-da-lei* building method, school buildings were built from scratch with significant participation of students who were happy and proud to study there afterwards. This self-construction process may also be considered a predecessor of the educational system introduced later that involved part-time studying and part-time work.

In addition to regular primary schools and middle schools, professional schools were gradually established within a few years, specializing in geology, mineral exploration, agricultural mechanics, education, finance and economy, healthcare, etc. All of them complied with the practical demands of the overall settlement. In fact, during its most crucial period, roughly the first half of the 1960s, self-construction had been a basic and effective tool in shaping the initial physical landscape of Daqing's numerous settlements.

When female dependents started to arrive after the initial great campaign in 1961, women began playing an active role in settlement construction. Following an organized group study and some labor (such as collecting organic manure to make fertilizers), the first women's production brigade was formed in the spring of 1962 to convert the grassland into agricultural land. By the end of 1962, records show that there were already 3,800 family dependents in the workforce, forming 182 production teams. They converted 4,000-mu (266.7 hectares) of land and yielded 330,000 kg of grain and 375,000 kg of vegetables. When more dependents arrived in 1963, the total working population increased to 14,000 in 398 production teams. Besides working on grain and vegetables, they also started planting orchards and raising chickens, pigs, and cattle, which allowed the locals to enjoy homegrown rice, vegetables, fruit, poultry, eggs, meat, and even milk. With support from nearby industry, some 200 female agricultural mechanics were trained, and their working tools developed from simple to semi-mechanized.[14]

Besides conventional agricultural production, women also played important roles in other services. One good example is the sewing and mending workshop. Started with three veterans and five female dependents in the winter of 1960, the workshop was responsible for washing oil workers' dirty clothes, mending and taking apart old ones, and making new ones. The major purpose was to fully utilize the materials by recycling old clothes into new ones in a rough "two-old into one-new" proportion. Growing from the initial workshop equipped with only simple tools collected from home into a small-scale factory with dozens of sewing machines, the workers also managed to rebuild the initial working space into a new workshop based on the pipelining principle.[15]

Meanwhile, as more and more new buildings were built to accommodate community facilities such as canteens, daycares, kindergartens, barbershops, clinics, and primary schools, some family dependents also joined other female employees in these services. By the end of 1965, more than ninety-five percent of the family dependents in Daqing had joined the workforce in one way or another.[16] As revealed in the Ivens/Loridan documentary, many women were proud to talk about their participation in house construction and agricultural activities when interviewed by the filmmaker. According to them, it was necessary and exciting for them to get involved in building activities, which had traditionally been perceived as men's work. In their own words, by participating in both farming and construction, they proved what they were capable of. And they were even happier when their husbands no longer looked down on them but showed more respect. As some explicitly stated, these experiences helped them become more confident to pursue equality in their relationships with their husbands.[17]

4. Typological Change

Before the overall planning approach was decided, some modest and down-to-earth practices had already been adopted to provide immediate housing to workers and their families from the very beginning. Constrained by financial and material scarcity, yet inspired by local building tradition and technology, designers working for the Daqing Oil Group were able to develop the so-called *gan-da-lei* housing model after continued experiments during the early 1960s. As the basic spatial unit shaping people's everyday lives in these settlements, a close reading of its layout is necessary to better understand how people actually lived in such a settlement.

14 *Daqing jianshi* (Daqing Brief History), 78–79.
15 Song, *Gongye xue Daqing shimo*, 114–18.
16 Ibid., 114.
17 This interpretation is based on an episode of the film in which a group of women sitting in front of their homes in the Foundation Making Settlement were interviewed. Ivens et al., *A Petroleum Field: Daqing*.

Following the dwelling tradition in rural areas in northern China, each house comprises a series of fixed spatial elements: a cooking/heating stove, a large built-in bed (*kang*), and a firewall connected to the chimney. The stove plays a dual role for both cooking and heating to endure the long harsh winter.

Unlike the conventional method of placing the stove and the kang in the front part of the house, in the new plan the stove was placed towards the middle in the entrance hall, and the kang was pushed farther away from the window to the back. This change must be viewed considering the changing lifestyles. Traditionally, placing the kang right next to the front window made the big kang area the most comfortable domestic space in addition to providing the sleeping function during the night. Usually it was two by three meters with the best possible natural lighting, ventilation, and heating. By placing a small low table on top of it during the day, this became the central area where family activities such as eating, sewing, and homework took place. Mostly located in small villages, sometimes in the central village, three to five of such houses were constructed as one building with slightly different layouts according to family structures and population. Families with two generations were often given big and small bedrooms either with an independent or a shared kitchen. Married couples without children often lived in a one-bedroom house with a shared kitchen.

6. Communal Living in Daqing's Everyday Life

Single workers were generally accommodated in large dormitory rooms located in the central village. According to the numbers of cups and basins shown in a sketch of the interior of a worker's dormitory dated March 1964, each room was likely to host ten to twelve people. The division between the sleeping area and the everyday storage area was similar to those often seen in school or army dormitories. As described in a short note next to the drawing, the fact that items like quilts, towels, washbasins, cups, and books were always neatly lined up suggested a communal lifestyle that had been practiced by those who were working or studying away from home at that time.

Without any kitchen facilities, single workers had their meals served in a communal cafeteria nearby. Meals could also be bought ready-made or partially made and be eaten at the canteens or taken back home. Often a large cafeteria was also used as a multifunctional space where big meetings were organized, operas were performed, and films were shown. Families were free to choose between daycare and twenty-four-hour care for their young children. During the busy farming season, babies were often brought to their mothers who were working in the fields to be breastfed. Although probably with limited frequency, buses ran along major roads that provided essential transportation links between each settlement. For settlements where fixed public facilities were not yet available, mobile staff and teams were then organized to provide services such as healthcare, haircuts, and grain products. In short, efforts were made to provide communal services in the shortest range possible so that residents could have their basic needs met without leaving their settlement.

The immediate benefits of such a communal working and living system were reflected in several ways. No rent was collected for housing, as most residents had participated in construction and maintenance. Free medical care was provided for those who were injured during working hours without any deduction from their wages. Both daycare and education were provided for very low fees paid by families. The introduction of a new educational system—part-time studying, part-time working (participating in either industrial and/or agricultural activities)—to all middle schools and vocational schools in Daqing in 1964 was another effort aimed at producing future generations equipped with both industrial and agricultural production knowledge to continue developing these settlements under the same principle.

In the documentary film made by Ivens and Loridan, a group of female residents openly expressed their feelings and attitudes towards such communal living in interviews.[18] Speaking honestly, some admitted that in the beginning many of them acted like common housewives whose worldview only included her own family, husband, and children. But as soon as they participated in communal work such as farming and home building, the immediate outcome made them feel the difference. Paid according to the wage system based on labor credits, participation in the collective work enabled them to earn independent income and achieve self-liberation through labor as envisioned by the communist leadership. This shift in mentality certainly did not occur overnight, nor was it easy. With the increasing participation of women in all kinds of collective work ranging from agriculture to social services, "women supporting half the sky" became a quite accurate conclusion for what happened in Daqing's settlement development.

18 According to Ian Mundell's study of Ivens and his films, the use of "cinema direct" techniques in this series of China documentaries was discussed extensively. In Mundell's view, this technique and approach helped Ivens and Loridan explore and capture life in China after the Cultural Revolution close up. As he suggests, "This is perhaps why they suffer more than usual from accusations of construction and their proximity to the official line. However [...] there is a sense that these Chinese documentaries show a spectacle that would be taking place even if the camera was not there. They also return to Ivens's enduring themes of work, the elements, and a people trying to build a new way of life." Ian Mundell, "Joris Ivens," *Senses of cinema* 37 (October 2005), http://www. sensesofcinema.com/contents/directors/05/ivens.html.

As analyzed earlier, with the increasing time and energy devoted to the new communal work and lifestyles of both men and women, the space, role, and meaning of the individual's house/family/home was also considerably transformed. Although it is imaginable that such a new way of living must have been resisted and challenged by old conventions and habits from time to time, the intense participation in communal affairs was certainly a vital and prominent aspect in everyday life at Daqing's numerous settlements during the 1960s and 1970s.

7. "Learning from Daqing" Campaign

Daqing's achievement was summarized in an official report prepared by the Petroleum Ministry at the beginning of 1964. After listening to a two-and-a-half hour presentation given by the petroleum minister, Yu Qiuli, about his personal experience, Mao Zedong immediately made a positive comment and suggested that Chinese industry should learn from Daqing. The comment appeared on the front page of *People's Daily* on January 25, 1964, which clearly marked the beginning of the nationwide campaign, "Learning from Daqing."

This resulted in Wang Jinxi, a model worker from Daqing with the nickname "iron man," being selected to be a people's representative and attend the national congress in 1964. He was also invited to attend a special birthday dinner for Mao Zedong on December 26 of the same year with other model figures from different areas.[19] If Wang represented the best of the Daqing workers, then Xue Guifang represented Daqing's family dependents, when she attended a national conference held by the All Chinese Women's Federation (ACWF) on International Women's Day (March 8) in 1965. A play performed by Daqing's women about their life experience helped spread the story about how Daqing settlements were constructed and developed in a balanced way with both urban and rural features. Yet it was the publication of the *People's Daily* article on April 2, 1966, and the republication in the *Journal of Architecture* that reinforced Daqing's contribution to planning and architecture in a more explicit way.

This campaign had a positive impact on both architectural and planning practices, such as more innovative design proposals for family houses and dormitories with local materials, techniques, and typologies, and more integrated collaboration between designers, engineers, builders, and end users through the promotion of on-site design. Also, more professionals started reflecting on the general ignorance of planning and construction in small cities and towns, the lack of regional planning to balance existing urban and rural relations, and the lack of flexibility in housing design.[20] Yet, when "learning from Daqing" became simplified and narrowed down to a way to save money and empower non-professionals over professionals, the negative consequences were also obvious.

8. Summary

The early modest approach to finding proper housing forms and building techniques was Daqing's legacy in the field of spatial planning and building construction and fit right into the pragmatic and ideological concerns of the day. The unassertive attitude and down-to-earth working method of early design staff involving countless consultations with vernacular builders and trial-and-error experiments finally resulted in the *gan-da-lei* building. The success of this typology in Daqing lies in its honest expression and the relationship between the building materials, techniques, and forms, which were deeply rooted in its geo-cultural context.

Above all, great efforts were made to manage and coordinate different aspects of social life based on limited resources in regard to the socio-spatial organization within each settlement in Daqing. The development of Daqing settlements was inspired by Mao's earlier guideline from 1957 that large state-owned enterprises "should engage in agriculture, trade, education, and military training, as well as industry," and was also in accordance with the People's Commune principles of the early 1960s. They provided another example of how industry, agriculture, commerce, education, healthcare, and civilian self-defense could be incorporated into both spatial planning and social organization.[21]

However, the earlier indigenous approach and attitude, which led to the introduction of *gan-da-lei* buildings through careful studies of and experiments with local materials and building techniques, seemed to have been largely ignored in the construction of new buildings in Daqing's later developments. Despite the introduction of new building materials and techniques, little effort was made to find new solutions for the crucial insulation issue or put into the search for the rationale between new materials such as bricks, tiles, and cement, their techniques, and their corresponding forms. When the earlier *gan-da-lei* approach and method was oversimplified and reduced to a cost cutter while

19 It was the first and last time that Mao made his birthday celebration a public event by inviting several key figures of the time, including Dong Jiagen and Xin Yanzi as male and female models of educated teenagers who volunteered to build the countryside, Chen Yonggui as the model farmer from Dazhai, Wang Jinxi as the model worker from Daqing, Qian Xuesen as the model scientist, who was later remembered as the "father of Chinese missiles," etc.

20 Hua, *Chongjian Zhongguo*, 118–123.

21 Shan-hao Chiang, "Daching Impressions (IV): Combining Urban and Rural Life," Peking Review, no. 27 (1977): 24; Yaolin Ding, "Daqing Oilfield Today," *Beijing Review*, no. 13 (1983): 23–25.

ignoring its success in meeting basic comfort and durability needs proven in innovative experiments, the consequences were severe. Large numbers of highly economical buildings of poor quality, such as those built in later years in Daqing itself, were produced all over the country in the following decade.

The formation and development of Daqing settlements between the 1960s and 1970s provided both legacies and lessons for settlement planning and related social organizations aimed at responding to industrialization and urbanization in a more balanced way. Spatial features such as a dispersed and decentralized structure, mixed land use, and self-construction, which were prominent during early stages of development, had proved to be an effective approach and strategy to cope with practical difficulties in funding, material, and manpower. More importantly, such small-scale settlements also helped shape family and social life, where everybody was stimulated or urged to participate more in public life and self-management.*

Literature

Chiang, Shan-hao. "Daching Impressions (IV): Combining Urban and Rural Life." *Peking Review*, no. 27 (1977): 24.

Ding, Yaolin. "Daqing Oilfield Today." *Beijing Review*, no. 13 (1983): 23–25.

DQJS editorial board. *Daqing jianshi* (Daqing Brief History). Contemporary China Press, 1991.

DQTPJ editorial. *Daqing tupian ji* (Collection of Daqing Photography), People's Fine Arts Press, and Heilongjiang People's Press, 1977.

DQXM editorial. *Daqing xinmao* (New Image of Daqing), People's Fine Arts Press, 1976.

DQZJ editorial board. *Dui Daqing jingyan de zhengzhi jingji xue kaocha (A Political and Economical Research on Daqing's Experience*). People's Press, 1979.

Dwyer, D. J. "Urban Housing and Planning in China." *Transactions of the Institute of British Geographers*, New Series, vol. 11 no. 4 (1986): 479-489.

Editorial Committee of Daqing City Record Office. *Daqing shizhi* (*Daqing City Record*). Nanjing Publishing House, 1988.

Hoa, Léon. *Réconstruire la Chine: Trente ans d'urbanisme, 1949–1979*. Paris: Moniteur, 1981.

Hua, Lanhong. *Chongjian Zhongguo: Chengshi guihua sanshi nian, 1949–1979 (Reconstructing China: Urban Planning in Thirty Years, 1949–1979)*. SDX Joint Publishing Company, 2006.

Ivens, Joris, and Marceline Loridan. *A Petroleum Field: Daqing* (one of the 12 documentary films under a general title *How Yukong Moved Mountains*), 1976.

Kwok, Reginald. "Architecture et urbanisme 1949–1979." *L'Architecture d'Aujourd'hui*, no. 201 (February 1979): 8–14.

Kwok, Reginald. "Da-qing et le modèle urbain." *L'Architecture d'Aujourd'hui*, no. 201 (February 1979): 54–57.

Mundell, Ian. "Joris Ivens." *Senses of cinema*, Great directors, 37 (October 2005). Accessed July, 2006. http://www.sensesofcinema.com/contents/directors/05/ivens.html.

Song, Liansheng. *Gongye xue Daqing shimo* (*The Beginning and End of the Campaign of Learning from Daqing in Industry*). Hubei: People's Press, 2005.

* This paper is a revised version based on the contents of Chapter 6, 8, and 9 of my doctoral dissertation entitled "Socio-Spatial Transformation in Mao's China: Settlement Planning and Dwelling Architecture Revisited (1950s–1970s)," completed at KU Leuven, Leuven, Belgium in 2007.

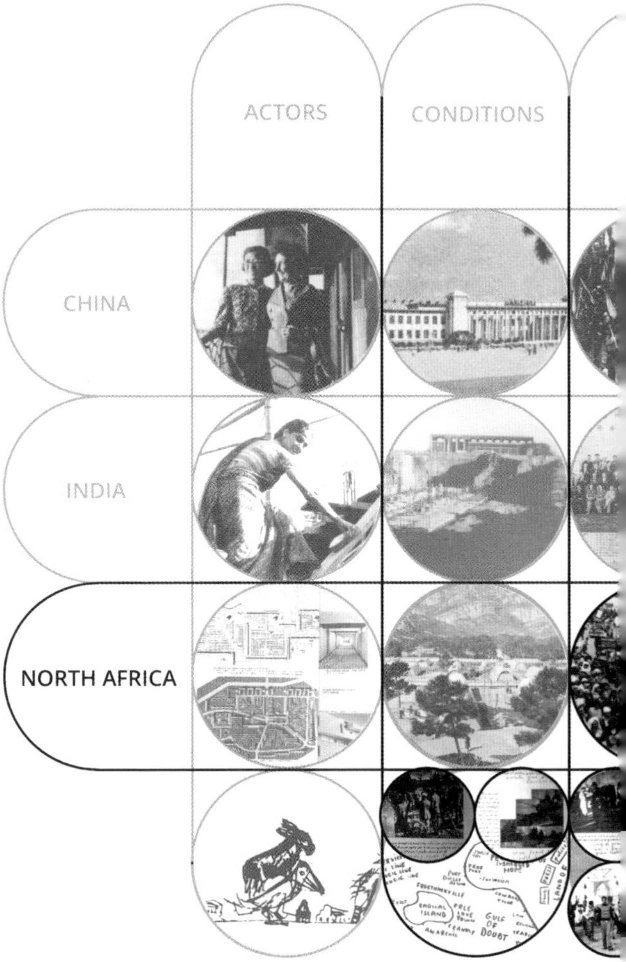

From Casablanca To Be’er Sheva

DEBATES & DISCOURSES

CONCEPTS

ART & RESEARCH

THEORIES

The Beehive Metaphor

Morocco 1952

×

Anti-Colonialism

Casablanca

Decolonization

From/ To Casablanca Beer Sheva

Morocco

Starting in 1952, general strikes and several protest demonstrations organized mainly by inhabitants of the Bidonvilles in Casablanca were violently suppressed. As the new settlements were erected, the military became increasingly present in everyday city life. After years of anticolonial struggles, Morocco gained its independence in 1956.

© Photo: Private Collection.

Non-Pedigreed Architecture

Felicity D. Scott and Marion von Osten in Conversation

Marion von Osten: In the Western and non-Western architectural practices of the 1950s and 1960s, cultural expressions and techniques, which had hitherto not been regarded as modern but as pre-modern, were assiduously studied by architects and planners. One path of this movement was to "learn from" vernacular architecture, to acknowledge the pre-industrial city as well as dwelling practices of nomadism as major influences for new methods of design and planning. Such references were also to be found in the influential exhibitions "Mostra Di Architettura Spontanea" by Giancarlo de Carlo held in Milan in 1951; or in "This is Tomorrow" at the Whitechapel Gallery London in 1956 as well as in the influential show "Architecture Without Architects" by Bernard Rudofsky at MoMA in New York in 1964. Theoretical writings by Sibyl Moholy-Nagy, such as the influential book *Native Genius in Anonymous Architecture* (1957) or *The Matrix of Man* (1968) are vivid signs for a discourse that can also be interpreted as crisis of modernist authorship in architecture and posed the pressing question: who builds? But Rudofsky's approach turned out to be one of the most popular of its time.

Felicity D. Scott: I think there were many factors informing the resurgent interest among architects in pre-industrial architectural vernaculars and nomadic structures in the 1950s and 1960s, some of which help explain the enormous popularity of Rudofsky's 1964 exhibition, others do not. Although the specific conditions driving this shift in discourse vary across different contexts and with different protagonists—the Italian discourse being quite distinct from the French, British, or American, for instance—one key underlying factor haunting the architectural imagination was, I believe, the recent experience of war in Europe. Beyond the significant destruction of urban environments on account of bombing, the massive displacements of populations in inter-war, wartime, and postwar Europe exacerbated the experience of uprootedness and environmental insecurity that had long been a condition of modernity. Driven by processes of industrialization and the forces of capitalism, rural to urban migration had, of course, been taking place for generations in Europe. Yet the rising tide of nationalism during this period, and the racially motivated claims to a "native place" or authentic mode of belonging that often accompanied nationalist politics, was for many a truly (and often quite literally) unsettling phenomenon. The pre-industrial village, with its supposedly organic social relations and material connection to traditional culture, thus emerged as a rather paradoxical cipher for this condition; it stood at once for a lost (and to many minds better) form of life and a challenge to identitarian models of form-function-place relations that had long been assumed by architects. It raised the question not only of how an architect was supposed to operate within such a condition of deracination or unsettlement but also of modern architecture's proximity to, even participation within, industrialized violence and environmental destruction.

Architects now asked: had modernism's embrace of new technologies for their capacity to advance enlightenment ideals of progress unwittingly served to turn those ideals on their heads? Following the end of World War II, the threat of violence remained, of course, on people's minds, whether on account of escalating fears of atomic warfare or of military conflicts born of Cold War divides (notably the Korean War, which received only limited attention from Europe and the United States, and the war in Vietnam). Beyond the task of reconstructing cities damaged by war, that is, this connection between technological advancement, warfare, environmental destruction, and displacement was a profound legacy of the devastating wars of the first half of the twentieth century, a legacy that I believe served to condition this shift in discourse. Coupled with growing evidence of environmental devastation wrought by industrialization (popularized by the 1962 publication of Rachel Carson's *Silent Spring*, followed by Stewart L. Udall's *The Quiet Crisis* the next year) and the sense of failure associated with large-scale urban renewal projects in American and European cities, architecture's relation to the environment, and to capitalist industrialization, was being profoundly reconsidered.

Modern architects had, of course, long been interested in vernacular and mobile forms—we need only think of Ludwig Mies van der Rohe, Le Corbusier, or Hannes Meyer during the inter-war period—so in many regards the fascination with Mediterranean hill towns and mobility was not new. Indeed, the fascination with architectural vernaculars was distinctly modern. What was new, as you indicate, was the enormous popularity of Rudofsky's exhibition, which after closing at MoMA in New York traveled nationally and internationally to more than eighty locations, for over a decade. It was so popular that MoMA had to fabricate a second, condensed version of the traveling show to accommodate the demand. Sibyl Moholy-Nagy's 1955 book, *Native Genius in Anonymous Architecture*, or the many important Italian exhibitions on regional vernaculars simply did not enjoy the scale of success of Rudofsky's polemical show and its accompanying catalog, even if they were known and appreciated by many architects. And it is perhaps important to mention that Rudofsky's fascination with vernacular architecture and mobility itself dated back to the 1920s but did not receive widespread attention until he packaged it in a seductive visual format with the catchy title, "Architecture without Architects." Indeed, to understand its popular success I think we need to understand the manner in which both the exhibition and publication embodied a media strategy that the architect developed over many decades and in many institutional contexts. While that story is too complex to recount in detail here, a short account of the images displayed in *Architecture without Architects* and the polemics to which they spoke will hopefully help elucidate aspects of this phenomenon.

The exhibition consisted of seventy-five large photographic panels, with forty-five smaller panels accommodating both photos and text, along with a title panel and one containing the introductory wall text. At MoMA the panels were installed within a labyrinth-like aluminum frame, with some presented vertically, some horizontally, some titled, some recessed, etc. In many instances the images were at a distance from the captions referencing them, an organization that produced for some viewers an annoying disassociation while for others gave rise to a complex set of associations among and between the images. Like his earlier work for the United States pavilion at the 1958 Brussels Fair, Rudofsky deployed a decidedly open-ended or non-narrative approach that encouraged the visitor to wander in an aleatory manner amidst the three-dimensional lattice of images, hence producing their own set of associations.

There was, however, a set of ordering devices at work in the selection of images and organization of the show, which was carefully crafted in order to resonate with modern architecture and its aesthetic logic. Indeed, radically decontextualizing the buildings or environments depicted in the photographs from their cultural and geographical contexts (about which he often knew very little), Rudofsky divided the material into thematic sections such as prefabrication, standardization, flexibility, portability, etc. He also carefully selected the images to resonate with modernist aesthetics and even sometimes with particular works of modernism, aiming to elicit a profoundly unstable resonance between the vernacular and the modern.

The 122 panels and demountable frame then traveled to subsequent venues in a single box to be reconstituted according to desired or possible layout at the next site. In other words, this was not fixed in advance. The panels could, for instance, even be hung more conventionally on a wall, although it would remain evident that they were designed for circulation. The publication itself largely repeated the visual material used in the exhibition, along with their witty and often ironic captions. Designed by Rudofsky himself, the book was presented as a "prelude" to a larger study, which appeared in 1969 as *The Prodigious Builders*, but enjoyed nothing like the reception of *Architecture without Architects*.

While to many at the time the exhibition and book seemed to be offering models for contemporary design, Rudofsky was adamant that he had no such instrumentalizing ambition, and repeatedly refused the suggestion that vernacular architecture offered simple models for architects. In fact, he insisted repeatedly that the show operated in the register of a parable or allegory. In many ways it was exactly the same set of conditions, anxieties, and desires which made the subject matter so appealing that led to the profound misunderstanding (that it offered solutions), and hence its success. Finally, that Rudofsky's show received such a divided reception—being hailed by some in the critical and architectural establishments as an important intervention into contemporary debates yet considered by others to be a severely misguided and nostalgic retrieval of pre-industrial forms and a romance with the "exotic"—and that it was launched from a bastion of modern architecture in America, also helped fuel the fire of its visibility and fame. With its catchy title and visually captivating photographs achieving near-global circulation, *Architecture without Architects*—both catalog and exhibition—proved among other things an auspicious vehicle for disseminating images of pre-industrial structures and rural vernaculars into diverse contemporary debates. All this to say that I think many factors informed the success of Rudofsky's show—from its ability to resonate with issues regarding architecture, technology, and the environment that were on so many people's minds to its media-savvy visual realization.

MvO: In the writings and projects by the Swiss architect André Studer in North Africa in the early 1950s, a proposal for a new synthesis between the modern and the pre-modern is expressed. Designs relate to a concept of a north-African kasbah and international modern architecture. In the housing complex Sidi Othman built in 1952 on the outskirts of Casablanca, these concepts were implemented in the design and building process. Another path of this "vernacular modernism" started in North Africa with the locus of anti-colonial liberation movements—the *bidonvilles*—and from there a new perspective developed that focused on dwelling practices and was critical of previous modern approaches to dwelling. As a dwelling environment, the *bidonvilles* was not only the locus of the first encounters and negotiations with the modern city for a lot of people coming from rural areas, it was also the spatial expression of a non-planned way of organizing an urban environment. European architects like Georges Candilis and Shadrach Woods declared the *bidonvilles* a subject of study and investigated this environment with an anthropological approach. They "learned" from the inhabitants of the *bidonvilles* how everyday dwelling practices made an urban neighborhood possible through self-organization. This line of architectural debate recognized the self-built environment in the colonial city as valuable housing practices from which European planners would need to learn. The studies in Casablanca or John Turner's similar studies on self-built housing in the shantytowns of Peru also influenced a generation of "non-planned" and participatory strategies. This led in part to a new role for the architect and architecture in urban planning in the 1960s. Do you see certain genealogies and particular developments that need to be drawn from here?

FDS: If you are asking whether Rudofsky was engaged with or could be considered to be part of this genealogy of architectural research and practice during the 1950s, the answer is largely "no." He was certainly a reader of Fumihiko Maki's *Investigations in Collective Form* (1964) and Oscar Newman's *CIAM 59 in Otterlo* (1961), and he was familiar with aspects of Yona Friedman's work, so it was not that he was unfamiliar with studies of *bidonvilles*, self-built environments, colonial cities, and participatory strategies. But in many ways he remained a distinctly modern architect when compared to these discourses and practices: the plan remained important to him, and the "subject" of his concerns was not populations displaced by the violence of colonization or forces of industrialization but the contemporary European or American city dweller. In fact, one of the most astounding aspects of researching Rudofsky is how rare it is for him to even acknowledge colonialism, let alone liberation struggles and the process of decolonization. I certainly wish one could more forcefully make this connection, but the archival evidence is simply not there.

MvO: This would also speak for the modernist discourse of the "vernacular" as an agent that wanders through different localities and time zones. Thus, the study and usage of the vernacular need to be understood as a contextual concept, as its meaning shifts within concrete architectural practices embedded in specific political and local conditions. Like in the French colonies, the vernacular-modern synthesis varied from the re-ordering of the *bidonville* (restructuration) to temporary rehousing (relogement) and finally to the creation of new housing estates (habitations à loyer modéré) based on the standard Écochard grid that consisted of a standard two-room patio house. Also, the patio house gained kind of a model status for international postwar architects. It can be found in Israel's Development Towns like Be'er Sheva for example, but also as a basic structure in tourist resorts or villa architecture in the Mediterranean. Often it is argued that the patio house is a response to specific climate conditions. How would you—in the context of Rudofsky's work—understand this trend?

FDS: Rudofsky's use of the patio house or courtyard house typology was in fact one of the most fascinating, and contradictory, aspects of his work. With his earliest published patio house design, a sketch for "Haus B. auf Capri" of 1934, we find for instance that the photo collage he produced uses an image of the Greek Island of Santorini as its base, not one from Capri. The house designed the following year for himself and Berta Doctor (soon to be Berta Rudofsky) for the island of Procida, also off the coast of Naples, would in some senses appear to be closer to a conventional use of vernacular architecture by a modern architect. But when one reads Rudofsky's 1938 account of the house, as it appeared in *Domus* under the title "Non ci vuole un nuovo modo di costruire, ci vuole un nuovo modo di vivere" (We don't need a new way of building but a new way of living), what you find are a series of concerns that depart significantly from such paradigms. In addition to musings on the affinities between modern architecture and Mediterranean forms of life, and familiar polemics against architectural fashions and styles, we find in this text a series of peculiar but persistent obsessions regarding the naked foot and the idea of bringing the occupant down to the very surface of the house in order to produce an intimacy with the floor. Moreover, following the Anschluss in March 1938, which motivated his departure from Italy, Rudofsky repeatedly used the Mediterranean typology in other contexts, such as Brazil and the United States. Indeed, the patio house quite literally came to serve as something like a mobile infrastructure for an uprooted life, providing the basis of an intimate mode of dwelling wherever one might be and hence a form of (primarily psychological) defense against external conditions.

As I argue in my forthcoming book, *Cartographies of Drift: Bernard Rudofsky's Encounters with Modernity*, the patio house served as the key term in his formulation of a mode of domesticity that might enable the subject to dwell while adrift, to be at home anywhere. It becomes a device for mediating between the international aspirations of high modernism with its footholds in vernacular architecture, and the technical and geopolitical conditions informing deracination; it served as a demonstration of a post-regional, even post-national formulation of architecture, an architecture of unsettlement. When Rudofsky's patio houses in Brazil were included in Philip Goodwin's 1943 MoMA exhibition, "Brazil Builds," this non-regional idiom was noted by Henry-Russell Hitchcock, for whom the designs seemed "less acculturated" than they might have been, to him a very problematic quality. It might also be noted that Rudofsky's very first publications following his arrival in the United States were two texts on patio houses that appeared in *New Pencil Points*, "Notes on Patios" and "Three Patio Houses," the latter an account of his three major houses in Brazil in which he polemically insisted that the type was strictly not indigenous to the region. "Notes on Patios" returned to the subject of a 1938 text in *Domus*, "Quattro esempi di giardini," and stressed again that the patio house was not regional but universal. But more unexpected is his implicit argument tying the emergence of the patio type in the United States to the use of the stockade by European settlers, and hence to questions of colonizing operations on foreign territories and with them the need for defense. Hence we find ourselves at quite a distance, conceptually speaking, from the figure of authentic, or climatically appropriate modes of dwelling often attributed to this typology.

Patios, Carpets, and No Pavilion
Model Housing in Morocco and Israel

Marion von Osten

In 1956, the artists Nigel Henderson and Eduardo Paolozzi, and the architects Alison and Peter Smithson, all members of the Independent Group, created the "Patio and Pavilion" installation for the famous "This Was Tomorrow" exhibition at the Whitechapel Art Gallery in London. In photographs documenting "Patio and Pavilion," found and faulty materials and objects are loosely displayed on sand, strewn over the gallery floor. In the center of the set, a three-walled shack was installed, topped with a translucent roof and fenced in by a precarious aluminum-plywood wall. Unlike other participations, the "Patio and Pavilion" area was not a proto-pop statement like other group exhibits, for example, the contributions by Richard Hamilton, John McHale, and John Voelcker. Instead, the mixture and collage of different images and objects in the "Patio and Pavilion" installation highlighted the more profane aesthetics of everyday life together with vernacular building practices. As an artistic strategy, all materials and objects were displayed "as found."[1] But as Ben Highmore argues, the "Patio and Pavilion" exhibit was not just an installation of different objects, materials, and panels, but also a "conglomeration of references." For him, "Patio and Pavilion" was "enough like a house in an Algerian Bidonville, enough like a shed in Bethnal Green, enough like a post-nuclear ruin, enough like a rural dwelling, enough like a smashed-up shop, enough like an ur-form dwelling. [...] But it was also enough not like previous architectural pavilions, enough not like a celebration of consumerism."[2]

Combining the pavilion—a site of Asian and European garden architecture, world fairs, and exhibitions—with the vernacular courtyard house, the patio in the installations title also related to empirical and anthropological studies of the time on Western and non-Western localities. On the one hand, it referred to the many self-built shelters that were part of the urban fabric of the bombed European cities in the early years after the Second World War, and, on the other hand, to the emerging urban-anthropological studies conducted in working class districts. In addition to the Independent Group's shift to popular cultures and the everyday, the Smithsons had also been participants of the ninth CIAM Congress and were involved in the discussions around architectural studies in North Africa, which focused on the building practices of slum dwellers. These studies marked a shift in postwar modern building approaches, as the self-built environments of the shantytown dwellers were presented as models for understanding the interrelation between the public and the private sphere. This was an emerging intercultural debate that formed new architectural approaches, in which the Smithsons, as founding members of the group Team 10, were central actors.[3]

1 Claude Lichtenstein and Thomas Schregenberger, *As Found: The Discovery of the Ordinary: British Architecture and Art of the 1950s* (Zurich: Lars Müller Publishers, 2001).

2 Ben Highmore, "Rough Poetry: Patio and Pavilion Revisited," *Oxford Art Journal*, no. 29 (2006): 269–90.

3 Marc Crinson, "From the Rainforest to the Streets," in *Colonial Modern: Aesthetics of the Past, Rebellions for the Future*, eds. Tom Avermaete, Serhat Karakayali, and Marion von Osten (London: Black Dog Publishing, 2011), 98–111.

The GAMMA Grid

At the ninth CIAM (*Congrès International d'Architecture Moderne*) meeting in Aix-en-Provence in the summer of 1953, these shifts from single architecture solutions to larger concepts of city planning were expressed in a new guideline, the Charta of Habitat.[4] Here, a younger generation of modern architects presented ideas that were critical of the functional separation within urban planning between housing, work, leisure, and transportation. In an amendment to the 1933 Athens Charter, which was developed at the first CIAM meetings, they called attention to the interconnectedness of housing, street, district, and city. Next to other factors, one context for this dispute was the presentation of three visual urban studies (so-called "grids"): the "GAMMA Grid," presented by the Groupe d'Architectes Modernes Marocains, guided by Michel Écochard in Casablanca, the "Mahieddine Grid," a study of a shantytown in Algiers presented by Roland Simounet, and the "Urban Re-Identification Grid," by Alison and Peter Smithson, a collage of photographs, children's drawings, and an urban analysis of street usage in East London's working class and colonial migrant district, Bethnal Green.[5]

The GAMMA section of the CIAM meeting 1953 consisted of Michel Écochard and a group of young architects, including students of Le Corbusier who were working in the ATBAT Afrique office in Tangier, Algiers, and Casablanca. Michel Écochard, director of the Morocco Department of Urban Planning in Casablanca from 1946–52, had developed a large-scale program under the name "Housing for the Greatest Number," with the aim of addressing the Moroccan proletariat that had settled in the city's outskirts. For his master plan, he applied a grid structure as the main planning instrument for the new urban neighborhoods that were to replace the numerous *bidonvilles* (tin can cities). Gaining knowledge of the social and physical characteristics of the field was a prerequisite for his planning method. Écochard introduced sociological and building surveys to investigate "human groups in all of their daily realities, as well as cartographic and statistical analyses, used to identify 'the city's fundamental tendencies.'"[6] Instead of showing single examples of modern architecture, the GAMMA group presented an analysis of the social conditions of a shantytown in the suburbs of Casablanca, an area that had thus far been treated as a misery that needed to be eliminated. Their detailed grid presented in Aix-en-Provence included different sources such as aerial photographs alongside sociographic charts and documentary images about the modern, industrialized and rural, traditional aspects of daily life in the so-called *bidonvilles*, the self-built settlements where new migrants, arriving mainly from the Atlas Mountains, were forced to live. The study proposed cleaning up *bidonvilles* by relating to European discourses of hygiene, and presented a new urban scheme that included a low-rise patio house grid and a few experimental high-rise buildings. But the grid also proposed—as a side effect—that modern architects should take the opportunity to learn from vernacular architecture as well as the self-built environments and dwelling practices of local populations. Thus, the study created an image of conditions determined by self-organization and small-scale interventions by the dwellers themselves. As a dwelling environment, the *bidonville* was not only the locus of the first encounters and negotiations with the modern city for many people coming from rural areas; above all, it was the spatial expression of an unplanned way of organizing an urban environment. This focus on the everyday life of the inhabitants and builders of the *bidonvilles* was a radical challenge to the abstract rational parameters of the earlier CIAM congresses, which would have considered this ad-hoc urbanism a pre-modern phenomenon that modern architecture would radically overcome.[7]

Presenting self-built environments or street usage in working class districts as models for understanding the interrelation between the public and the private sphere was an alternate interpretation of the CIAM concept of "habitat" by the younger, more international generation. These new proposals caused heated debates and marked a first sign of the dissolution of CIAM as an international organization of the modernist movement. The ninth CIAM meeting ended in conflicts with the congress' older generation of founding members, such as Le Corbusier, Gropius, and Giedion. The dispute included the constitution of a group of younger architects from different local backgrounds who would later meet under the name Team 10, as they were charged with organizing of the tenth CIAM congress in Dubrovnik, Yugoslavia.[8]

4 In her article "The Concept of Habitat: Écochard in Morocco," published in the above-mentioned *Colonial Modern: Aesthetics of the Past, Rebellions for the Future,* Monique Eleb argues that the notion of "Habitat" "was borrowed from ethnologists, geographers and anthropologists, who addressed the issues of shelter, housing and environment, the concept of geography and terrain, and the links with civilisation as opposed to rural areas." She states that before the 1950s, the term habitat was already in use during colonial rule to refer to non-Western societies, 156.

5 Mustafa Baghdadi, "Changing Ideals in Architecture: From CIAM to Team X," in *Architectural Knowledge and Cultural Diversity*, ed. William O'Reilly (Lausanne: Comportements, 1999), 22–56; Zeynep Çelik, "Learning from the Bidonville: CIAM Looks at Algiers," *Harvard Design Magazine*, (February 2003): 476–79; Marion von Osten, "Learning from...," in *In der Wüste der Moderne. Koloniale Planung und danach*, ed. Haus der Kulturen der Welt (Berlin: *taz* supplement for the same-titled exhibition, 2008), 3.

6 Michel Écochard, *Casablanca, le roman d'une ville* (Paris: Edition de Paris, 1955), 105.

7 Tom Avermaete, *Another Modern: The Post-War Architecture and Urbanism of Candilis-Josic Woods* (Rotterdam: NAi Publishers, 2005); Gwendolyn Wright, *The Politics of Design in French Colonial Urbanism* (Chicago: University of Chicago Press, 1991).

8 Eric Mumford, *CIAM Discourse on Urbanism, 1928–1960* (Cambridge, MA: MIT Press, 2000); Alison Smithson, *Team 10 Primer* (Cambridge, MA: MIT Press, 1968); Paul Rabinow, *French Modern: Norms and Forms of the Social Environment* (Cambridge, MA: MIT Press, 1989).

Moreover, the detailed study of the GAMMA Group produced for the ninth CIAM Congress also resulted in new experimental buildings and already existing new urban schemes. Two architects from the group, Georges Candilis and Shadrach Woods, later leading Team 10 members, were able to present a completely planned and realized building that they had constructed as an experimental high-rise structure: the Cité Verticale was built next to what was one the largest *bidonville* settlements at the time—and still is today—the Carrières Centrales in Casablanca. They transferred the collective analysis of vernacular architecture and the hut settlements directly onto an exceptional modernist architectural project.[9] The result was a design that integrated the *bidonvilles'* everyday vernacular practices, local climatic conditions as well as modernist ideas of educating people on becoming modern.[10] On a formal level, the buildings can be seen as a synthesis of a traditional building—the patio house—translated into a stacked block of apartments with balconies. One of the three high-rise buildings of the Cité Verticale was named the "beehive"[11] in the architects' plans.

"Habitat Musulman"

The building models and shantytown study from Casablanca had a lasting influence on a younger generation of architects, who witnessed modernism appearing to adapt to local climatic and "cultural" conditions, thus slightly deviating from its universalist path. My interest in this crisis of planning principles is manifold, and provokes many questions that are the subject of this article and further research on the patio house scheme and its implementation in other regions of the world. A central question for the Casablanca case is how the European relation to the colonized, and the phantasms of Arabian culture are expressed in the "culturally specific" master plan and translated into the modernist typology of the modernist patio house. The question that follows is how the cultural misrecognition that informed this modernist synthesis through hierarchic power relations can still be incorporated and interpreted by inhabitants of the building structures in the era of decolonization and after. Implemented until 1984, the low-rise scheme of the Écochard patio house grid was the most prevalent planning structure in Casablanca's suburbs after Morocco's independence in 1956, and is still visible today. Since its emergence in Morocco, it has also been adapted in other cities in North Africa and the Middle East.

From the 1950s onward, housing programs in the French colonies attempted to take certain specific local, regional, or cultural conditions into account, but these conditions turned out to be much more complex after decolonization than previously thought. The single-floor, mass-built modernist patio houses, intended to facilitate the control of Moroccan workers, have been so significantly altered that one can now no longer distinguish the original base structure. The builders simply used the original design as a foundation upon which to construct three or four floors of apartments. The many ways in which people appropriate space and architecture can also lead to the assumption that both colonialism and the postcolonial government never managed to assume complete power over the population. This is an aspect I highlighted in my article "Architecture without Architects," which appeared in the *e-flux* journal in 2010.[12] When investigating the implementation of the patio as a modernist typology in other localities, it is necessary that a further aspect of this planning principle be foregrounded, namely "clustering and class-making."

In fact, the large-scale housing programs were attempts by the French protectorate to build modern settlements for the colonized in the very moment of emerging anti-colonial sentiment, as Morocco gained independence in 1956. In this moment of resistance, the strategies of the French-led Service de l'Urbanisme varied from the re-organization of the *bidonville* (restructuration) to temporary housing (*relogement*) and finally to the creation of new housing estates (*habitations à loyer modéré*), all based on the Écochard grid. His master plan applied notions of "culturally specific" dwellings, taking—in their interpretation—local building practices as a point of departure for developing a variety of dwelling typologies for different categories of inhabitants. These categories were still confined to existing definitions of cultural and racial difference. However, it was only under colonial rule that these categorizations were reinforced and turned into a means of exercising governmental power. The Écochard plan divided the city into different residential zones for European, Moroccan, and Jewish residents, as well as for industry and commerce. The housing estates for Muslims were built far from the "European" colonial city, creating a so-called Zone Sanitaire surrounded by circular roads and the motorway. This spatial division was also a legacy of the colonial apartheid regime, in which Moroccans were forbidden from entering the protectorate city unless they were employed as domestic servants in European households, and likewise constituted a strategic measure, facilitating military operations against possible resistance struggles.[13] Special neighborhoods were also developed for the Moroccan-Jewish population of Casablanca. Built

9 Jean-Louis Cohen and Monique Eleb, *Casablanca: Colonial Myth and Architectural Ventures* (New York: Monacelli Press, 2002).

10 Janet Abu-Lughod, *Rabat: Urban Apartheid in Morocco* (Princeton: Princeton University Press, 1980).

11 Like the notion "habitat," the "bee hive" metaphor is borrowed from ethnologists and serves an important planning reference in the work of Le Corbusier as well as Arial Sharon. See also Fahim Amir's entries about the "Bee Modern" and "Biopolis" at http://www.transculturalmodernism.org/page/58?layer=14 and Juan Antonio Ramírez, *The Beehive Metaphor: From Gaudí to Le Corbusier* (London: Reaction, 2000).

12 See http:/www.e-flux.com/journal/architecture-without-architects—another-anarchist-approach.

near the seaside, the El Hank district is one of the largest neighborhoods in Casablanca. These buildings were also placed in a sort of intermediate zone, but within sight of the French population, located on the Corniche, between the exclusive residential area of Anfa and the old Medina, very close to the colonial city center of Casablanca. The spatial organization of the residential and urban planning projects was highly hierarchical. It divided the Moroccan population into religious groups (Jews, Muslims), while the Europeans remained a universal category. Thus, the master plan itself was not just an expression of, but also in itself constitutive for, the Euro-American principle of a white, middle class, nuclear family ideal. Teaching the local population to "become modern" meant not only studying "their habits" and "culturally specific" building, but also trying to create modern living habits based on European preconceptions of ethnic and religious differences. Here, the master plan divided the populations along constructed strata, in which the Berber and Arab population were placed into the frame of the poor working class. The so-called culturally specific low-rise building programs like the Écochard patio grid were developed for the Moroccan proletariat, meanwhile high-rise housing projects were created for the so-called Évolués, which was, according to French ideology, a local group that already spoke French, followed French laws, and usually held white-collar jobs (although rarely higher than clerks). As Frantz Fanon argues:

> In the early days of colonisation, a single column could occupy immense stretches of country: the Congo, Nigeria, the Ivory Coast and so on. Today, however, the colonised countries' national struggle crops up in a completely new international situation. After a phase of accumulation of capital, capitalism has today come to modify its conception of the profit-earning capacity of a commercial enterprise. The colonies have become a market. The colonial population is a customer who is ready to buy goods.[14]

The so-called "Housing Grid for Muslims" measured eight by eight meters, and consisted of two rooms and a large outdoor space, which, according to Écochard corresponded to an Arabic patio. The grid was dimensioned according to a courtyard dwelling typology, believed to be the appropriate *habitat adapté* for the future inhabitants, the former *bidonville* dwellers.[15] This modernist patio house was based on existing and newly conducted colonial studies of Moroccan habitats as well as on the appropriation of the US neighborhood unit concept, and included streets and infrastructure.[16] Part of the ensuing sixty-four square meter patio house grid or "carpet" plan was organized in an intricate ground-level structure of patio-dwellings, alleys, and public squares. A single house in this grid consisted of two or three rooms, with a patio as entry space. Using a variety of combinations, it was designed to be flexible enough to eventually accommodate the creation of other types of housing (individual or collective), states architectural historian Catherine

Blain.[17] The patio house in Écochard's vision allowed the possibility for "growing" through usage. As Monique Eleb stated at the "Colonial Modern" conference, the patio reference was not a copy of a traditional courtyard house, but a European (mis)interpretation thereof. On the other hand, the patio house structure in the French colonies must be understood as a modernist synthesis, a Eurocentric translation with the pedagogical intention of teaching people the modern ways of industrial production and consumerism.[18] Moreover, the patio references are also a sign for an "anthropological turn" in architecture discourse against the background of heavy geopolitical drifts and ruptures.[19] It combines Orientalist studies on the Arabic house and its functions with modernist studies on the *bidonvilles'* self-builders, and adapts the grid, historically a colonial planning strategy, for its building concept, combining it with neighborhood concepts established in the United States. The rationales that served as a basis for the Athens Charter (the industrialization of building) and for the concept of building for the "Existenz Minimum," (constructing a great number of functional and cheap housing) are also articulated in the modernist patio house grid. The grid plan is also a territorial strategy for settling and expanding as fast as possible.

From the outset, the new urban strategies were situated in the field of tension between the emancipatory aims of improving inhabitants' everyday lives and the search for governing tools that complied with these intentions. In 1952, an important demonstration, organized by the Istiqlal Party, the national liberation movement, and other anti-colonial forces, took place in the *bidonvilles*

13 Jean-Louis Cohen and Monique Eleb, *Casablanca: Colonial Myth and Architectural Ventures* (New York: Monacelli Press, 2002); Janet Abu-Lughod, *Rabat: Urban Apartheid in Morocco* (Princeton: Princeton University Press, 1980).

14 Frantz Fanon, *The Wretched of the Earth* (London: Penguin Books, 1963), 51.

15 Monique Eleb, "An Alternative Functionalist Universalism: Écochard, Candilis and ATBAT Afrique," in *Anxious Modernisms: Experimentation in Postwar Architectural Culture*, eds. Sarah Williams Goldhagen and Réjean Legault (Cambridge, MA: MIT Press, 2000), 55–74.

16 In the course of the 20th century, the Neighborhood Unit scheme became a leading tool in town planning, not only in the United States, where it was first applied to the designs for Sunnyside gardens and Radburn, New Jersey by Henry Wright and Clarence Stein, cf. Chart Habitat / Develop / Neighborhood Unit: http://www.transculturalmodernism.org. Accessed February 9, 2013.

17 See http://www.team10online.org/research/papers/delft2/blain.pdf.

18 Pierre Bourdieu, *In Algerien. Zeugnisse einer Entwurzelung* (Graz: Camera Austria, 2003); Brian Ackley, "Blocking the Casbah: Le Corbusier's Algerian fantasy," *Bidoun*, no. 6 (2005): 13–39, http://www.bidoun.org/magazine/ 06-envy/blocking-the-casbah-le-corbusiersalgerian-fantasy-by-brian-ackley.

19 Moreover, the courtyard or patio house was also an important planning issue in the new town planning of Chandigarh in India. When Margarete Schütte-Lihotzky traveled to China in 1956, she also did an in depth study of the traditional courtyard houses, the Siheyuan (see Christina Linortner's contribution in this book). One year later, Werner Hebebrand published a proposal for a new model housing settlement, based on traditional yards, in the German *Werkbund* magazine.

of Carrières Centrales and was brutally suppressed by the French rulers. Thus, the construction of the new housing plan took place in the midst of military actions, with tanks and heavily armed troops, arrests and killing. It must have been virtually impossible to not recognize the conflict, as it happened on the very site of the building construction itself. The basic capacity for the young Team 10 architects to fully accomplish an experimental settlement in Morocco and Algeria was fundamentally bound to the circumstances of colonial occupation and anti-colonial resistance.[20] These circumstances were reflected in the research, exhibition, and publication project *Colonial Modern. Aesthetics of the Past. Rebellions for the Future.*

The intention of the architects and urban planners working under colonial rule in Morocco who wanted to revise modern architectural and planning approaches by integrating knowledge on dwelling practices and habits into urban planning and architecture was ambivalent because ethnographic knowledge is ultimately based on specific production conditions—on conditions that might even lead to a fundamental epistemological "misrecognition." This assumption is sound to the extent that colonialism creates an "ethnographic state." In other words: it subjugates the colonized on the basis of ethnographic knowledge.[21] For the modern architects, learning from the inhabitants was mainly a matter of adjusting their planning and architecture design according to ethnological findings. Their concept of observing everyday dwelling related uncritically to already existing ethnological and anthropological studies and Orientalist narratives of African space, which included perspectives similar to those used for studying the working class in Europe.[22] In addition, while new concepts of postwar architectural modernism strongly related to the everyday practices of population groups that had become mobile, they were also used to regulate and control, employing the planning instrument of an architecture for the "greatest number." Moreover, modernist architecture and housing projects in non-Western contexts in times of anti-colonial uprisings also played a highly symbolic role in shifting the concept from a "civilizing" to a "developing" colonial modernity. At the moment of decolonization, towards the end of the Second World War, the "civilizing" discourse turned into a "development" discourse.[23] After the independence movements in the global South, development discourse became even more dominant within high-modernist concepts of new town planning. Many architects who had built under colonial rule were now asked to create housing projects and public buildings for the newly independent states under specially created "development programs" initiated by the former colonial powers.[24] Michel Écochard himself applied these principles later in his career, for planning new towns and town extensions in the newly independent states of Guinea, Lebanon, Pakistan, Senegal, Cameroon, the Ivory Coast, and Kuwait.[25]

The Carpet Settlement in Be'er Sheva

Following an invitation by Michael Gross from the Bauhaus Center Tel Aviv, I first visited Israel in 2008. There, I met the architect and curator Zvi Efrat, who does research, publishes, and organizes important exhibitions on 1950s and 1960s architecture in Israel and the so-called Development Towns. Since I had done work on the ATBAT Afrique housing settlement projects in Casablanca for the exhibition "In the Desert of Modernity. Colonial Planning and after" (Berlin, Casablanca 2008/2009), he strongly recommended I travel to the desert city Be'er Sheva and visit several spectacular Israeli Brutalist buildings, particularly the so-called "Model Neighborhood Mishol Girit," built in Be'er Sheva by a group of young Israeli architects in the late 1950s. On this visit, I also recognized a number of modernist patio structures. The "new town" of Be'er Sheva emerged within the context of the comprehensive urbanizing program of establishing "development towns" in the Negev Desert during the late 1950s and early 1960s. The master plan had been designed by Ariel Sharon as part of the project of Zionist socialism, which also brought about the Kibbutz. The majority of "development towns" however had been built in the Galilee region of northern Israel and in the north part of the Negev Desert of southern Israel. Thus, even today, they are still the outposts of Israel's borders with the surrounding Arab states.[26]

In this larger context, the "Model Neighborhood" in Be'er Sheva was the first attempt to create an alternative to the standard public housing projects in Israel's Development Town program after 1948, which had mainly been based on the Garden City principle. The Model Neighborhood was meant as an experiment that would translate ideas of the neighborhood unit into new climate-specific approaches. A group of young architects including Avraham Yaski, Amnon

20 See Georges Candilis, *Bauen ist Leben. Ein Architekten-Report* (Stuttgart: K. Krämer, 1978).

21 See Nicholas Dirks, *Castes of Mind: Colonialism and the Making of Modern India* (Princeton: Princeton University Press, 2001); Arjun Appadurai, *Modernity at Large: Cultural Dimensions of Globalization* (Minneapolis: University of Minnesota Press, 1996).

22 Johannes Fabian, *Time and the Other: How Anthropology Makes Its Object* (New York: Columbia University Press, 1983).

23 Aram Ziai, "Zur Kritik des Entwicklungsdiskurses," Aus Politik und Zeitgeschichte, APuZ, no. 10 (2010): 23–28; Mark Crinson, *Modern Architecture and the End of Empire* (Aldershot, Hants, England and Burlington, VT: Ashgate, 2003).

24 See Udo Kultermann, *Neues Bauen in Afrika* (Tübingen: E. Wasmuth, 1963); Jaqueline Tyrwhitt, *Report on the Seminar on Housing and Community Planning*, given to the UN by Jaqueline Tyrwhitt, 1954, Archive School of Planning and Architecture, New Delhi; Okwui Enwezor, ed., *The Short Century: Independence and Liberation Movements in Africa, 1945–1994* (Munich: Prestel, 2001).

25 See http://halshs.archives-ouvertes.fr/docs/00/42/45/44/PDF/EUHConference-Verdeil-Michel_Ecochard.pdf.

26 Anna Minta, *Israel Bauen. Architektur, Städtebau und Denkmalpolitik nach der Staatsgründung 1948* (Frankfurt am Main: Reimer, 2004), 248–53.

Alexandroni, Nahum Zolotov, Daniel Havkin, and Ram Karmi were commissioned to find new local solutions for a settlement with 3000 residential units. Yaski and Alexandroni designed the large "quarter kilometer block," a reference to contemporary architectural ideas by Le Corbusier. The architects Nahum Zolotov and Daniel Havkin, who were also part of the planning team, designed the modernist patio house grid, the "The Carpet (Hashatia) Settlement," which consisted of a patio house grid that was integrated into the larger master plan.[27] This modernist patio house grid, also referred to as the "Carpet Settlement," resembles an almost identical base and ornamental grid plan structure as the "Housing Grid for Muslims" in Casablanca that Michel Écochard developed in 1951.

Thus, based on this first visit, I asked myself how and why an architectural or urban building concept from North Africa, which had been planned for Berbers and Arabs in Morocco during colonial rule, could make its way to Israel for the construction of houses for newly arriving Jewish settlers. On the one hand, an exchange of ideas might be easily explained by the fact that European architects traveled between America, Asia, Africa, and Europe and were agents of a global transfer of knowledge, propagating modernist ideas that were then internationalized. Many architects from the Middle East, Latin America, and Asia participated in the international CIAM congresses and were in intellectual and personal contact. In addition, architectural and urban planning experiments in Africa, Asia, and South America didn't go unnoticed. Numerous international architecture journals kept up with the projects that had developed under colonial and postcolonial conditions. The French magazine *L'Architecture d'Aujourd'hui* was an important player in the dissemination of this knowledge. On the other hand, Israeli architects like Artur Glikson, head of the planning department of the Ministry of Labor's Housing Division, had a significant influence on the planning discourses in Israel during the 1950s and 1960s. Glikson had designed a prototype of a modern patio house, laid out as a *habitat adapté* in a "carpet form" in Kyriat Gat shortly before the Model Neighborhood in Be'er Sheva was realized. Glikson also did intense research on vernacular architecture, not so much in Israel, but on Crete, where he created a regional planning method, modeled after a Mediterranean vernacular typology. He was an influential teacher at the Technion in Haifa, where he passed on his knowledge to a younger generation of architects. Since he was closely connected to Team 10, he also knew about the urban experiments in Morocco, seeing as members of Team 10, namely Georges Candilis and Shadrach Woods, were central protagonists in this endeavor. Glikson was also in close contact with Clarence Perry and Lewis Mumford, and connected to the ideas of Patrick Geddes. As a central protagonist within the regional planning and vernacular architecture discourse, he had a major impact on his younger colleagues when they were asked to develop their ideas for experimental housing proposals.[28] Both Artur Glikson and Ariel Sharon articulated important conceptual ideas on new urban models and were involved in the international debates around the concept of "Habitat" and the discourse on vernacular modernism.

However, the question that remains unanswered in this transfer of architectural designs and concepts from Morocco to Israel is how the "culturally specific" studies conducted in Casablanca—which had led to heated debates in Aix-en-Provence in 1956 and to the segregation of the local population in Morocco, and are closely related to this planning model—could be excluded from the Israeli "Patio Plan," in favor of a climate specific mode of construction. After all, the relationship to the vernacular appears to point the Israeli Patio House Settlement in an utterly different direction than its Moroccan predecessor had taken. Though Zvi Efrat calls attention to the fact that architects in Israel might have had an eye on the old Ottoman center of Be'er Sheva when planning the model neighborhood, this cannot be viewed as research on vernacular architecture.[29] The "old" city center of Be'er Sheva was planned and constructed as a colonial grid structure by civil engineers from the German imperial crown at the beginning of the twentieth century, by order of the Ottoman Empire. German military architects had translated the spatial order of a medina into a settlement structure, which is popularly known today as the "Arabic Kasbah." During the Ottoman Empire, Be'er Sheva had been a key strategic military base en route to the Suez Canal. It was laid out in a grid that resembled an administrative outpost for the military. It was here that, near the end of the First World War, the last sultan of the Ottoman Empire fought against the British Army with his German and Austrian allies, ultimately leading to the loss of control over Palestine and consequently also of the entire Middle East. Due to this military alliance, Austrian and German orientalists had conducted research on local architecture and archeological diggings.

The history of this place and the archeological discoveries made there were crucial in the Zionist discourse on the plans for the territory, because they were used to authenticate its biblical ties. This was a development that led to a very specific regionalism following the Six-Day War of 1967, which deliberately interpreted the past in terms of a specific desire for the future, reflecting a discourse as well as a practice that Eyal Weizmann has termed the "politics of verticality."[30] The Model Neighborhood in Be'er Sheva is perhaps the first

27 Noam Dvir, "Magic carpet," http://www.haaretz.co.il/hasite/spages/1082108.html. Avraham Yaski, foreword in A. Hirsch and R. Sharshevski, *Occupants' reactions on the planning of apartment and neighbourhood in the Experimental Housing Project in Be'er Sheva*, 1–5, Ministry of Housing, Unit of Social and Economic Research, 1968.

28 James M. Mayo, "The Ideologies of Artur Glikson," *Journal of Architectural and Planning Research*, no. 21 (2004): 99–101.

29 See the conversation with Zvi Efrat in this publication.

30 Eyal Weizman, *Hollow Land: Israel's Architecture of Occupation* (London and New York: Verso, 2007).

harbinger of this "situated modernity" after 1967. At the time of the foundation of the state, Zionist socialism also aimed to renew the previously existing social structures and did so by employing a very specific form of collectivism, one that, taking into consideration its history of immigration, imagined and set out to form a collective that was not based on national origin, but on the Jewish faith, coupled with a commitment to modernity. The Palestinian locals and the nomadic population became a minority within the new state. At the same time, the Sharon Plan pursued a politics of settlement in the regions where these "minorities" lived. However, this did not engender a new "culturally specific" form of architecture, like in North Africa during French colonial rule; instead, the Israeli planning discourse focuses on the formation of community(s) and, architecturally, on "clusters."

Thus, in current discourses surrounding the "Carpet Settlement" of Be'er Sheva, the influence of vernacular Palestinian or Arabian architecture on the development of the patio house's specific design vocabulary has partially been addressed, but also highly relativized.[31] While the Israeli modernist patio houses resemble a climate-sensitive approach, the term regional is not meant to describe a specific local population or building practice, as it refers neither to Bedouins nor to Palestinians. Rather, in recent discourses, Interbau Berlin's influence has been cited as having had an impact on the planning discourse of the development towns, although the roots of the modernist patio house or "Carpet Settlement" cannot be directly traced back to the Hansaviertel in Berlin. Instead, the Israeli patio house grid—the "Carpet Settlement"—is still a product of a transnational knowledge transfer, carried out by journals, the CIAM congresses from 1928 onwards, and personal encounters. Above all, the modernist patio house is an expression of a Eurocentric discourse on Arabic secular buildings, situated within the modernists' construction of tradition and modernity, and the phantasmic binary of the Occident and the Orient. The modernist patio house as a planning principle thus tries to simultaneously embrace and overcome the vernacular by recreating and shifting it into a modernist rationale, which can be both filled with and emptied of any concrete meaning.[32]

Becoming Arab

Some names on the doors of the Be'er Sheva patio house settlement show that the transnational relationship between the settlements in Morocco and Israel is clearly marked by the post-1948 emigration of Moroccan Jews to Israel. At the end of the Second World War, the Moroccan-Jewish population was forced to leave Morocco, which had a long history of religious tolerance. In her publication *Not the Enemy. Israel's Jews from Arab Lands*, Rachel Shabi notes that the Moroccan Jews had not been a discriminated group under the French Protectorate in Morocco. However, during the first large uprisings against the

French Protectorate in 1952 and the emerging movement of decolonization, the anti-colonial fighters portrayed the Jewish population as colluding with the French. Many Jewish authors have noted that the moment Morocco gained independence, a wave of anti-Semitism also ensued.[33] Thus, it could also be argued that this estrangement was an effect of the "culturally specific" zoning of Écochard's plan and the urban apartheid policy of the French colonial powers, as mentioned above. However, in the 1950s, large waves of Jewish emigrants from Morocco arrived in Israel. Prior to the mass exodus of Jews between 1948 and 1967, the Jewish population in Morocco had been over 250,000.

The strategy of new town planning in Israel was also called "population decentralization," which included a "Judaization" of the new national territory. In this context, there was also talk of the "exigencies of national security" and the "conquering of the frontiers." After their arrival in Israel, many Jewish-African emigrants were confronted with settlement politics that were termed "From Ship to Frontier." These entailed the relocation of a majority of the Mizrahi Jews to transit camps, as well as direct relocation to the newly built development cities.[34] Oren Yiftachel introduces the term "ethnocracy" to describe a type of regime that promotes social segregation and enables the government to categorize different ethnicities and (re)produce uneven class relations. As Yifachtel argues:

> Largely absent from the planning discourse of the time, as appearing in documents, plans and books, was an examination of the social consequences of this ambitious project. Population dispersal goals, historical rationales, territorial strategies, design criteria and economic development proposals took centre stage, with only scant reference to the plight of the (mainly Mizrahi) people about to be housed in the new towns, or to their needs and aspirations. This can be partially explained by the social positions of most Israeli planners of the time, being European educated, middle- or upper-class Ashkenazim. This group of highly capable professionals, many of whom worked for the government, fused their own vision and interests with

31 Hadas Shadar, "Vernacular Values in Public Housing," *Architectural Research Quarterly*, Cambridge 8, no. 2 (2004): 171–81; Robert Oxman, Hadas Shadar, and Ehud Belferman, "Casbah: a brief history of a design concept," *Architectural Research Quarterly*, Cambridge, no. 4 (2002): 321–36.

32 V. Y. Mudimbe, *The Invention of Africa: Gnosis, Philosophy and the Order of Knowledge*, (Bloomington: Indiana University Press, 1988).

33 See: Maurice Roumani, *The Case of the Jews from Arab Countries: A Neglected Issue* (Tel Aviv: World Organization of Jews from Arab Countries, 1977), 32–33; Said Ghallab, "Les Juifs vont en enfer," *Les Temps Modèrnes*, no. 229 (April 1965): 2247–51.

34 Roy Kozlovsky, "Temporal States of Architecture: Mass Immigration and Provisional Housing in Israel," in *Architecture and Politics in the Twentieth Century*, eds. Sandy Isenstadt and Kishwar Rizvi (Seattle: University of Washington Press, 2008), 139–60.

> that of the state. Their plans were thus represented as reflecting 'national' or 'state' objectives, although they mirrored the views and interests of specific powerful elites.[35]

The modernist patio house grids in Casablanca and in Be'er Sheva are thus not only interconnected by the migration of an urban planning grid or by their comparable expansion-oriented planning parameters, but most significantly by the mass migration movements within the Mediterranean world following the Second World War, and by the regulation and control of these movements. In Morocco, the increase in those moving from rural areas to cities gave rise to the planning. In Israel, the planning resulted from diverse forms of emigration from around the globe following the Shoah and the founding of Israel in 1948. Today, Jewish families who emigrated from the Maghreb and Middle East still live in the modernist patio houses of the Carpet Settlement in Be'er Sheva. Their diasporic history is linked to utterly diverse forms of orientalist inscriptions, to processes of re-Arabization and being rendered a minority. The discrimination and the social and spatial segregation that this caused also brought about resistance in the early 1970s. Following a visit to Israel by Angela Davis, a group of young Mizrahi Jews founded the Israeli Black Panthers to mobilize against the social discrimination of Mizrahi, also in Be'er Sheva. Determined to resist the ethnocratic regime, they identified as politically "Black."

35 Oren Yiftachel, *Ethnocracy: Land and Identity Politics in Israel/Palestine* (Philadelphia: University of Pennsylvania Press, 2006); Oren Yifachtel, "Trapped Voices: Mizrahim between Marginalization and Colonialism," in *Mizrahi Voices*, eds. Guy Abutbul, Lev Greenberg, and Pnina Mutzafi Haler (Jerusalem, 2006): 384–97; Leonard Downie Jr., "Israel Builds," The Alicia Patterson Foundation, New York, 1971, http://aliciapatterson.org/stories/israel-builds.

Literature

Abu-Lughod, Janet. *Rabat: Urban Apartheid in Morocco*. Princeton: Princeton University Press, 1980.

Ackley, Brian. "Blocking the Casbah: Le Corbusier's Algerian fantasy." *Bidoun*, no. 6 (2005): 13–39.

Appadurai, Arjun. *Modernity at Large: Cultural Dimensions of Globalization*. Minneapolis: University of Minnesota Press, 1996.

Avermaete, Tom. *Another Modern: The Post-War Architecture and Urbanism of Candilis-Josic-Woods*. Rotterdam: NAi, 2005.

Baghdadi, Mustafa. "Changing Ideals in Architecture: From CIAM to Team X." In *Architectural Knowledge and Cultural Diversity*. Edited by William O'Reilly, 22–56. Lausanne: Comportements, 1999.

Bourdieu, Pierre. *In Algerien. Zeugnisse einer Entwurzelung*. Graz: Camera Austria, 2003.

Candilis, Georges. *Bauen ist Leben. Ein Architekten-Report*. Stuttgart: K. Krämer, 1978.

Çelik, Zeynep. "Learning from the Bidonville: CIAM Looks at Algiers." *Harvard Design Magazine* (February 2003): 476–479.

Cohen, Jean-Louis and Monique Eleb. *Casablanca: Colonial Myth and Architectural Ventures*. New York: Monacelli Press, 2002

Crinson, Mark. *Modern Architecture and the End of Empire*. Aldershot, Hants, UK: Ashgate, 2003.

Crinson, Marc. "From the Rainforest to the Streets." In *Colonial Modern. Aesthetics of the Past. Rebellions for the Future*. Edited by Tom Avermaete, Serhat Karakayali, and Marion von Osten, 98–111. London: Black Dog Publishing, 2011.

Dirks, Nicholas. *Castes of Mind: Colonialism and the Making of Modern India*. Princeton: Princeton University Press, 2001.

Downie Jr., Leonard. "Israel builds." Alicia Patterson Foundation Newsletter of Leonard Downie Jr., New York 1971. Accessed May 1, 2013. http://aliciapatterson.org/stories/israel-builds.

Dvir, Noam: Magic carpet. Accessed July 18, 2011. http://www.haaretz.co.il/hasite/spages/1082108.html.

Écochard, Michel. *Casablanca, le roman d'une ville*. Paris: Édition de Paris, 1955.

Eleb, Monique. "An Alternative Functionalist Universalism: Écochard, Candilis and ATBAT-Afrique." In *Anxious Modernisms Experimentation in Postwar Architectural Culture*. Edited by Sarah Williams Goldhagen and Réjean Legault, 55–74. Cambridge, MA: MIT Press, 2000.

Eleb, Monique. "The Concept of Habitat: Écochard in Morocco." In *Colonial Modern. Aesthetics of the Past. Rebellions for the Future*. Edited by Tom Avermaete, Serhat Karakayali, and Marion von Osten, 142–161. London: Black Dog Publishing, 2011.

Enwezor, Okwui (ed.). *The Short Century: Independence and Liberation Movements in Africa, 1945–1994*. Munich: Prestel, 2001.

Fabian, Johannes. *Time and the Other. How Anthropology Makes Its Object*. New York: Columbia University Press, 1983.

Ghallab, Said. "Les Juifs vont en enfer." *Les Temps Modernes*, no. 229 (April 1965): 2247–2251.

Highmore, Ben. "Rough Poetry: Patio and Pavilion Revisited." *Oxford Art Journal*, no. 29 (2006): 269–290.

Kozlovsky, Roy. "Temporal States of Architecture: Mass Immigration and Provisional Housing in Israel." In *Architecture and Politics in the Twentieth Century*. Edited by Isenstadt, Sandy and Kishwar Rizvi, 139–160. Seattle: University of Washington Press, 2008.

Kultermann, Udo. *Neues Bauen in Afrika*. Tübingen: E. Wasmuth, 1963.

Lichtenstein, Claude and Thomas Schregenberger. *As Found: The Discovery of the Ordinary: British Architecture and Art of the 1950s*. Zurich: Lars Müller Publishers, 2001.

Mayo, James M. "The Ideologies of Artur Glikson." *Journal of Architectural and Planning Research*, no. 21 (2004): 99–101.

Minta, Anna. *Israel Bauen. Architektur, Städtebau und Denkmalpolitik nach der Staatsgründung 1948*. Frankfurt/Main: Reimer, 2004.

Mudimbe, V.Y. *The Invention of Africa. Gnosis, Philosophy and the Order of Knowledge*. Bloomington: Indiana University Press, 1988.

Mumford, Eric. *CIAM Discourse on Urbanism, 1928–1960*. Cambridge, MA: MIT Press, 2000.

Oxman, Robert, Hadas Shadar, and Ehud Belferman: "Casbah: a brief history of a design concept" *Architectural Research Quarterly*, Cambridge, vol. 6, no. 4 (2002): 321–336.

Rabinow, Paul. *French Modern. Norms and Forms of the Social Environment*. Cambridge, MA: MIT Press, 1989.

Ramírez, Juan Antonio. *The Beehive Metaphor: From Gaudí to Le Corbusier*. London: Reaction, 2000.

Roumani, Maurice. *The Case of the Jews from Arab Countries: A Neglected Issue*. Tel Aviv: World Organization of Jews from Arab Countries, 1977.

Shadar, Hadas. "Vernacular Values in Public Housing." *Architectural Research Quarterly*, Cambridge, vol. 8, no. 2 (2004): 171–181.

Smithson, Alison. *Team 10 Primer*. Cambridge, MA: MIT Press, 1968.

Tyrwhitt, Jaqueline. *Report on the Seminar on Housing and Community Planning*. By Jaqueline Tyrwhitt given to the UN, 1954. Archive School of Planning and Architecture, New Delhi.

Von Osten, Marion. "Learning from..." In *In der Wüste der Moderne. Koloniale Planung und danach*. Edited by Haus der Kulturen der Welt, 3. Berlin: Taz-Beilage zur gleichnamigen Ausstellung. 3. Berlin, 2008.

Von Osten, Marion "In Colonial Modern Worlds." In *Colonial Modern. Aesthetics of the Past. Rebellions for the Future*. Edited by Tom Avermaete, Serhat Karakayali, and Marion von Osten, 16–37. London: Black Dog Publishing, 2011.

Weizman, Eyal. *Hollow Land: Israel's Architecture of Occupation*. London/New York, Verso, 2007.

Wright, Gwendolyn. *The Politics of Design in French Colonial Urbanism*. Chicago: University of Chicago Press, 1991.

Yaski, Avraham. Foreword in Hirsch, A. and R. Sharshevski *Occupants' reactions on the planning of apartment and neighbourhood in the Experimental Housing Project in Be'er Sheva*, 1–5. Ministry of Housing, Unit of Social and Economic Research, 1968.

Yiftachel, Oren. *Ethnocracy: Land and Identity Politics in Israel/Palestine*. Philadelphia: University of Pennsylvania Press, 2006.

Ziai, Aram. "Zur Kritik des Entwicklungsdiskurses." *Aus Politik und Zeitgeschichte, APuZ*, no. 1 (2010): 23–28.

An Architectural Overdose

On Planning Discourses of Late 1950s and Early 1960s Architecture Projects in Israel

Zvi Efrat and Marion von Osten in Conversation

Marion von Osten: We are sitting here in the southern part of the Hansaviertel in Berlin that was constructed from 1953 to 1960 as part of the "Internationale Bauausstellung" (IBA), which took place in 1957. Israeli architects came and visited the event. You mentioned once that the Hansaviertel served as a model for the Development Town programs in Israel.

Zvi Efrat: For lack of sufficient historiographical documents and critical writing, my research on the Israeli new town planning had to frequently draw on interviews I conducted with the major protagonists of the period. Regarding the relationship between the IBA and experimental housing in Israel, the influence has been mentioned in many testimonies. The 1957 Berlin IBA certainly served as a direct model for the Israelis, but it was also criticized and argued that it would need to be improved for the Israel housing program. The Hansa ensemble was initially constructed as a fairground or an exhibition of a sort. A collection of renowned architectural figures created a number of exemplary architectural objects, which were embedded in certain environmental and social settings that didn't prove to work well in Israel. Essentially, Hansaviertel was still entrenched in the garden-city paradigm, in the pastoral reform of the urban, in the promise of a slow and soft modernism.

But, in Israel of the late 1950s and early 1960s the garden city was already more a locus of discontent than a tale of hope, due to the fact that most of the new towns, or development towns as they were often called, established in the first decade of Israeli statehood from 1948 throughout the fifties, were all built according to the model of the garden-city or even of the garden-suburb. And they mostly failed. Their misery was already reverberating within professional and political circles in the late 1950s. Evidently, the implementation of a spacious, porous, and vegetative (anti-)urbanism was totally inadequate for the peripheral towns, which, on top of their geographic marginalization, were further injured by the compulsory lack of urban density and cohesion and the subsequent prohibition to develop habitual street life. At least in some recorded instances, British postwar new towns or garden-suburbs were simply replicated and transplanted in the Israeli desert. So, from 1959 on, Israeli architects were trying to find new paradigms, which would be denser and which would fit in a more specific way, and this is when the Model Housing projects, like the housing experiment in the town of Be'er Sheva, which claimed to articulate the particular parameters of desert architecture, enter the local discourse and praxis.

MvO: And the Department of Housing formed a group of young architects to work on this solution.

ZE: Yes, in Israel, housing programs after 1948 were initiated and sponsored almost entirely by government authorities, at that time by the Department of Housing at the Ministry of Labor. And just like the generic programs of mass housing, the more idiosyncratic model housing projects were also motivated and controlled by the housing authorities. So, in fact, we are witnessing experimental architecture, which presents a critique or even negation of the state apparatus, endorsed by the state and promoted as its highlight.

And yes, it was state bureaucrats who deliberately chose young architects, mostly Israeli born and trained (in the Technion in Haifa, the only local school of architecture by then), bypassing the older generation of European immigrants. Such top-down avant-gardism whereby the official state initiative would entrust twenty-eight- to thirty-two-year-old architects with a large-scale construction enterprise may seem peculiar, but for a state that venerated modernism or zeitgeist as its highest values, the younger generation better represented the premise of migration of ideas. The native Israeli architects were up-to-date and well aware of experiments in North Africa, the Écochard project, the ATBAT Afrique, and the Casablanca carpet structures. They were critical of early modern architecture in Palestine, so-called Bauhaus Architecture, prevalent not only in the cities of Tel Aviv, Haifa, or Jerusalem, but surprisingly also in the Jewish rural settlements. For them, it was "architecture of migrants," because it was not localized; it was too plastered, too white, too aestheticized. Somehow, their contemporaneous European style of Brutalism seemed to them more authentic, contextual, and sincere, less generic, derivative, and superficial. Reiterating "white" Le Corbusier was now contemptible, while venerating "grey" Le Corbusier and literally copying his latest Béton Brut style was considered a moral act. In spite of the difficulty to travel abroad, they managed to be informed, and some of the international actors of the postwar discourse were in touch with this generation of Israeli architects.

MvO: Thus they could only read about new discourses and projects in magazines.

ZE: There were three or four architectural magazines that were distributed in Israel in the 1950s, certainly *L'Architecture d'Aujourd'hui* and *Architectural Design*. Basically, they read the magazines that wrote about them. And some traveled, not to North Africa at the time, but mainly to England and France.

MvO: As well to the CIAM conferences?

ZE: Yes, a few went regularly, and they were definitely aware of the Team 10 projects, which were quite famous in Israel. Urban and typological concepts were readily flowing in and appropriated, always with a certain critical twist, adapting them to the local conditions and technologies. In retrospect, during such moments of instantaneous (mis)appropriation architecture becomes really interesting; it mutates.

MvO: And what was their model for a proper urbanism in Israel?

ZE: First I have to say something general about model projects. It is certainly true that the Israelis were importing ready-made methods and formats, but more significant to our conversation is the fact that the notion of a model project, or prototype-making, is not at all a new phenomenon of the 1950s, but may be regarded as the very essence of the Zionist mind-set since its inception in late nineteenth century. Zionism was always preoccupied with planning and with setting and testing new urban layouts and new building types. Since there were no particular indigenous Jewish or Hebrew building traditions or dwelling practices, and since Zionism was born in the age of social and environmental reform, Israeli urbanism could later imagine a tabula rasa ("a State without a people, for a people without a State"), turn itself into a machine producing new towns, and base its scheme on the double-negation of the native Arab town and the big industrial city. In this sense, the garden-city paradigm served Zionism perfectly and helped the European immigrants to adapt climatically to the Levant but ignore it physically and culturally. Generally speaking, surviving the local conditions meant transforming them.

But here the model housing project in Be'er Sheva is an exception and signals a new sensibility. The chosen group of young architects came up with a layout that seemingly, at least, had to do with what they studied in Casablanca and other projects in North Africa, but also in Be'er Sheva itself, the grid formation of the old city, which was ruined and abandoned during the war of 1948. Ironically, the "old city" of Be'er Sheva was indeed an Arab city but had nothing to do with an indigenous kasbah-like formation. German planners designed the grid layout during Ottoman rule at the beginning of the twentieth century. For the young Israeli architects, it was an authoritative model of desert urbanism. So the new quarter of the model housing project emulates the old gridded city and subdivides it into smaller units; each would have its own public center and tower to mark it. There was a main axis crossing the entire neighborhood, connecting it to a commercial center and distributing public facilities along it such as schools and synagogues. The architecture of the housing was split between two main types: the block, or super-block, located on the margins of the site to provide a protective wall, as it were, against desert sandstorms; and "mat housing" with their various takes on the ideas of "urban textiles" and "patio houses." Usually, mat housing was two stories, and the top story hovered over the public pathway, shading it. There was also an integrated backyard to these houses, presumably allowing an expansion of the apartment. So a "patio house" was theoretically often also a "growing house."

In retrospect, when we come to evaluate the Israeli experiment of model housing projects, we can definitely acknowledge the coordinated group effort and the genuine attempt to reach integrated urbanism, but there is a heavy price to such professional solidarity: architecture becomes a flattened typology, and typology is reduced to a limited number of recurring building types.

MvO: The Be'er Sheva patio houses from 1959 have almost the same ground floor plan as in the Écochard grid built for Muslim workers in the outskirts of Casablanca in 1951. Michel Écochard appropriated the neighborhood unit concept for his large-scale housing projects. Did the international discussion about the neighborhood unit developed by Clarence Stein have an influence on the Israeli planners as well?

ZE: Yes, but it had a local interpretation. In fact, the neighborhood unit was the building principle of the new towns in Israel. Each neighborhood unit was supposed to be self-sustaining and based on separating pedestrians and motor vehicle traffic, so children would walk free of the danger of cars. Each unit had its own small center of commerce and services, a few units had a major center, and so on. It was a hierarchical system aggregating ostensibly autonomous units into urban clusters. The contours of the units were biomorphic and supple to suggest a natural setting and to counter the modernist orthogonal grid. There was not a straight axis or angle in these neighborhood units, and of course, no traditional street with typical mixed use. In many ways, we can identify in the neighborhood units a transposition of the concept of the kibbutz, the Zionist rural communal settlement, which was based on zoning, separation of urban functions, and no parceling of land into private lots. Yes, I suggest considering the Israeli new town not only as a derivative garden city but also as a blow-up of an entirely original, and rather radical, social and architectural construct.

MvO: At the "Colonial Modern" conference in Berlin (2008) Monique Eleb stated that Michel Écochard would have invented the notion of the habitat for his new town plans in Casablanca to describe the concept of this new social housing program. I saw the habitat chapter in your book on development towns. I'm very interested in how the concept of "habitat" developed in Israel.

ZE: Yes, habitat was a big word in Israel from the late fifties well into the seventies, and it is probable that it came directly from Écochard. However, in my opinion, it was largely hollowed of its anthropological reference and social performance. In Israel, habitat assumed a mainly morphological meaning. It became a general framework for geometric experimentation, motivated, as it were, by the critique of modernist figure-ground urbanism and generic architecture. If it signaled any paradigm shift (at least in the eyes of its practitioners), it was a shift from the oversimplified orthogonal grid to the complex polyhedral matrices. In other words, it was not at all a new sensibility towards the vernacular, but quite the opposite, an attempt to cure the built environment through an architectural overdose.

Interestingly enough, it was possible to look at indigenous North African building patterns but apparently not at the Palestinian village. That was too close to see. The distant model could easily be turned into a formal composition and modified into an academic discourse. In fact, most of the Israeli habitats had little to do with social housing. They could be a faculty building on a university campus, a military base, a resort, a city hall, or a lavish apartment building. In some instances, they were indeed designed as social housing, but they performed so poorly as such that they were soon turned into hostels for new immigrants or for orthodox Yeshiva students.

The main figure behind the habitat trend in Israel was Alfred Neumann, a former student of Peter Behrens and Auguste Perret. He became Dean of Architecture at the Technion in Haifa and had many followers amongst his students. Neumann formed one of the most creative firms in the sixties together with two of his former students: Zvi Hecker and Eldar Sharon. For Neumann and his followers, notions of organic or spontaneous structures were catalysts for their so called "system theories" or "space packed architecture," which was equipped with promising rhetoric of open-ended accumulative patterns and slogans such as "change, growth, and uncertainty." Yet the result was not a kind of soft free-form architecture, better adaptable to specific geographies or ethnographies, but rather a very rigid, formalized, and idiosyncratic clustered architecture with no material elasticity and certainly no political agenda. I think that precisely because it had no agenda other than formal, it remained an almost anecdotal "avant-garde," and it was readily appropriated immediately after the war of 1967 and the ensuing occupation of the Palestinian territories by the builders of the large scale housing projects, especially in the "greater Jerusalem" neighborhoods. Now, the agglomeration of ever-growing modular clusters became very useful for expansionist policies. The reference to the diversified organic community, so pertinent to the notion of habitat, was all forgotten and taken over by the passive-aggressive clustered community.

MvO: In an interview with Yona Friedman in Paris in 2011, he said it was highly relevant for him not only to study vernacular architecture, but also vernacular building cultures during his time in Israel. He was very much interested in how a local community builds, not only morphologically, but also how the building process is organized collectively. He was writing his doctoral thesis on vernacular building practices of local Palestinian communities when he was still in Israel, but his Technion professors did not agree on this approach. Would you say there was a division between the people that were translating the vernacular aesthetic on a formal level and a generation that was highly interested in how communities were actually built?

ZE: Friedman may have genuinely been interested in vernacular building practices, and so were a few other Jewish architects from the early decades of the twentieth century to this very day. But, by and large, Zionism was remarkably blind to vernacular building practices. Even the British colonial work was more attuned to native traditions and to the local landscape. Such ideological blindness allowed Zionism to be highly innovative and productive in formulating ever-new urban and especially rural typologies. These new types corresponded to original and often quite radical social formations such as collectivist or communal settlements. Perhaps Zionism's preoccupation with novel and ideally planned social forms explains the rejection of spontaneous architectural traditions. What is left then is the captivating image of natural complexity, and of course the opportunity for the pre-fabrication of repetitive elements, randomly arranged, as it were, to form an artificial topography and a "beehive" community. The first to fully capitalize on this understanding and to fossilize the ultimate habitat is, of course, Moshe Safdie with his "pavilion" for the 1967 Expo in Montréal.

MvO: This is certainly the most important example of its time internationally.

ZE: Yes, but I can see Safdie's ideas developing within the peculiar context of Israeli architecture. Paper habitats and built habitats produced by Neumann and his disciples proliferated in the Israel of the early sixties and inspired Safdie, as they have Friedman. I believe that Safdie acknowledged the influence of Neumann's ideas upon him.

As we discussed in the beginning of our conversation, some of the Israeli habitats, especially the "mat structures," expressed serious explorations into site-specific conditions and indigenous traditions; others pursued morphological complexity in itself and played their periodic role in the historic process of industrialization and commodification of the dwelling unit.

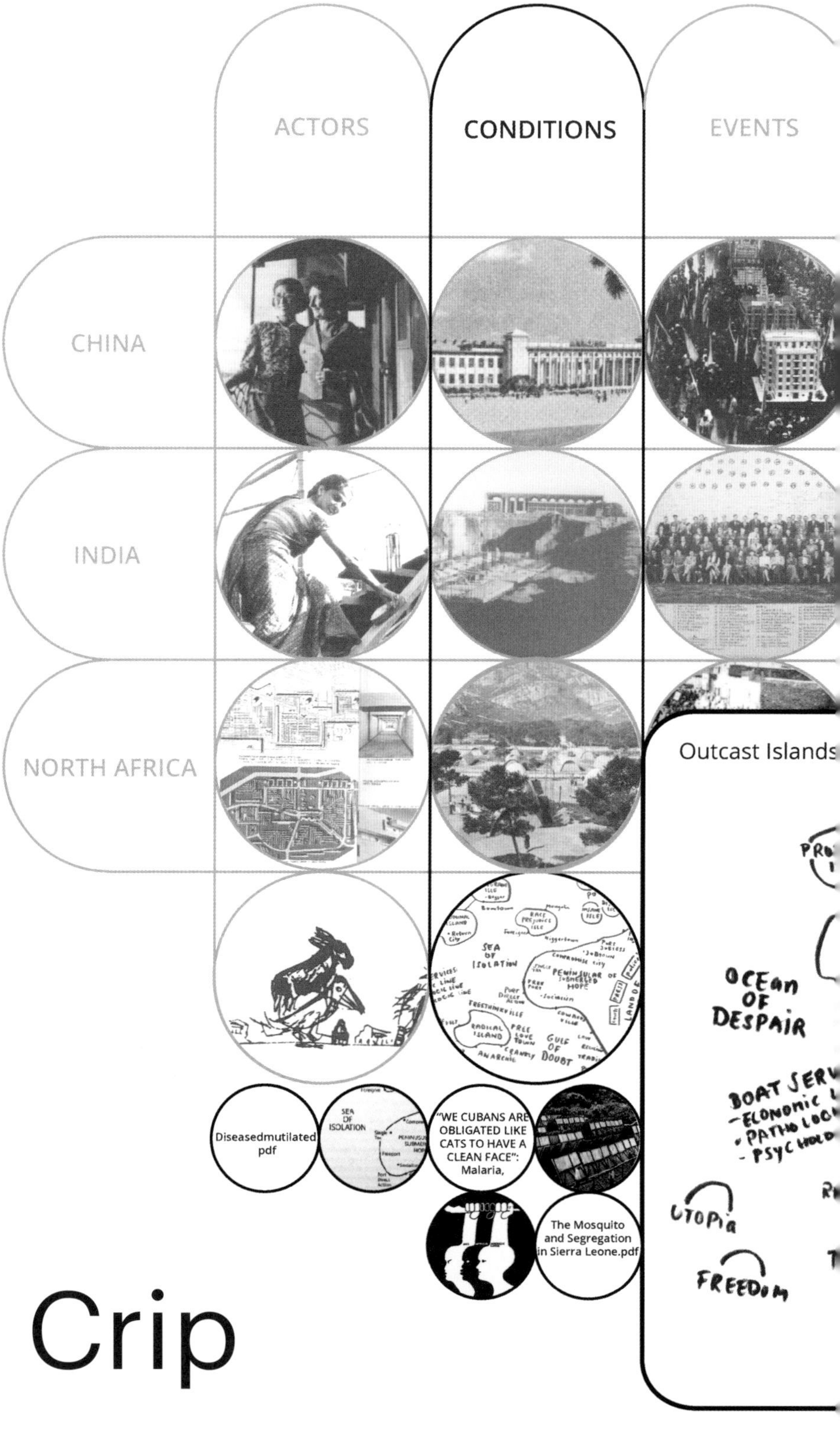
ACTORS
CONDITIONS
EVENTS
CHINA
INDIA
NORTH AFRICA
Outcast Islands
SEA OF ISOLATION
GULF OF DOUBT
Diseasedmutilated pdf
"WE CUBANS ARE OBLIGATED LIKE CATS TO HAVE A CLEAN FACE": Malaria,
The Mosquito and Segregation in Sierra Leone.pdf
OCEAN OF DESPAIR
UTOPIA
FREEDOM

And Crip

BATES & OURSES

CONCEPTS

ART & RESEARCH

THEORIES

based on Ben Reitman's map from 1910

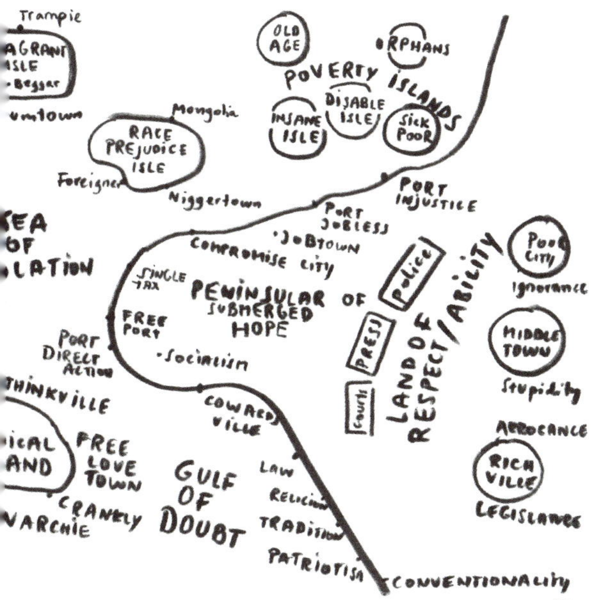

- Ableism
- Access
- And Crip
- Biopolitics
- Chicago
- City Beautiful
- City Planning
- Disability
- Disableism

Buildings That Fit Society
The Modernist Ideal and the Social Production of Ableist Spaces

Rob Imrie and Eva Egermann in Conversation

Eva Egermann: Your book, *Disability and the City* (hereafter DC), is an in-depth analysis of the context within which the status of disabled people is experienced, the interrelationships between disability, physical access, and the built environment. It explores the socio-cultural and political processes around the social construction and (re)production of "states of disablement." Donlyn Lyndon suggests that architecture ought to be a thoughtful structuring of places to inhabit and that it should be enabling. His book, *Rethinking Architecture*, documents a collaborative project between design students and people with physical impairments in Berkeley, California, initiated by the architect and the disability rights activist Raymond Lifchez. While Lyndon's observations seem to point to the relevance of universal design and emancipatory architecture, he critically notes that architectural education's primary goal is "to educate people who will tend to the making of buildings that fit society," and architecture therefore "handicaps those who are exceptionally different in behavior or appearance or physical ability."[1] So, the perpetuation of disablist space is linked to the socio-institutional practices of architects and the wider design professions, as you also write in DC. How would you describe these relationships?

Rob Imrie: My thoughts on these relationships have changed over the years and the characterizations embedded in DC have been read by some as implicating architects and other agents as the primary purveyors of disabling spaces. In some ways this characterization holds, but only if one situates such agents' actions in the broader socio-cultural and political contexts that shape, in a recursive sense, their dispositions, mentalities, and values. Lyndon's observations are well made and the very best architects understand that the legacy of their work is dependent precisely on it enabling human activities, and being part of a sociability that is defined by universal values relating to shelter, habitability, and well being. However, architects, and other design professionals, do not operate outside broader ideological frameworks that disregard impairment and which, historically, have led to the incarceration of many disabled people into separate contained spaces. While the integration of disabled people into society has been much more to the fore in recent years, design discourses are implicated in creating barriered and bounded places that, while not state sanctioned places of incarceration, have the effect of limiting where disabled people are able to go to, who they are able to interact with, and how their rights to citizenship may be experienced and curtailed.

There is no single actor or individual to blame for this state of affairs,

1 Donlyn Lyndon, "Preface," in *Rethinking Architecture. Design Students and Physically Disabled People*, ed. Raymond Lifchez (Berkeley: University of California Press, 1987), xii.

although each individual, in their acting, ought to reflect on what the sources and motivations of their actions are, and, in so doing, at least provide themselves with the possibilities of (self-)transformation. In and of itself this will never be enough to create non-disabling socio-cultural formations because of the embedded, and systemic, nature of ableism that, for its dissolution, will require a broader collective series of political practices and actions to emerge. This is where Lyndon's point about the making of buildings that fit society is interesting. By highlighting architectural education as one of the sources of the socio-cultural (re)production of disablism in design discourses, the coercive power of educational practice in the (re)production of disciplinary fields is brought to the fore.

What is interesting is that, already over 2000 years ago, the Roman architect Vitruvius was lamenting the paucity of architects' engagement with the materialities of the world. He suggested that those "who relied only upon theories and scholarship were obviously hunting the shadow and not the substance," a comment about architects' lack of knowledgeability and engagement with the prosaic processes of construction.[2] Fast-forward and the American architect Frank Lloyd Wright was saying something similar by exhorting trainee architects to learn about the building process in its fullest sense as a prerequisite for good practice. As he observed about the estranged nature of architectural knowledge: "go into the field where you can see the machines and methods at work [...] stay in construction direct and simple until you can work naturally into building design from the nature of construction."[3] Indeed, Frank Lloyd Wright was scathing about the architectural schools of the time and the splintering of education into discrete, individualized parts, observing that "the educational fabric has been so far departmentalized, over standardized."[4]

The perceived irrelevance of much of architects' education is also shaping the contemporary debate. I like to think there are parallels here with disability and design relating precisely to architects' perpetuation of design knowledge of/about building users that do not equate with, or respond to, the manifold possibilities of bodies' spatial interactions. However, this is not an "architect thing" per se, but much more about the social relations of the design and construction process, insofar that only to target architects as in need of re-education is to miss the point and purpose of what needs to be done. Indeed, one needs to challenge, and change, not only the pedagogic basis of society, but the broader systemic nature of disablism that is part of the social fabric of institutions and their practices.

EE.: There are several examples of the conjunction of formal, aesthetic, and body-related concerns in urban planning. For example, the neighborhood unit proved to be a persistent concept of modernist city planning. It was ad-

opted all over the world. A precursor was Ebenezer Howard's conception of the "Slumless, Smokeless Garden City" which involved a construction of health that assigned the "insane," the "inebriates," and the "epileptics" to segregated places outside the main center. Urban problems, such as disease, crime, and pollution were also addressed through the concept of "beautification."

In 1925, Le Corbusier developed the Modulor. Based on the proportions of the human body, it represents a schema of human proportions to aid designers in the design and construction of buildings. The Modulor outlines a series of standard measures relating to the proportional relationships between human beings and buildings. The measure for this schema is a strong, muscular man standing upright with no sign of physical or mental impairment, 183 cm in height.

Devising a certain "standard" was influential for the modern importance of function and, as Le Corbusier argued, essential to architectural forms, which he defined as being "determined by the dimensions of man [sic] and the space he occupies."[5] Buildings, in a way, became a site for teaching self-optimization and standardization with the effect of the projection of normality as one of able-bodiment. Can the functional, moral, and economic imperatives underlying modern planning efforts also be termed "ableist social relations" as they point to "standardization" that relates not only to spatial but also social settings?

RI: My original characterization of Le Corbusier's Modulor man was, perhaps, overstated. It provides a powerful, visual representation of the human body, and at first glance it appears to be reductive in projecting a body type or typology of the body that is unable to capture the complexities of bodily form and performance. However, the Modulor may be regarded as an "ideal type" or a representation to aid the design process. It is not necessarily a definitive or absolute projection of bodies but rather an instrument or tool to guide how different body parts interact in combination with material artifacts. So, there are multiple interpretations that one can make about Le Corbusier's Modulor man, although there is no doubt that, as a representation, it is static by providing no real sense of the senses or the sensuous nature of buildings, spaces, and the materials that comprise them. This reflects a broader orthodoxy in architecture in which the objective is filling in space with objects and connecting them

2 Vitruvius, *The Ten Books of Architecture* (New York: Dover Publications Inc., 1960), 5.

3 Frank Lloyd Wright, *Frank Lloyd Wright: An Autobiography* (New York: Longmans, 1932), 241.

4 Ibid., 312.

5 Rob Imrie, *Disability and the City: International Perspectives* (London: Paul Chapman Publishing, 1996), 81.

as geometric structures.
So, my feeling is that Le Corbusier's Modulor man is a tool or instrument to aid designers to (pre-)figure dimensional standards, and that such standards, if following the directives of the Modulor, provide scope to incorporate a broad range of human-types or potentialities in relation to body-environment interactions. This is not to say that I am in favor of just geometrical proportions as a means of defining and seeking to shape such interactions or the delimitation of body-environment interchanges solely by recourse to pre-set standards. In fact, however we delimit or standardize, it will not necessarily shape anything or pre-determine action or outcomes, because actions are what they are through their unfolding, including the combinations of things that tend to make every interaction of bodies in place unique in some way. We cannot escape from geometry either, nor should we seek to, because it is no more than one sense of how materials connect to one another or are placed relative to each other or in combination.

Perhaps the reaction to the Modulor man is less the limits of geometry and more the representation that it appears to be. The Modulor is an ahistorical, instrumental tool, devoid of context and seeking to propagate an image of the body that is at odds with what we all encounter daily, that is, the diversity of bodies and the messiness of bodies-in-space. Here, one can draw parallels with Pérez-Gómez's[6] observations about designers' use of computer imaging as a decontextualized and decontextualizing experience or, as he says, "a complete disregard for history and embodied consciousness." In this respect, the Modulor is part of the broader, fragmented nature of modernism, where social experiences appear to be divisible and discrete. Gellner describes this as characteristic of modern human agency, in which we are all constituted as "a Modulor," seeking to put together, in piecemeal fashion, different versions of ourselves. Kallinikos[7] suggests that this is a "response to the demands raised by the distinct institutional realms of modern life."

EE: Let's come back to the term and discourse of "ableism" that constantly references and reproduces normativity. The Disability Studies author Lennard Davis[8] notes that the social process of disabling arrived with industrialization and practices that are connected to late eighteenth and nineteenth century notions of nationality, race, gender, criminality, and sexual orientation. Identities of the abled person have been reproduced throughout history and within different fields, "whether it be the 'species typical body' (in science), the 'normative citizen' (in political theory), the 'reasonable man' (in law)."[9]

In DC you describe how the modern "axiom of human domination of nature," the domination of scientific values and of human rationality, have been

important influences on the modern movement, and that the aesthetics were relying upon an abstract purity of rational geometric forms and mass-produced industrial technology.[10] You explain how the architectural styles of modernism in particular are generating forms that seemed to deny differences in bodily experiences and suggest that the modern ideal equates to an ableist space.

RI: There are many issues that are raised here concerning the relationships between styles of architecture and conceptions of the form and performance of the human body. I think an important point is not to reduce ableist socio-spatial relations, in and of themselves, to something we describe as "the modern ideal." That the modern ideal may equate to the crafting and (re)production of ableist spaces is not to sideline or discount the interplay between other non modern design discourses and the disabling nature of socio-spatial relationships. So, I would insist on situating the understanding of the "modern ideal" and its projection of the hetero-normative, able-bodied citizen within a broader historical critique of contrasting socio-cultural systems and their dispositions towards the body, environment, and society. There is much to be done to provide research about how far disabling design processes are evident in cross-cultural and different historical contexts.

As much as there is a need to document the cross-cultural nature of disablism, there is a need too to recognize that modernism is characterized by, potentially, a positive, forward-thinking conception of human subjects. The values of modernism were built upon a sense that buildings ought to facilitate human action and be responsive to a perceived need for efficient living. Modernist design values propagate a critique of society and provide a basis for political reform based on, arguably, a progressive betterment of society by improving the circumstances of human kind. At least this was the stated ambition of those who subscribed to modernism. While the anthropogenic focus of modernism is a cause for concern, modernist values do not, in and of themselves, preclude the possibilities of a liberating future for human beings. However, the difficulty is the way that the potential humanism of modernism, or at least its liberating possibilities, has been sidelined by social experiments that have

6 Alberto Pérez-Gómez, "Polyphilo's thresholds: alternatives for nomadic dwellings," in *Transportable Environments*, eds. Robert Kronenburg and Filiz Klassen (London: Taylor and Francis, 2006), 4.

7 Jannis Kallinikos, "Work, Human Agency and Organizational Forms: An Anatomy of Fragmentation," *Organization Studies*, no. 24 (2003): 597.

8 Lennard Davis, "Constructing Normalcy," in *The Disability Studies Reader*, ed. Lennard Davis (New York: Routledge, 1997), 3.

9 Fiona Kumari Campbell, *Contours of Ableism: The Production of Disability and Abledness* (Basingstoke, Hampshire: Palgrave Macmillan, 2009), 44.

10 Imrie, *Disability and the City*, 80.

propagated the discourse of scientism and the belief in technology and expertism as the basis of/for social progress. We see this in the rise of the rehabilitation industries with the emphasis on the repair and rehabilitation of disabled people as part of a process to make them "normal."[11]

This is the perpetuation of a universal subject or a projected ideal of the citizen characterized by social and physiological features that are counterpoised to those that, so it is argued, disabled people lack. The fixation of modernism with de-differentiation and the commonality of humanity is the (continuing) basis for an assimilationist ideology to take hold, in which the only deal for disabled people appears to be to fit their defunct bodies to societal norms, including putting up with inaccessible design or, otherwise, to accept their outside status as deficient and "not normal" beings. If one part of the "modern ideal" is the application of instrumental rationality, what Schmitt describes as "a blind domination of nature," one cannot be surprised by designed outcomes that are less than sensitive to the manifold nature of the body. The modernist proclivity to the suppression and domination of nature, often by the application of a technological apparatus, provides little scope for "not normal" bodies to be part of mainstream culture or to partake in daily undertakings.

This is evident in practically every aspect of the designed environment. This ranges from the standardized "fit out" of kitchens, where cupboards and tabletops are often placed out of reach of people who use wheelchairs, to the re-engineering of street environments that encourage, in many European cities, a sharing of space between automobiles and pedestrians. A consequence of such space sharing in urban areas is that this may create hazardous places for, for example, vision impaired people. I have been documenting the spread of shared space design in England, and it reflects, in part, the mentalities of highways and transportation planners in deploying an engineering rationality to influence the behavioral patterns of different street users. A top-down vision, expert-led, concerned primarily with creating efficiencies of movement and mobility in street spaces and expecting people to negotiate the use of space through eye contact with one another. This is nothing short of a dystopian spatial formation, and it is no surprise that vision impaired people report disliking shared spaces and feel that they are adding yet another "no-go" area in the built environment.[12]

EE: This assumption that spaces are characterized by the constant interaction of different actors under unequal conditions implies another perspective of agency. In our project we follow the assumption that the built environment is not just simply built or lived in, but formed in and through interactions with the political, social, technological, and economic conditions, public discourses,

concepts, artistic and scientific production with the given conditions. As you also mention, it would be unfair to characterize architects and modernists as "disablist" in as much that there was recognition of what was regarded as the "subversive" potential of people.[13] (Le Corbusier, for instance, said, "It's life that's always right and the architect who's wrong."[14]) I would like to ask: In what sense would you say that affirmation of architectural forms and spaces took place through the intervention of different "not normate" or disabled bodies?

RI: The messy and contingent conditions of human life provide one with sufficient reason to guard against claims that assert the determinate nature of social actors and actions ascribed to them. Le Corbusier's understanding of the interactions between everyday material life and the designed environment were realistic and echo what most architects are thinking, even if they don't publicly acknowledge it. Some of the most influential architects have acknowledged the improbability of achieving the synthesis of form and use, a sentiment expressed by Frank Lloyd Wright[15] in relation to the design of furniture: "Soon I find it difficult, anyway, to make some of the furniture in the abstract. That is, to design it as architecture and make it human at the same time—fit for human use." Recurrent throughout Frank Lloyd Wright's work is the struggle to create organic forms in which it was never a choice between aesthetics and use or usability, but about the total environment oriented towards the bodily needs of human beings. In echoing, and reproducing, some of the ideas of the Chinese philosopher, Lao Tzu, Frank Lloyd Wright maintained that the essence of any building is not in the materiality of the roof, walls, or ceilings but is part of the lived spaces within.

Close study of architects and their practices show that they do not necessarily propagate disabling and disableist design discourses. I have been spending some time in archives looking at the writings, correspondences, and drawings of Frank Lloyd Wright to gauge how far his design conceptions were sensitized to the manifold interactions of bodies-in-space. There is surprisingly little research of this type, and it is too easily assumed that architects are unthinking about the body's emplacement in space.

11 Barbara Gibson's excellent work is exemplary in deconstructing, and subjecting to critique, the relationships between disability and rehabilitation. I recommend looking at her portfolio of publications. See http://www.hollandbloorview.ca/research/scientistprofiles/gibson.php.

12 Rob Imrie, "Auto-Disabilities: The Case of Shared Space Environments," *Environment and Planning A* 44, no. 9 (2012): 2260–77.

13 Imrie, *Disability and the City*, 86.

14 Charles Jencks, *Le Corbusier and the Tragic View of Architecture* (Harmondsworth: Penguin, 1987), 74.

15 Lloyd Wright, *Frank Lloyd Wright: An Autobiography*, 145.

The case of Frank Lloyd Wright may not be typical, but it does indicate how one of the most influential architects of the modern era was influenced by the interrelations between the building context, particularly the physical location and content of the site, and the potential for any architecture to be human-centric and sensitive to sensory experiences. For Frank Lloyd Wright and other architects such as Alvar Aalto, what was paramount was precisely a multi-sensory architecture that contained the potential to respond to what you have termed "not normate" bodies.

EE: A range of scholars have called for the development of a non-ableist, non-essentialist sociology based upon the understanding of sensory feelings and physiological impairments in their socio cultural contexts. Judith Butler, for instance, argued that physiological impairments, in and of themselves, are a constraint on specific types of action, and it is impossible to derive a social theory which is dismissive of, and independent from, the situatedness of the body of its pedagogical and/or physiological state, the historicity you referred to before.[16] What would a non-ableist theorization look like, in your sense?

RI: Non-ableist formulations require, as a principle, an openness to the manifold interactions between bodies and the material world and sensitivity to the diversity of ways in which people sense space and, subsequently, come to practice and know the world. What I find frustrating is that there are data available about the interrelationships between senses, spaces, and practice, yet much of it is ignored, sidelined, or rendered as irrelevant by design practitioners. There is, therefore, a need to "mainstream" knowledge of/about the body as a precursor to non-ableist practices emerging, and this will involve professionals' exposure to a range of learning environments. I would like to see much more inter-institutional activities emerging as I see little evidence of design and building professionals interacting with, for example, people with dementia or those with learning difficulties. Indeed, there appear to be few opportunities, either in educational systems or design practice, for practitioners to learn about the body's manifold presence in space and the ways in which it ought to be regarded as co-constitutive of the designed environment.

There have to be theorizations of ableism that unpick and explain the different ways in which social relations (re)produce the impaired body as an aberration and "not normal." So, a non-ableist theorization of society requires, necessarily, a theorization of ableism as a precursor to creating progressive, non-ableist, conceptions of society and space. This task requires a thorough transformation in systemic ideas, values, and practices, and here I agree with Tony Fry, who suggests that this will require making design "overtly and proactively political." [17] Urban planning, architecture, and design is too often presented and understood as an aesthetic, technical activity, standing above and beyond politics or the murky world of values. This is what Fry calls a delimited view, a focus on taste and style. The struggle then, as a precursor to developing non disabling discourses in society, is a thorough politicization of design or what Fry refers to as a "political ontology wherein politics becomes a lived mode of being that infects its institutional forms."[18]

16 Judith Butler, *Bodies that Matter* (New York: Routledge, 1993).
17 Tony Fry, *Design as Politics* (Oxford: Berg, 2011), 7.
18 Ibid., 79.

Literature

Butler, Judith. *Bodies that Matter*. New York: Routledge, 1993.

Campbell, Fiona Kumari. *Contours of Ableism: The Production of Disability and Abledness*. Basingstoke, Hampshire: Palgrave Macmillan, 2009.

Davis, Lennard. "Constructing Normalcy." In *The Disability Studies Reader*. Edited by Lennard Davis, 3–19. New York: Routledge, 1997.

Fry, Tony. *Design as Politics*. Oxford: Berg, 2011.

Gellner, Ernest. *Conditions of Liberty: Civil Society and its Rivals*. London: Penguin, 1996.

Howard, Ebenezer. *Garden Cities of Tomorrow*. London: S. Sonnenschein & Co., Ltd., 1902.

Imrie, Rob. *Disability and the City: International Perspectives*. London: Paul Chapman Publishing, 1996.

Imrie, Rob. "Auto-Disabilities: The Case of Shared Space Environments." *Environment and Planning A*, vol. 44, no. 9 (2012): 2260–2277.

Jencks, Charles. *Le Corbusier and the Tragic View of Architecture*. Harmondsworth: Penguin, 1987.

Kallinikos, Jannis. "Work, Human Agency and Organizational Forms: An Anatomy of Fragmentation." *Organization Studies*, no. 24 (2003): 595–618.

Lloyd Wright, Frank. *Frank Lloyd Wright: An Autobiography*. New York: Longmans, 1932.

Lyndon, Donlyn. Preface in *Rethinking Architecture. Design Students and Physically Disabled People*. Edited by Raymond Lifchez, xi-xv. Berkeley: University of California Press, 1987.

Pérez-Gómez, Alberto. "Polyphilo's thresholds: alternatives for nomadic dwellings." In *Transportable Environments*. Edited by Robert Kronenburg and Filiz Klassen, 2–9. London: Taylor and Francis, 2006.

Schmitt, Carl. *The Crisis of Parliamentary Democracy* [1923]. Cambridge, MA: MIT Press, 1985.

Vitruvius. *The Ten Books of Architecture*. New York: Dover Publications Inc., 1960.

Unlikely Encounters in the Fog

Crip Connections Within the Project Model House

Eva Egermann

> **_Cripple_, _gimp_, and _freak_ as used by the disability community have transgressive potential. They are personally and politically useful as a means to comment on oppression because they assert our right to name experience.**[1]
>
> **—Simi Linton**

Introduction

Experiences of embodied difference are closely entangled with space, the built environment and architecture. Authors from various fields have continuously argued for a politicization of space and for a view of space that reflects its social production. In *The Production of Space*, Lefebvre describes that space and spatial politics are the expressions of social relations and react upon them.[2] This notion implies "a socio-spatial dialectic," so to speak, "which sees society and space as mutually constituting material dynamics."[3]

Disability Studies authors have pointed out that the social and cultural construction of disability in the history of Western modernity functioned as the projection of "normality" as one of "able-bodied-ness."[4] As Mathias Danbolt states: "Ideologies of progression legitimized the containment of *deviants* on a moral ground by presenting racial, gendered and sexual others as a threat to the development of the society."[5] "Crip subjects" were seen as "slowing down the progress of Modernity."[6]

Assuming "able-bodied-ness" as the standard within social and spatial relations, ideas, practices, processes, and institutions is termed "ableism," a way of thinking that constantly references and brings about normativity. Lennard Davis describes that "the normal" is a configuration that arose "in a particular historical moment. It is part of a notion of progress, of industrialization, and of ideological consolidation of the power of the bourgeoisie. The implications of the hegemony of "normalcy" are profound and extend into the very heart of cultural production."[7]

1 Simi Linton, *Claiming Disability Knowledge and Identity* (New York: New York University Press, 1998), 17.
2 Henri Lefebvre, *The Production of Space*, trans. Donald Nicholson Smith (Oxford: Blackwell, 1991).
3 Brendan J. Gleeson "A Geography for Disabled People?" *Transactions of the Institute of British Geographers* 21, no. 2 (1996): 391.
4 See Rob Imrie, *Disability and the City: International Perspectives* (London: Paul Chapman Publishing, 1996); Susan Schweik, *The Ugly Laws: Disability in Public* (New York: New York University Press, 2009).
5 Mathias Danbolt, "Disruptive Anachronisms: Feeling Historical with N.O. Body," in *Temporal Drag*, eds. Pauline Boudry and Renate Lorenz (Osterfildern: Hatje Cantz, 2011), 1986.
6 Ibid.
7 Lennard J. Davis, *Enforcing Normalcy: Disability, Deafness, and the Body* (London: Verso, 1995), 49.

Conceptions of unproblematic geographic spaces have been further critiqued with Parr and Butler: "space cannot adequately be conceived of as a mere blank surface on which uncritically to map medical and *deviant* subjects."[8] Moreover, critical geographers such as Golledge and Gleeson have described disabled people as creators of space who inhabit "distorted spaces," for example.[9] They are equipped with agency and "seen actively to transform the general geographic landscape in their everyday lives and reproduce this as their own experimental world."[10]

There are many different examples of the conjunction of formal, aesthetic, and body-related concerns in the history of modernist urban planning. To see "crip subjects" "as entirely subsumed by modernist ideology" would be "a terrible mistake, offering them yet again no loop-hole," as Susan Schweik explains later on in this book.[11] Likewise, different ways in which social relations (re-)produce the impaired body as an aberration and as "not normal" are revealed and discussed in a conversation with Rob Imrie.[12] It requires "a theorization of ableism as a precursor to creating progressive, non-ableist, conceptions of society and space," Imrie argues. And this again requires a transformation in systemic ideas and values as well as making architecture and design "overtly and proactively political."[13]

Resistances, negotiations, the place of encounter, and the in-between are a focus of the *Model House* project. Architectural modernity itself is seen as conflictual terrain, with manifold connections and entanglements. Therein, an understanding of the built environment as emerging from a set of conditions is viewed as a relevant research approach. "The project chose for a praxeologic perspective, assigning agency to all that is there." (*Model House*) Questions on embodied difference taken from Disability Studies and Crip Theory broadened our discussion on Transcultural Modernisms. Architectural spaces were disassembled into single components such as the home, the street, the settlement, the neighborhood—or the "habitat." Throughout the research, we tried to pick apart some of these spatial conceptions. Places and concepts such as the Chinese *danwei* work unit, Le Corbusier's Modulor, the 1950s neighborhood unit, whose environment functioned to meet the industry's needs, or its precursor, Ebenezer Howard's 1898 conception of the "Slumless, Smokeless Garden City," and others were mapped out and clarified, as well as terms such as "ugliness," "beautification," or "ableism," among others.[14]

The following passages offer some further connections to the research project, based on anarchist doctor Ben Reitman's radical mapping of Chicago from the year 1910. It documents repression against various deviant and "other" subjects in the early twentieth century. Negotiations and resistance that took shape later on were already anticipated in the map.

Departure: An Unusual Mapping of a City in 1910

On this map we can see a landmass with a peninsula and several islands that either form archipelagos or stand on their own. At the bottom left are two mountainous islands, which are marked "Freedom" and "Utopia." Large areas of sea and ocean (the "Sea of Isolation," the "Ocean of Despair," and the "Gulf of Doubt") cover most of the map. Three different ferry lines serve to connect the different places (the "Economic Line," the "Pathologic Line" and the "Psychologic Line").

The islands nearest the mainland are called "Orphans," "Sick Poor," "Disable Isle" (at the center of the archipelago), "Insane Isle," and "Old Age." Together they are called the "Poverty Islands." The nearest port to the Poverty Islands on the mainland is Port Injustice. Next to the "Poverty Islands" is the isolated "Race Prejudice Isle" with its different towns, located opposite "Port Jobless" and "Port Injustice."

Also in the "Sea of Isolation": "Vagrant Isle" with the cities of "Hoboville," "Bumtown," "Trampie," and "Beggar." It is connected to Prostitute Isle and Criminal Island with its "Return City." "Radical Island" is at the bottom of the map and is separated from the mainland/"Richville" by the "Gulf of Doubt." "Freethinkville," "Freelovetown," "Crankly," "Anarchy," "Tolstoy," and "Revolt" are the towns on "Radical Island," which is located closest to "Port Direct Action."

Three cities are located on the mainland in the right hand margin of the map: "Poor City," "Middle Town," and "Richville." The towns are based on classical class-based identities (i.e., working class, middle class and upper class). These areas form the "Land of Respectability." The remaining mainland is identified as the "Peninsular of Submerged Hope" and is separated from the "Land of Respectability" by three different blockades or barricades: the "Courts," the "Press," and the "Police."

8 Ruth Butler and Hester Parr, *Introduction to Mind and Body Spaces: Geographies of Illness, Impairment and Disability* (London: Routledge, 1999), 11.

9 Reginald Golledge, "Geography and the disabled: a survey with special reference to vision impaired and blind populations," *Transactions of the Institute of British Geographers* 18, no. 1 (1993): 64.

10 Brendan J. Gleeson, "A Geography for Disabled People?" *Transactions of the Institute of British Geographers*, vol. 21, no. 2 (1996): 389.

11 See the conversation between Susan Schweik and Eva Egermann in this volume. "Searching for the International Deformed Nation, or 'Too Loud in its Patterns.'"

12 See the conversation between Rob Imrie and Eva Egermann in this volume. "Buildings that Fit Society: The Modernist Ideal and the Social Production of Ableist Spaces."

13 Ibid.

14 See glossaries by Amir, Hille, Linortner, Kravagna, and von Osten on http://www.transculturalmodernism.org.

Several ports are found on the mainland coast. These are possible entry points, but also points of departure for the islands. "Port Injustice" and "Port Jobless" point towards ways in which people are excluded from the islands on the "Sea of Isolation." Lower down the coast, close to "Richville," there are piers and points that provide ways and entry points into the "Land of Respectability." These are the formal and informal mechanisms of acceptance and affirmation such as "Law," "Religion," "Tradition," "Patriotism," and "Conventionality."

The "Outcast Nights" and the Context of the Map

The map shows Chicago in the year 1910 and was presented on November 17, 1910 at the Pacific Hall on West Broadway, New York, at the so-called Outcast Night, an event organized by Reitman himself. Tim Cresswell described this event as follows:

> Anarchist intellectuals, including [Emma] Goldman, witnessed a discussion of various types of social outcasts including hobos, prostitutes, 'homosexuals' and criminals. The hall was crowded and the event attracted the press. The audience was treated to a number of appearances by various outcasts from Hippolyte Havel, the outcast psychologist, to Arthur Bullard, the outcast moralist, and Sadakichi Hartman, the outcast poet. At the end of the evening, Reitman took the opportunity to reveal his 'social geography'—a talk based on a large map.[15]

Whilst the text of the lecture was not found, the diagram—originally drawn on a bed sheet—is now preserved at the Reitman Archive at the University of Illinois, Chicago.

Ben Reitman was a social reformer, doctor, and anarchist activist in the United States in the late nineteenth and early twentieth centuries. He was the founder of the March of the Unemployed in 1908, organizer of Outcast Nights, and a contemporary of the Chicago School of Sociology. Having been a hobo himself, he formed hobo colleges in Chicago and was jailed several times for his anarchist activities. He was later trained as a doctor and opened clinics in Chicago for the treatment of venereal diseases, including syphilis.

The Ugly Laws and the Managing of Deformed Bodies

Ben Reitman's map depicts Chicago and we can see that the poor, the sick, the disabled, the insane, the homeless, the prostitutes, the non-white, the old, the orphaned, and the politically radical, etc., all live on islands disconnected from the mainland. Here, "social geography" illustrates a series of points relating to the exclusion of a number of groups in early twentieth-century Chicago.

Susan Schweik calls this period (1867–1920) "the era of the unsightly."[16] It was the time in which Ugly Laws were drafted and introduced into most western and mid-western cities in the United States. Also known as the "unsightly beggar ordinances," these statutes prohibited "unsightly" people, beggars, and people with disabilities from visiting public spaces. "No person who is diseased, maimed, mutilated or in any way deformed so as to be an unsightly or disgusting object, or improper person to be allowed in or on the public places in this city, or shall therein or thereon expose himself to public view."[17] Many states' Ugly Laws were not repealed until the mid 1970s. Chicago was the last to repeal its Ugly Law, in 1974.[18]

This period was also the era that saw the rise of eugenics. In addition, state institutions concerned themselves with new pressures in respect of behavior in the city, of the conduct of people in the streets and public places. "Deformed" people were "seen as problems that would have to be managed as much as architecture or street layout."[19] Modern urban planning and maps for the City Beautiful were developed. Besides being a site for labor unrest, reformist progressive scrutiny, and the Ugly Law, Chicago became a main model of modern city planning and important example of the era of the City Beautiful.

The City Beautiful Movement was a North American urban planning movement, which began in 1893 at the World Columbian Exposition Chicago, had its heyday between 1900 and 1919, and consequences that lasted until 1929. The concept of "beautification" was applied to tackle urban problems, which were defined in terms of disease, crime, and pollution, as a reaction to the population increase in North American cities in the nineteenth century. The idea of beautification was influenced by the neo-classical style of the École des Beaux Arts, which emphasized monumental architecture, large avenues, and parks. The so-called beautification of a city can also be understood as an educational institution, since it was not intended for bringing about a better life for the poorer classes, but rather for teaching moral and civic values and increasing the productivity of the urban economy.[20]

15 Tim Cresswell, "The Peninsular of Submerged Hope: Ben Reitman's Social Geography," *Geoforum* 29, no. 2 (May 1998): 208.
16 Ibid.
17 City of Chicago Ordinance, 1911, Chicago Municipal Code, sec. 36034 (repealed 1974).
18 Schweik, *The Ugly Laws*, 290.
19 Ibid., 67.
20 Eva Egermann and Moira Hille, *Beautification*, http://www.transculturalmodernism.org. Accessed March 1, 2013.

Hence, it seems no coincidence that the Ugly Laws were introduced into most western and mid-western US-American cities during the heyday of the City Beautiful Movement. Though it is clear that this idea of the ideal city was one without "unsightly," disabled beggars and other deviants on the street, histories of urban development and the City Beautiful Movement have not yet addressed the relationship to the history of the Ugly Laws, as Schweik emphasizes.[21]

Radical Mappings and Unconventional Knowledge

Cartographies construct a territorial understanding of space, which assumes the existence of borders and demarcation lines instead of social relations, inclusions, or individual traces. There has been much critique of topographic, scientific cartographies and their claims to objectivity. The cartographic gaze has been described by Peter Spillmann as

> a placeless perception of space, in which the vast reality becomes a manageable world surface, upon which each spot has coordinates and each object is recorded in an index. The cartographic view makes the arrangement of populations visible and tangible, populations as the composition, consolidation, and dilution of certain criteria, which emerge, for example, through different rasters or shaded colorings. The cartographic view reveals borders as dotted, dashed, or drawn-out lines, as edges of colliding, differently colored territories.[22]

Ben Reitman's cartography does not offer a definite, demarcating, and objective perspective, but rather a very unconventional approach to connecting and visualizing spatial politics and social relations. Reitman's knowledge of the excluded was itself excluded from mainstream social science. His depiction differed from contemporary views of society in important ways. As Tim Cresswell emphasizes, his mapping and social geography "points to post-structuralist/ social geography of the 1990s, emphasizing marginalization, amplifying marginal voices, and pointing to the forces that produce marginalization in the first place. [...] Reitman produced and advocated knowledge that led him into conflict with scientific disciplines as he transgressed the boundaries of acceptable thought and action."[23]

The Land of Respectability is a place signified by arrogance, ignorance, and stupidity—"not a social space to aspire to, nor one that inevitably assimilates all difference. It is a space which consistently excludes and rejects, creating islands of outcasts."[24]

Contemplating Relations, Traces, and the "The Right to Opacity"

Islands represent places of desire and figures of thought. An island could also be defined as a place of movement, "whose historical documentation of mobile patterns and vectors remain continually available," notes Ottmar Ette.[25] "In its occidental tradition, the history of the island semantically functions as an ambiguous figure—on the one hand it stands for an island world spatialized in its entirety and insularity [...] On the other hand, the island also presents itself as part of an island world, representing the fragmentary, the splintered, the mosaic-like, characterized by diverse interior connections and constellations."[26]

When looking at Reitman's cartography, we can see other associations. The map with its connected archipelagos, the peninsula, the boat services that connect the different cities and ports are reminiscent of the appearance and cartographies of existing islands and archipelagos. The Caribbean Sea and its islands, for instance, were theorized by the postcolonial writer Édouard Glissant as an open sea, full of encounters, traces, and relations. He described it as a place of permanent Creole reality with countless forms of hybridization. Based on this perception, Glissant developed a concept of archipelagic thinking and demanded the "Right to Opacity":

> If we look at the process of *understanding* beings and ideas as it operates in western society, we find that it is founded on an insistence on this kind of transparency. In order to *understand* and therefore accept you I must reduce your density to this scale of conceptual measurement, which gives me a basis for comparisons and therefore for judgments.[27]

In Glissant's sense, understanding appears as the construction of the "other" as an object of knowledge, and opacity would therefore be a strategy of active resistance. "We must fight against transparency everywhere. [...] We demand for all the right to opacity, the right not to be understood."[28]

21 Schweik, *The Ugly Laws*, 70.
22 Labor k3000 and Peter Spillmann, "Der kartografische Blick versus Strategien des Mapping," in *Grenzregime. Diskurse, Praktiken, Institutionen in Europa*, eds. Sabine Hess and Bernd Kasparek (Hamburg: Assoziation A, 2010), 282.
23 Cresswell, "The Peninsular of Submerged Hope," 208.
24 Ibid.
25 Ottmar Ette, "Von Inseln, Grenzen und Vektoren. Versuch über die fraktale Inselwelt der Karibik," in *Grenzen der Macht – Macht der Grenzen. Lateinamerika im globalen Kontext*, eds. Marianne Braig et al. (Frankfurt am Main: Vervuert, 2005), 148.
26 Ibid., 137.
27 Celia M. Britton, *Édouard Glissant and Postcolonial Theory: Strategies of Language and Resistance* (Morgantown, WV: The University Press Virginia, 1999), 19.
28 Ibid.

Claiming the "Crank," the "Crip," and the "Outcast"

The history of embodied difference, as Homi Bhabha has conceptualized it, is a story "not of unilateral domination but of uncertainty, hybridity and ongoing conflict and negotiation."[29] When looking at the map, we can see how impairments, injuries, and deviations—as well as appropriations and resistances—have consistently acted as a countercurrent to dominant normative orders.

One of the places on the map is of special interest to me. It is the "Town of Crankly," situated on "Radical Island." The word, which is derived from the German word "krank" (Engl.: ill, sick), was used at the time for "odd or eccentric persons," according to Susan Schweik, a derogatory term that was applied to anarchists, freethinkers, and proponents of free love. On this map, I associate the way it is used in a re-signifying manner—in the sense of claiming a degrading discourse: claiming the "crank" (the ill, the feigning ill, the one who begs, and the collapse of the distinction between the three). Opacity and the "right to not be understood." Blurring the borders and demarcation lines—or as Schweik puts it: "Every space on this map, including 'Disable Isle' and 'Crankly,' is [...] a venue [...] for political organizing toward the dissolution of out-casting."[30]

29 Homi K. Bhabha, *The Location of Culture* (New York: Routledge, 1994), 19.
30 Schweik, *The Ugly Laws*, 73.

Literature

Bhabha, Homi K. *The Location of Culture.* New York: Routledge, 1994.

Britton, Celia M. *Édouard Glissant and Postcolonial Theory. Strategies of Language and Resistance.* Morgantown, West Virginia: University Press Virginia, 1999.

Butler, Ruth and Hester Parr. Introduction to *Mind and Body Spaces: Geographies of Illness, Impairment and Disability.* Edited by Ruth Butler and Hester Parr, 1–25. London: Routledge, 1999.

Cresswell, Tim. "The Peninsular of Submerged Hope: Ben Reitman's Social Geography." *Geoforum,* vol. 29, no. 2 (May 1998): 207–216.

Danbolt, Mathias. "Disruptive Anachronisms: Feeling Historical with *N.O. Body.*" In *Temporal Drag.* Edited by Pauline Boudry and Renate Lorenz, 1982–1990. Osterfildern: Hatje Cantz, 2011.

Davis, Lennard J. *Enforcing Normalcy. Disability, Deafness, and the Body.* London: Verso, 1995.

Egermann, Eva and Moira Hille. *Beautification.* Accessed March 1, 2013. http://www.transculturalmodernism.org.

Ette, Ottmar. "Von Inseln, Grenzen und Vektoren. Versuch über die fraktale Inselwelt der Karibik." In *Grenzen der Macht – Macht der Grenzen. Lateinamerika im globalen Kontext.* Edited by Marianne Braig, Ottmar Ette, Dieter Ingenschay, and Günther Maihold, 135–180. Frankfurt/Main: Vervuert, 2005.

Gleeson, Brendan J. "A Geography for Disabled People?" *Transactions of the Institute of British Geographers.* New Series. vol. 21, no. 2 (1996): 387–396.

Golledge, Reginald. "Geography and the disabled: a survey with special reference to vision impaired and blind populations." *Transactions of the Institute of British Geographers,* vol. 18, no. 1 (1993): 63–85.

Imrie, Rob. *Disability and the City. International Perspectives.* London: Paul Chapman Publishing, 1996.

Labor k3000 and Peter Spillmann. "Der kartografische Blick versus Strategien des Mapping." In *Grenzregime. Diskurse, Praktiken, Institutionen in Europa.* Edited by Sabine Hess and Bernd Kasparek, 281–287. Hamburg: Assoziation A, 2010.

Lefebvre, Henri. *The Production of Space.* Translated by Donald Nicholson Smith [First published in French in 1974]. Oxford: Blackwell, 1991.

Linton, Simi. *Claiming Disability Knowledge and Identity.* New York: New York University Press, 1998.

Model House–Mapping Transcultural Modernisms. Accessed March 1, 2013. http://www.transculturalmodernism.org.

Schweik, Susan. *The Ugly Laws. Disability in Public.* New York: New York University Press, 2009.

Searching for the International Deformed Nation Or "Too Loud in Its Patterns"

Susan Schweik and Eva Egermann in Conversation

> I got polio when I was three years old. I have two different-sized legs [raises pants leg] and a limp. I am disabled.
> Being disabled is a strike against you when you look for work. I ran into trouble when I decided to become an actress...
> Actually there is a long line of disabled performers—beggars, fools, freaks in a carnival sideshow—they all earned their living by performing.
> But the excitement of the performance was in the hump on the back, the withered arm, the scarred face.
> I am not a performing cripple. I'm limited on the stage by my limp. But if I concentrate really hard I can sometimes walk without a limp. [demonstrates walking and then does a somersault]
> Did you notice? Did you notice my limp? [begins signing] But why should I hide it. I am disabled... The cripples are coming out of hiding!
> I applied to a theater school in New York City. They refused to admit me because of my limp. They said, 'You could train to be a director ... have you ever considered costuming? ... We need some help in the office.'
> Actually I don't blame them. If they had allowed me to perform they might have been breaking the law. It's true—there is a law in some cities of the United States today, which reads:
> 'No person who is deformed or mutilated in such a manner so as to be a disgusting object shall be allowed to display themselves to public view.'
>
> —Passage from a monologue by the American performer Victoria Ann Lewis as part of the US feminist theater collective Lilith, during a European tour in 1980)[1]

Eva Egermann: As part of our research for the *Model House* project, we are interested in influences and appropriations of architectural modernity, the relationships and actors involved in the realization of planning processes. The notion of the habitat indicates culturally defined dwelling practices. We are looking at conditions and different agencies of actors whose contributions were often underrepresented, e.g., workers whose labor made architecture and urban planning materially possible, figurations and living beings whose forms of production and supposed way of life became productive ideals in certain contexts, and city-makers who adapted modernist urban spaces to their needs through dwelling, working, or straying practices.

The character of modernist ideas is often described as "ableist," as suggested by its concept of functionality based on assumed "sameness" or "normality."

1 Susan Schweik, *The Ugly Laws: Disability in Public* (New York: New York University Press, 2009), 13.

But different bodies and deviations—as well as appropriations and resistances—have also acted as a countercurrent to dominant normative orders. Your book *The Ugly Laws. Disability in Public* examines bodily norms in the public sphere, architecture, and culture much earlier. Did disabled people and people with physical differences in history solely serve as a kind of negative definition to modernist ideals, and to what extent did "crip" subjects have agency within transcultural modernism?

Susan Schweik: As you can tell, I like stories and examples better than generalities. Down on the streets of the orderly modern city, beneath the "logic of the grid" (in James Scott's great phrase), people lived their lives and found their ways, developed their—I love your words—dwelling, working, and straying practices. My favorite guy Arthur Franklin Fuller, the great disability street historian, offers numerous examples (he went around the country collecting stories of agency as well as of oppression from fellow "unsightly beggars"). For instance, here's his account of his conversation with a man named Kaase in Trinidad, Colorado about how Kaase negotiates the grid of the city's modern built environment, legal landscape, and bureaucracy:

> He was partially reclined in a wheelchair. He could not walk, wash, or dress himself. He showed lack of care. His hair was gnarled and face unshaven. His hands and limbs and back were twisted. His affliction had been rheumatism, followed by arthritis deformans. He could sit up, had good eyes, a fair education ... "I see you sell gum, laces, novels, and pencils. Do you have any trouble getting to work as you travel from place to place?" "More every year. Cripples are not supposed to have anything else to do but run around getting permits," he returned. "Do you ever have people ask you why you don't give it up and enter some of the places provided for people such as you?" I asked. "Yes, I get that every once in a while. It makes me wild, too. They cannot know what they are talking about or else are heartless."

Then there are several pages of transcription of Kaase's testimony about abusive and dangerous conditions in almshouses and county hospitals and inmates' unsuccessful struggles to stop them. Fuller's interpretation rounds it off: "So, kind reader, you see the purpose of modern legislation is to fix it so there is no technicality, no loophole, no chance for an unfortunate [...] The Law is ready to refer you to the places provided—to the charities and the poor house or county hospital." He concludes by quoting an English friend: "If this thing is not lawful, it is certainly AWFUL, which makes an 'ELL OF A DIFFERENCE." Telling their stories, passing them on, Fuller and Kaase are making their own kind of difference—to see them as entirely subsumed by modernist ideology is, I think, a terrible mistake, offering them yet again no loophole. In the end, what interests me most is the loophole in the knot of disability.

EE: In 1911, Chicago ratified the Ugly Law being introduced in many American western and mid-western cities. It included the quote by Victoria Ann Lewis above. *The Ugly Laws: Disability in Public* is an evocative examination of disability norms in the public sphere, municipal law, and culture by way of analyzing the phenomenon of the Ugly Law (or unsightly beggar ordinance) that prohibited diverse abject groups from appearing in public space and public view.

Many authors emphasize the conjunction of disability and poverty. Rosemarie Garland-Thomson notes that the most enduring form of segregation for disabled people has always been economic and that "the history of begging is virtually synonymous with the history of disability."[2] How did this law enforce this and criminalize people's lives?

SuS: Let me take one example I didn't have space to include in *The Ugly Laws*, except for a brief reference in the chapter on "mendicant literature" (my favorite chapter). That chapter was the place where I tried hardest to trace a history of agency and protest on the part of the subjects of the unsightly beggar ordinances. The "crip" contestations there (as we might now call them, following Robert McRuer) take more conventionally and visibly political and activist forms than elsewhere in the book, where the harder, messier, stranger truths of the situation dominate: that is, that in general it didn't take arrest under the law to cripple a "cripple." Was it hard for people to fight back against it, hard for people not to take it in, hard for people whether or not they ran directly afoul of a cop and a judge, just plain hard for people? Yes.

The example I'll offer here is a story of a woman—as Gayatri Spivak famously put it, within her "effaced itinerary [...] the track of sexual difference is doubly effaced." Disabled writer Kitty Smith wrote a mendicant autobiography, *Yours Truly Kitty Smith*, that reduplicated those effacements. Born "of poor parents" in 1882 in Chicago, at the heart of the Ugly Law, Smith lost her arms as a child when they were burned against a hot stove so badly they had to be amputated. Smith's alcoholic father was charged with having deliberately held her against the stove, and she was removed from the home by Children's Aid officials. We know this from the surrounding documents, not from her. In her "little history," illustrated with photographs ("The position of my feet when I write"; "These two

2 Rosemarie Garland Thomson, *Extraordinary Bodies* (New York: Columbia University Press, 1996).

views show how I handle a saw. I can saw a board in two almost as rapidly as others can with their hands"), Smith exposed herself to public view "to aid myself in securing a modest and humble living," asking people to buy the book to support her. In Spivak's landmark essay on the subaltern, "speech" at its most urgent is bodily, nonverbal, the story told by a woman's menstrual period: "Bhuvanesari attempted to 'speak,'" Spivak writes, "by turning her [menstruating] body into a text of woman/writing." So, too, the exposed bodies of the subjects of the Ugly Law "spoke," and Smith presented her photograph ("The position of my feet when I write"), turning herself into text: woman/cripple/writing. But like Spivak's famous Bhuvanesari's, Smith's writing took place under circumstances that rendered it largely illegible. The sensational narrative of the stove-burning and paternal abuse is—can be—neither confirmed nor denied by this autobiography, which exhibits so much else. Like the sati stories about which Spivak writes, Smith's story of her burning is choked by two sentences that get imposed upon her by a history of repression. Between "benefactors are saving poor girls from poor men" and "I am my father's daughter" lies an unwritten narrative. I did my best in the chapter on the autobiographies of disabled street people to show how much they had to say about their situation, but Kitty Smith's story shows the ways in which Spivak was right: the unsightly beggar cannot speak. Within my book, the moment I think that most clearly illustrates how profoundly, how pervasively, and how subtly the Ugly Law ruled the land for disabled people, whether it was enforced or not, is a citation from another woman's autobiography: deaf, working class writer Pauline Leader's *And No Birds Sing*. I'm glad to mention this book, because I think it deserves a place in disability studies curricula. Leader describes how her mother would make up stories telling her "of the policeman who said that I must not be allowed out." She knows the stories are made up, but still, she says, "They enter me." How did this law work? It entered people. Of course, as Leader's writing shows, people also found exit routes.

EE: Disease, crime, and pollution were addressed at that time through the concept of "beautification." The City Beautiful Movement was a planning movement in North America from 1893–1929. The idea of "beautification" was influenced by the neo-classical style of the École des Beaux Arts, which emphasized monumental architecture, large avenues, and parks. The architectural planning of Chicago as the "ideal," "alabaster," and "White City" was developed. The beautification of a city can also be understood as an educational institution; it was not intended to bring about a better life for the poorer classes, but rather to teach moral and civic values and to increase the productivity of the urban economy.

Hence it seems no coincidence that during the heyday of the City Beautiful planning movement the Ugly Laws were introduced, as you emphasized. "Deformed" people were made to "embody what was wrong with the city, all that stood in the way of its greatness, its efficiency, its health, or its visual appeal," and they would have to be managed as much as architecture and street layout.[3] Chicago, which became a model of modern city planning and an important example of the era of the City Beautiful, also became an important site for the Ugly Laws, labor unrest, and reformist progressive scrutiny. The idea of the ideal city was one without "unsightly," disabled beggars and other deviants on the street.

"Ugliness and beauty." Modernity as controlled appearance and "Ugly ordinances epitomized how modern bodies were and must be seen as they engaged with city spaces."[4] The Ugly Laws targeted something "that appeared vulgar, dysfunctional, and too loud in its patterns," too loud in its patterns—an expression that I especially like.[5] What are the genealogies of contemporary body politics and aesthetic discourses?

SuS: Let me offer one recent example of the way the story of this antiquated law resonates with today's examples of body politics and their aesthetic components. I have been thinking in the last year about the relation between "disability" and "obesity." Here is a news article from the *San Francisco Chronicle* from April 16, 1910. I found out about it after I finished *The Ugly Laws* book.

> Detective Tim Riordan made the biggest capture in police annals yesterday. It was Jolly Trixie, otherwise known as Miss Kitty Plunkett, who tips the scales at a disputed 625 pounds, whose hips measure 92 inches, bust 84 inches, and calf 36 inches. She was arrested for allegedly violating the Penal Code, and is accused of being deformed and exhibiting her deformity [...] "This lady does not appear deformed to me," said Judge Shortall [...] Two physicians testified that Miss Plunkett was perfectly symmetrical and was by no means deformed. "Obesity is not deformity," said one of the medical heights sententiously. "Thank heaven for that," muttered Detective John Collins [...] "The case will be continued for advisement," said Judge Shortall. "I am far from convinced that this lady is anything but charming."

Kitty Plunkett, also known as Jolly Trixie, was a nationally known American "Fat Lady" on the sideshow circuit. (She's been written about in Sharon Mazer's essay in the *Bodies Out of Bounds: Fatness and Transgression* an-

3 Schweik, *The Ugly Laws*, 69.
4 Ibid., 86.
5 Ibid., 88.

thology published in 2001). Her day in court gives us a clear set of terms divided by a supposedly firm line: symmetry and charm on the one hand, deformity and disgust on the other. Unbeknownst to Kitty Plunkett, she had landed at the epicenter of the Ugly Law (San Francisco's was the first example of the city ordinance that swept the United States in the nineteenth and early twentieth century). As Kitty Plunkett's case illustrates, the law was one way of punishing women whose appearance violated aesthetic norms of femininity. What's most striking to me about the news story here is that the judge "continued" Kitty Plunkett's case "under advisement." Today the Ugly Law seems almost quaint in its extremity of oppression. But discrimination—casual and legalized—against people with anomalous bodies in our post-Ugly era is still remarkably widespread.

I recently testified about the uses of the Ugly Law against people labeled "obese" at a hearing of the California Fair Employment and Housing Commission, which is considering amending its disability regulations in ways that will have a deep impact on the civil rights of fat, disabled people in California—and eventually elsewhere if others follow California's lead. The question at hand was whether "obese" people should now be required to prove an underlying medical/ physiological cause for their weight-related impairment in order to be covered under the FEHC's mandate to protect people against disability discrimination. No other individuals identified as disabled have had to prove an underlying cause in order to be protected; evidence of impairment, not of approved forms of causality, has been sufficient. The point is not that "obese" people are "disabled"; the point is that people disabled by weight shouldn't be denied rights—for instance, the subject of our discussion here, the right to the city, access, accommodation—because of stigma, because of judgmental assumptions about the reasons for weight gain.[6] (It's important to note that we know very little, scientifically, about what causes greater weight—but that too isn't the point). The wonderful lawyers spearheading the attempt to block the FEHC's proposed change make the key point that the extra burden of proof that the commission would demand would disproportionately affect women and lesbians, because those groups statistically have high rates of "obesity"—and I would add poor people into the mix.

The confusion at this hearing on this question was striking. For instance, there was a risk that the commission's "obesity exclusion" might be backed by some fat rights activists worried (understandably) about an absolute equation between obesity and disability—even though the exclusion might mean, say, that a child whose weight prevented access to a local elementary school might be denied accommodation. The simple truth—that fat disabled people might be denied protection afforded to others—was so hard to see. It's as if, in very real ways, where appearance norms and the maintenance of "bodies of distinction" are concerned, we continue to waver in the space between disgust and charm, deformity and symmetry; we all live in continuance, under advisement. As I wrote recently, we need to seek an (international) DEFORMED NATION—in the original sense of the word deformed: from the medieval Latin "dis-forma," "of diverse forms." Let's recognize honestly and value systematically and creatively the global, deformed nation and the dis-formed people that we are.

EE: A librarian from a Chicago archive treats the Ugly Law as an urban legend. Although his archive contains the Ugly Law documents and traces, when approached he says quite confidently that the ordinance is a myth. How would you explain that reaction?

SuS: Good question! Let me answer it in the manner of so many "unsightly beggars": sidelong and kind of deviously. Aside perhaps from civic pride, my first thought is that that librarian's repudiation has something to do with the way in which the idea of fakery haunts the history of the law at every turn. For the story of the "fake cripple," there has to be a mock archive. An urban legend about that legendary urban con. It can't be the stuff of a serious historical record. It's got to be fake all the way down. After all, the obscure place where the real collides with the fake is the Ugly Law's turf.

In a way, though he set himself up as objecting to the false stories of the masses, that librarian was simply offering up one more set piece from US popular culture. The dynamics of the Ugly Law—the identification, repudiation, abjection, exclusion, arrest, punishment, and incarceration of unsightly beggars—become the stuff of twentieth century American popular story precisely when faking is at stake.

For instance, what faint traces I found of the Ugly Law in fictionalized memory showed up only in pulp fiction and popular films that depicted the Doctor's and the other "faker bars" I described in the book where "for-real" and pretend disabled people pooled their begging profits. That makes sense, because the sheer ugliness of the Ugly Law could simultaneously reveal itself in lowlife settings and veil itself in plots of fraud

6 Disabled by weight through social exclusion. The DPI (Disabled Peoples' International) defines disability as "the loss or limitation of opportunities to take part in the normal life of the community on an equal level with others due to physical and social barriers." Dan Goodley, *Disability Studies: An Interdisciplinary Introduction* (London: SAGE Publications, 2011), 8.

exposed and foiled. In these fictions, as in Charity Organization Society discourse, fakery justified the unsightly beggar ordinances or other forms of police harassment and control.

By the way, though, in pulp stories about "fake cripple" beggars the plot unfolded more unevenly; there are lots of gaps and twists. My favorite is a story called *Street of the Forgotten Men* by George Kibbe Turner (1922), made into a marvelously corny silent film by Herbert Brenon, starring the hunk love interest Percy Marmont, in 1925. Brenon's *The Street of Forgotten Men* self-referentially thematized the special effects of disability imposture—but it didn't do that, finally, to call filmic sham crippling into question. The film's reviews by critics all emphasized one feature: how "real" it all "seemed." Even post-production, the film provoked border skirmishes between real and fake. In a news story a year after its release, "Speakeasy Equips Beggar as Cripple: 'One-Armed Soldier' Reveals Scheme When Detectives Find an Arm Under Bandages," police interviewed by the reporter attributed the resurgence of the "cripple factory" where disreputable people costumed themselves as fake deserving disabled people to the inspiration of Brenon's *The Street of Forgotten Men*, and another begging crackdown on the New York City streets ensued—one that, as usual, rounded up for-reals with impersonators. The police in this case blamed actor Lon Chaney, whom they mistakenly thought played *Street*'s faker, for giving beggars ideas, in a triumph of fetishism of this sort: "I know it is a fake cripple influenced by Percy Marmont playing a faker playing a real cripple, but even so it is the Hunchback of Notre Dame."

Making and unmaking quasi-disability was Lon Chaney's specialty. The New York policemen who thought Chaney played the faker in *Street of Forgotten Me*n may have been confusing that film with yet another Chaney story of disability imposture, *The Miracle Man* (1919). That movie was based on Frank Packard's 1914 *The Miracle Man*, another text in which pulp fiction met the Ugly Law. The novel concerns an unsightly beggar who involves himself in a complex scheme to bilk visitors to a faith healer, a con in which he fakes first disability and then healing. In the film this scene became a legendary set piece; Paramount preserved it as Chaney's greatest acting moment, one duplicated later in *Man of a Thousand Faces* when Jimmy Cagney played Lon Chaney playing an imposter playing a healing cripple. Chaney's sham cripple roles called for him to shift repeatedly before the eyes from normate to deformed or maimed and back again, in ways potentially as illuminating (though not any less problematic) for Disability Studies as his famous *Hunchback of Notre Dame*. In the figure of Quasimodo, who is proven "real" by contrast with the film's imposter beggars, *Hunchback* mystified and essentialized impairment; but *Miracle Man*, at least until its ending, demystified and opened up a potential space of self-consciousness regarding celluloid disability.

But that's the grand height of representation of disability fakery. The low story is all around and much cruder. With all this faker-begging going on for decades, why wouldn't the Chicago librarian think the Ugly Law was all made up?

EE: In the history of "getting Ugly" in public space, different subjects intertwine. You describe how within the texts of the Ugly Laws the language of freak and beggar, "street and stage," intersect. Freaks and freak shows provoked the question of "human and/or animal" ("the human-faced donkey, the three-legged rooster, and the deformed hen and the leopard girl").[7] Furthermore, the fear of the unsightly beggar emerged concurrently with the fear of the tramp, and resistance to the execution by police officers of the Ugly Laws was taking place through the formation of ugly crowds on behalf of poor people. Immigration screeners spotted unsightly beggars, and the Ugly Laws in practice functioned "to sort people on the streets by race as well as disability."[8] What are further intersections of subjecthood and affiliate relations in the context of the law's meaning?

SuS: There are so many intersections and—I like your phrase—"affiliate relations." I touched on the conjunction of obesity and disability already. Here's another example, a linkage I only barely touched on in the book, a connection between the issues I explored there and transgender body politics (and also the politics of war) that centers in the word "maimed," one of the terms of the Ugly Law ("No person who is diseased, maimed"). "Maimed" is linked etymologically to the word "mayhem." We tend now to think of mayhem as chaos or havoc (I'm fond of the definition in *Webster's Third*, which glosses "mayhem" as "needless or willful damage, as in literary criticism or editorial activity," an explanation that links maiming with transgressions of writing). But "mayhem," as Nikki Sullivan has pointed out, emerged first in early modern England as the specific criminal act of evading military service by mutilating oneself. English mayhem statutes sought to deter and punish those who might deliberately cut off a hand or toe or any body part necessary for waging warfare; the crime was a capital offense.

In recent years these statutes have been cited primarily in discussions of whether doctors might be charged with mayhem for doing transsexual surgeries. The king "had a law enacted," Harry Benjamin commented in

7 Schweik, *The Ugly Laws*, 98.

8 Ibid., 167.

his landmark *The Transsexual Phenomenon*, "that forbade depriving a soldier of any part ... necessary for his defense [...] To visualize the male genitalia in this category is difficult."[9] Difficult, but not impossible, for as Sullivan explains, the amputation of any "healthy" body part constitutes a kind of symbolic decapitation of the king, a serious threat to "the body politic and its members, one which affects confusion, disorder, disability, the loss of integrity, the violent dismembering of bodies of flesh, bodies of knowledge, and social bodies."[10] This symbolic dismembering links the (sham) cripple and the trans.

Crimes of literal, statutory mayhem crop up now and then in the discourse of the unsightly beggar, particularly when the stories concern other countries than the United States—Italian children injured by sinister *padrones* in order to increase their begging capital, the stock manufactured cripples of India or China, etc. Far more common in the culture of the Ugly Law, however, is that state of near-mayhem we find in those faker bars that occupied so much space in my book. Next to an imposter, a for-real maimed person becomes the very model of bodily integrity. Imposters dwelled in the realm of twice-maimed maiming, of maiming on the verge of mayhem. The havoc they created is sufficient to delight a literary critic. But we have to remember, too, that disabled people, like trans people, bore the brunt of the backlash against mayhem.

9 Harry Benjamin, *The Transsexual Phenomenon* (New York: Julian, 1966), 94.

10 Ibid., 229–30.

Literature

Benjamin, Harry. *The Transsexual Phenomenon*. New York: Julian, 1966.

Fuller, Arthur Franklin. *Fifty Thousand Miles Back-Ridden*. Fort Worth, Texas: Anchor, 1915.

Garland-Thomson, Rosemarie. *Extraordinary Bodies*. New York: Columbia University Press, 1996.

Goodley, Dan. *Disability Studies. An Interdisciplinary Introduction*. London: SAGE Publications, 2011.

Imrie, Rob. *Disability and the City. International Perspectives*. London: Paul Chapman Publishing, 1996.

Leader, Pauline. *And No Birds Sing*. New York: Vanguard Press, 1931.

Schweik, Susan. *The Ugly Laws. Disability in Public*. New York: New York University Press, 2009.

Scott, James. *Seeing Like a State*. New Haven: Yale University Press, 1998.

Spivak, Gayatri Chakravorty. "Can the Subaltern Speak?" In *Colonial Discourse and Post-Colonial Theory: A Reader*. Edited by Patrick Williams and Laura Chrisman, 66–111. New York: Columbia University Press, 1993.

Spivak, Gayatri Chakravorty. *A Critique of Postcolonial Reason: Toward a History of the Vanishing Present*. Cambridge, MA: Harvard University Press, 1999.

Sullivan, Nikki. "Integrity, Mayhem, and the Question of Self-Demand Amputation." *Continuum: Journal of Media and Culture Studies*, no. 19:3 (2005): 325–333.

Wilson, William H. *The City Beautiful Movement*. Baltimore: Johns Hopkins University, 1989.

Climate Calculations

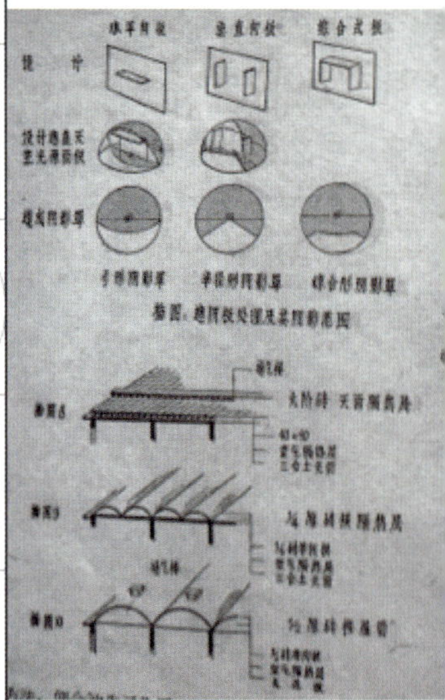

Epilogue

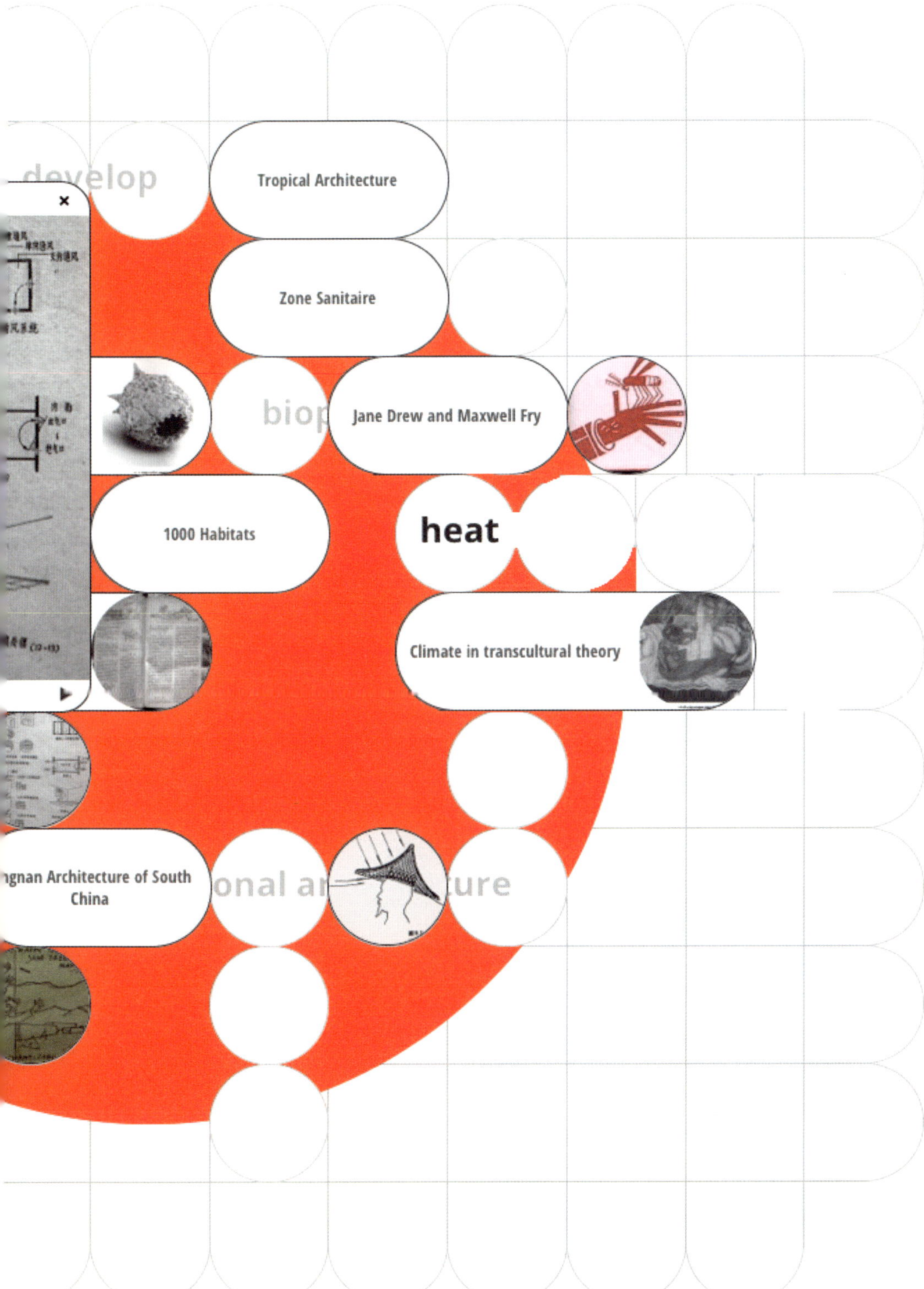
develop
Tropical Architecture
Zone Sanitaire
biop
Jane Drew and Maxwell Fry
1000 Habitats
heat
Climate in transcultural theory
gnan Architecture of South China
onal ar
ure

So Many Reports, So Many Questions

For Instance: Is There Such a Thing as Postcolonial Critical Planning?

Gabu Heindl

> **The young Alexander conquered India.**
> **/ Was he alone? / Caesar beat the Gauls.**
> **Did he not even have a cook with him?**
> **—Bertolt Brecht**

This is a selection of questions Bertolt Brecht poses in his 1935 poem "Questions from a worker who reads." After posing a number of productively naïve questions, he concludes the poem with: "So many reports. / So many questions."[1]

Brecht's "Questions from a worker who reads" are about colonization and hegemonic historical narratives. The questions repeatedly contemplate actors who have remained unnamed (like the cook), but by being ostentatiously singled out as individuals, they suddenly appear out of place. In today's research landscape, this Brechtian style critique is quite familiar. Nonetheless: at least in the field of architecture, people still snicker when (to use an example whose significance will soon be apparent), for instance, the notoriously naïve detective Columbo, in an episode ("Blueprint for Murder," 1972) of the TV series of the same name, asks a cocky architect "Hey sir, did you build that?" gesturing at the presentation model of the building project. Columbo's friendly question "only" refers to the model, prompting the architect to reply: "No, one of my staff did." Had the architect believed Columbo had meant the building rather than the model, he certainly would have proudly answered: "Yes."
What may appear a joke in a smaller fictional context is no joke in the greater scheme of reality. To this day, star and signature architecture à la Frank Gehry renders those who collaborate with architects invisible, making it seem as if they have no name or play no part in the discourses surrounding architecture or the production of cities and spaces. It is not uncommon to hear that the star architect not only "built" the Guggenheim Museum, but he also put the city of Bilbao itself (back) on the map. *Was he alone?*

"Who or what builds a city or a city district?" Like Brecht, the authors of the interdisciplinary research project *Model House* pose this question on the first page of their web cartography http://www.transculturalmodernism.org. The project and the question deal with urban planning and architecture during the time of decolonization in the 1950s and 1960s in North Africa, Israel, India, and China. The answer is not "one architect," but a multitude of human and nonhuman actors, many of whom have been left out of classical architecture history: women, political constellations, nonhuman actors, materials, etc. The

1 Bertolt Brecht, "Questions from a worker who reads [Fragen eines lesenden Arbeiters] (1935)," in *Poems 1913–1956*, trans. Michael Hamburger (New York: Routledge, 1979), 252.

program here is the relativization and examination of hegemonic historical narratives as well as the subjectification and equal recognition of actors and resistance movements: "The result of this constellation is a polylogical and multiperspectival narration by a number of speakers."[2] It's not about creating a "grand" historical and linear narrative, but about bringing together different histories, found objects, intertextualities, empirical detail studies, and narratives on the same map, which raises many new questions; some I will address in the following. *So many reports, so many questions*.

Habitat Chart: Why Not Charter? Why a Map and Not a Master Plan?

Let's start with form. Designing a master plan or postulating a new charter would go against the grain of the critical approach of a postcolonial endeavor. Using cartography as a form of notation, *Model House* maps the relations among the transformations of the afore mentioned (post)colonial spaces at a time when architectural discourse is largely concerned with questioning the dictates of modernity and countering universalizing claims by taking a closer look at regionalism, local contexts, culture or climate. Part of the project's comprehensive online database is the "Habitat Chart," which consists of a cartography of discourses, projects and projections surrounding postcolonial urban planning and its habitat concepts—modern concepts that change according to local and political contexts.

At the time the "Athens Charter" was passed in 1933, it presented a universal set of guidelines for urban planning under the assumption of worldwide universal and equal conditions. With regard to new questions of the habitat and a growing critique on modern urbanism the *Congrès International d'Architecture Moderne*, CIAM IX in 1953 and CIAM X in 1956 pursued the idea to draft another Charter: the "Charter of Habitat," an undertaking which, however, never came to fruition due to the strongly contrasting positions within the group, which also ultimately led CIAM to disband in 1959. The seminal act of creating another charter would have meant laying a foundation not everyone was willing to build upon. With historical distance, the *Model House* project's "Habitat Chart" does not attempt to make up for the charter that was never written but instead seeks to map out the circumstances and discourses that made the charter impossible and to offer a set of guidelines for understanding the relationships and backgrounds of existing structures, employing postcolonial and postfundamentalist critique in the process. Critique of the critique is inevitable in this context, seeing as some positions that sought to critique modernity did so on the basis of naturalizing and nostalgic notions of culture (culturalization) derived from colonial observations. The informal ways in which non-expert inhabitants utilized and defined their living spaces inspired the CIAM X architects: in these naturally evolving informal structures they saw a possibility for architecture to develop a new language; they hoped the vernacular architecture of colonized cultures would offer new input: "This work has allowed for a new architectural language to develop that had initially been created by the structures of inhabitation."[3] Maintaining a close proximity to power and to the market—these architectural perspectives have remained in place—from the era of colonialism and decolonization until today. As the colonies began to crumble, the new sensibility for local contexts made sure Western architects continued to have access to the market. Their purported knowledge about specific ways of life was used to justify racialized boundaries as well as the construction of segregated neighborhoods and class-based gated communities.

To add a further critique to the critique, the (self-)criticality of postcolonial studies also comes into play here: within an academic context, postcolonial studies may be emancipating and sensitizing, e.g. in light of democratization processes, but they are not part of a radical, de-colonial liberation movement. While we may not share the de-colonial impetus to separate the two, we are conscious of the fact that empirical and archive-based research perpetuates certain colonial structures: for example, the fact that European researchers use European research funds to do (self-)critical research on the history, spaces, and discourses of colonization and the potentials of decolonization, to conduct "field studies," which, due to the practical research conditions, are often too short and constrained by language and translation difficulties. Often, this does not allow for what Anthony King defines as an important premise for Postcolonial Studies: "knowledge of the local pre-colonial society, knowledge of the colonizer's society at home, and that of the colonized society."[4]

When addressing the issue of planning such (self-)criticality can also be employed to conceive of a more substantial notion of democracy within planning, particularly since "social sustainability" now plays such a tricky key role within planning discourse. It is again particularly within the context of postcolonial architecture, that a certain type of discourse reveals itself so clearly. To bring in an example: for nearly ten years now, the university project "SARCH" (Social Sustainable Architecture) has been building "necessary communal facilities in squatter settlements in developing countries," and the homepage

2 Fahim Amir, Eva Egermann, Moira Hille, Johannes Köck, Jakob Krameritsch, Christian Kravagna, Christina Linortner, Marion von Osten, and Peter Spillmann (2012): "Who or what builds a city or a city district?". http://www.transculturalmodernism.org. Accounted May 1, 2013.

3 Alison Smithson, ed., *Team 10 Primer* (Cambridge, MA: MIT Press, 1968). Quoted in: "Dwellers," http://www.transcultural-modernism.org. Accounted May 1, 2013.

4 See Jean-Louis Cohen, "Architectural History and the Colonial Question: Casablanca, Algiers and Beyond," *Architectural History*, no. 49 (2006): 349–68.

informs us that "European students" and the "local population" are working together on the projects. Within one semester, architecture students learn about the needs of people in "developing countries" or the architectural manifestation of the "necessary" development. (The project defines itself as "Vienna's contribution to the development goals established in the UN Millennium Declaration: eradicating poverty, encouraging sustainability and establishing universal primary education."[5] "Knowledge" of the "users'" ways of life and needs is an attitude imminent within the discipline of architecture. Even in cases where planners are more familiar with the situation and the predominant language surrounding their project, there are still translation difficulties or misconceptions concerning users and inhabitants, who are often neither listened to nor understood, despite a shared language. These situations are based on an understanding of the planning process that divides it into planners with "knowledge" and users with "needs." By contrast, within the context of democratic participation in planning, democratization consists of "democracy education" that takes place in these schools in which tools are developed for "interfering" in elitist planning practices or of the opportunity to formulate demands and debate planning and construction budgets in public forums (such as the participatory budgeting in Rio Grande do Sul and Porto Alegre).[6] All of these are themes currently, once again, being discussed within the field of critical architecture in the "West."[7]

Is Architecture Fundamentally Undemocratic?

The above-mentioned points of critique prompt us to contemplate who commissions architecture. Which political structure makes which design possible? Why does Nehru commission Le Corbusier to plan a top-down master plan for Chandigarh, as the symbol of a new democratic India, in 1947? Because (only) Nehru wants it that way? Who invited him? Who pays for it (both figuratively and literally)? What is ordered? Who builds the walls? *Model House* doesn't answer all these questions—we do however learn, among other things, about the architect Minnette De Silva, who has thus far not been considered part of the architectural history of Chandigarh,[8] about the transcultural influences or, about different actors and debates in South Asian modernity.

Back to the "face" of the tabula rasa planning of Chandigarh: Le Corbusier. The notion that one architect is given credit for the planning of an entire city is not only diametrically opposed to a radical understanding of democracy; it is also a far cry from any sensitivity for "collective planning." Also within postcolonial critique, the image of the "evil" planner emerges—architects who exert their power over the design in an authoritarian way. Though such cases exist, ultimately, architects never have absolute power within architecture or in urban planning. (Even "the Chandigarh Masterplan had many masters.")[9]

And yet it would also be too simplistic to claim architects are "merely" part of the system, or henchmen of those who commissioned the architect in the first place. What's more: often times the commissioners are not so easily identifiable. In the reception of architecture in which power relations are obscured and the decision-making processes untransparent, planners come in handy in terms of giving a "face" to the design that is seen as exerting and representing domination. Making architects the only ones accountable for the built form affirms a concept of absolute, hierarchical authorship (as if the form-building "masters" were the only ones responsible for built environments) that also fails to address power structures, capital relations, decision processes.

The anti-colonial resistance of the *bidonvilles* dwellers, the protests against the construction of Chandigarh as well as against urban planning based on segregation form the basis for yet another chart of *Model House*: "Dwellers," which maps different forms of resistance practiced by the dwellers, such as self-building, rebuilding, repurposing, self-organizing. It also includes reports of mosquitoes and malaria, of cows eating the plants of Chandigarh's landscaping, of donkeys disrupting construction. It talks about how the dwellers of the North African *bidonvilles* were used by Candilis-Josic-Woods as living "research objects" with which to study everyday urban life, and later by CIAM X architects who observed local routines and appropriations for their modernist plans of Casablanca (*Carrières Centrales, Cité Verticale/Horizontale*, 1952). These reports also lead to more questions: how problematic is a strategy of appeasement that continues to obscure the West's/modernity's unbroken dominance? How generalizable or resistant are local contexts? To what extent is modernity renewable and adaptable? How capable of appropriation are city districts that were planned to include appropriation processes?[10] How dominant is architecture?

Is Architecture not Fundamentally Colonizing?

Architecture is an art form that cannot be eluded,[11] as Margarete Schütte-Lihotzky, a modern architect who plays an important role in the *Model House*

5 http://sarch.twoday.net.

6 Bernhard Leubolt, *Staat als Gemeinwesen. Das Partizipative Budget in Rio Grande do Sul und Porto Alegre* (Vienna: LIT Verlag, 2006).

7 Gabu Heindl, "Solidarity. How do democratic spaces come into existence?" Lecture series curated for the Österreichische Gesellschaft für Architektur (2011/2012), http://www.oegfa.at.

8 Moira Hille, "Minnette De Silva: A Modern Regionalist Architect," Accessed May 1 2013. http://www.transculturalmodernism.org.

9 Fahim Amir, "Dwellers and Strayers: Multispecies Criminality in Postcolonial Worlds," Accessed May 1, 2013. http://www.transculturalmodernism.org.

10 For more on the appropriation of the "appropriated" housing settlement, e.g., the Cité Verticale, see Marion von Osten, "Architecture Without Architects—Another Anarchist Approach," *e- flux*, no. 6 (May 2009), http://www.eflux.com.

11 From a conversation with Margarete Schütte-Lihotzky. Christina Linortner, "Bamboo and the Courtyard House: Margarete Schütte-Lihotzky in China," http://www.transculturalmodernism.org.

project research on China, repeatedly pointed out.[12] In this respect architecture is dominant. Generally speaking, the architectural history of economic-political spaces is a history of power and committed social politics—especially regarding mass housing projects.[13] In a Gramscian sense, in non-dictatorial forms of government, successful architecture politics are almost automatically "hegemonic," because they are based on a consensus that creates and affirms dominance. While architects help to appease and "pacify." However, the moment an environment is (re-)designed or "simply" re-modeled, something else is always destroyed, the space is occupied in another way, becomes "colonized."

What does colonizing mean in this context? Building settlements, creating policies to populate certain areas, land grabbing are all concepts that are still familiar parameters of action for (colonizing) city planning, even if they are not defined as such: from the violent exploitation of economically "underdeveloped" regions to global capitalism profiting from gentrification projects—"here" as well as "there." Just as forms of colonialism persist in postcolonialism, planning practices remain colonial after colonialism—though under new political circumstances. Their discourse remained Eurocentric both within and following the CIAM X architects' attempts to create a new sensibility—in how Michel Écochard dealt with the informal structures of *bidonvilles* as director of Casablanca's city planning office, or how, in the early twenty-first century, Rem Koolhaas and his students at Harvard, much in the vein of the CIAM X "learning from" approach, researched precarious market economies in Lagos and described them as "working" economies.[14] In the film *Koolhaas Houselife* about Rem Koolhaas' *Maison à Bordeaux*, the filmmakers describe how the camera follows the housekeeper Guadalupe Acedo "and other people who look after the building." And further: "This experiment presents a new way of looking at architecture and broadens the field of its representation."[15] Here, only one of many actors who have a part in (re)producing the space is given a name and a voice—only because she is beneficial in terms of a new representation of the architecture.

Actors involved in building, rebuilding, using, and cleaning the space remain excluded from the network of representative architecture discourse. At the same time, also architects are struggling to be recognized for their efforts; while descriptions of new buildings in architecture magazines often cite the name of the photographer and the commissioner of the project, there is rarely any mention of any other names of people involved in the project. Recently, one of the largest commissioners in Austria responded to the question of why in their publications architects are not named by saying, "if we did, we would have to mention everyone's name involved in a project, even the person who lays the tiles." (This was meant as a self-explanatory argument, as in: "Nobody could possibly want that!"—so much for acknowledging multiple actors within the building sector.)

Back to the period the research in *Model House* focuses on: after decolonization, "development" discourse took the place of the notion of "occupation." Both are modernist concepts: the logical step after "occupying" a space imagined to be empty was the modernist idea of "forwards"—progressing towards modernity (paternalistically supported by modernity experts from the West). Developing, developers, development: these are all terms that are quite familiar within the architecture sector. In the architecture world, the expertocratic project development of a building far outweighs concerns of the inhabitants' use. Since fewer projects are being contracted due to the recent financial crises, architects gladly take on the role of developers themselves, initiating projects themselves that are geared toward the free market. Part of such initiatives is acquiring government funding for creative or economic projects where they can engage in urban or architectural developments (modernization) in "developing countries." North-South or "West and the rest" relations demonstrate architecture's inherent paternalism, which persists to this very day. Why have such projects remained so attractive for Western architects (aside from reasons of wanderlust and exoticism)?

In What Way is Architecture's Dominance Particularly Obvious in (Post)Colonies?

Tabula rasa—the realization of the pure form of a new urban master plan—is contingent on the circumstances surrounding property for it to be a possibility at all. Modernist urban planning is contingent on receiving access to vast stretches of land. New towns, carpet settlements, "habitat for the greatest number"—all large-scale, mass residential construction projects—are difficult to realize without an incredible amount of land available, even today.

> It was not only the land conditions that made colonies "testing grounds" for Fordist mass residential construction projects or for ways to structure massive urbanization. A cheap workforce enabled these to be carried out based on Taylorist organizational structures—at least as long as access to construction workers and *dwellers* was ensured.[16] With regard to his critique that such urban planning projects are however all too quickly labeled "testing grounds," new ideas or "laboratories" for experimenting with development (in the modern linear sense), Jean-Louis Cohen notes that "evaluations" of such projects are rare.

12 Georges Teyssot, *Die Krankheit des Domizils. Wohnen und Wohnbau 1800-1930* (Braunschweig: Vieweg, 1989).
13 Rem Koolhaas and Edgar Cleijne, *Lagos: How it Works* (Baden: Lars Müller Publishers, 2008).
14 http://www.koolhaashouselife.com
15 Cf. the film by Harun Farocki, Zum Vergleich (In comparison), Germany/Austria, 2009.
16 Cohen, "Architectural History and the Colonial Question."

The charge that the metaphor "laboratory" is brought into play too hastily applies to architecture in general, seeing as it is one of the few disciplines that does not have its own evaluation process methods, although in reality, prototypes are the only things being built.[17] Building large-scale habitats without previous testing and thus performing trials of residential concepts on a one-to-one scale does not require too much justification or explanation if it is "Not in My Backyard" (NIMBY). The physical distance between the Western planning centers and the colonies not only plays to the NIMBY mentality, it also maximizes the application of a "bird's eye perspective" for top-down planning or "North-South recommendations" the outcome of which can be seen well looking down from an airplane on the way to a vacation. By paying attention to daily routines and taking them as a foundation for new architecture, e.g., floor plans assigned to specific users, à la "European-style habitat" or Housing for the Arab population, it is once again clear how "identifying a target group" naturalizes and racializes an entire population—which is also reflected in discussions around social housing for migrants in the West.

Perhaps the most salient point in terms of dominant forms of urban planning is that (post)colonial planning does not encounter any obstacles through democratic circumstances. "Zones for experimentation [...] were only possible because local power structures hardly left any room for democratic debate."[18] This could also be viewed as an "ideal condition" for realizing any (modernist) building project. The inevitable fact that, within a democracy, there is always the possibility that demands may be raised to participate in the project; along with the concern that some would veto the project or that opposition, objection, resistance could prevent or delay the construction often results in planning being done in secrecy, in untransparent contracting procedures and in information being provided to the public for the shortest time legally possible. By speaking of an intervention as being "technically necessary," criticism is staved off and the fact that any intervention, any planning is political, and thus contestable, is concealed.[19]

Why Continue Developing Housing for the Middle Class While There Are Still Sans-Papiers?

During the financial crisis of the 1920s, architects bundled their creative energies to build minimal existence housing ("Wohnung für das Existenzminimum"), thereby proving to the market and to the modern residents that it was indeed possible to build housing on most minimal space (shown, for example, at CIAM's 1929 exhibition in Frankfurt). While this rendered the "minimal existence home" acceptable, according to architect Giancarlo de Carlo (also part of CIAM X), it did so without questioning the social circumstances that caused this "minimum."[20] Despite their sensibility towards context, climate, and lifestyle habits, also CIAM X architects working on mass housing projects "for the greatest number" within postcolonial contexts continued to plan in a fundamentally colonizing and paternalistic manner. The fact that the minimal existence home and the housing settlements in Carrières Centrales ultimately remained unaffordable for those in need[21] and for whom they had initially been built—at least according to the planners—is not only a farce, but inherent to the system. Then and now, "social housing" means building for a middle class with civil rights. In "Fortress Europe," social housing is available for those with citizenship rights who can afford "social" housing. While it is uncertain how many, a great number of *sans papiers* are "here [in Europe], because we were there" (and still are), and yet, (star) architects are still planning and building for authoritarian regimes or private clientele on the neoliberal capitalist market. Rhetorically savvy and along deconstructivist critique, Rem Koolhaas justifies his involvement in projects in China by claiming that the CCTV headquarters in Beijing (Koolhaas's iconic building for Chinese state television) could serve to foster greater democratization. This interest in democracy seems contradictory when critics rave about the building, emphasizing how it successfully "dominates" the city's skyline.

Speaking of dominance and urbanism: Nezar AlSayyad writes that dominance is "not exclusive to colonial cities, but [that] the use and manifestation of dominance in the colonial context is particularly blunt."[22]

Another contemporary example of the "bluntness" of White dominance up to outright cynicism, is the planning discourse surrounding New Orleans. Entire "colonial" tracts of urban land were flooded and destroyed by Hurricane Katrina, especially black neighborhoods located in stretches that were cheap to build on due to the high risk of flooding. The flood of projects initiated by architects from around the world to develop architectural solutions/answers for rebuilding the city ranged from architecture spectacles, to Brad Pitt's housing initiative "Make it Right," to cynical "white-washing" projects. The flood areas that had previously been home to a mostly African American population were

17 Cohen, "Architectural History and the Colonial Question," 356.

18 Ironically, planning policy in a city with a paternalistic policy style like Vienna currently includes demands for democratic participation, at a time when the financial and budget crises don't allow for much planning let alone building.

19 Giancarlo De Carlo, "Architecture's Public" [1970], in *Architecture & Participation*, eds. Peter Blundell Jones, Doina Petrescu, and Jeremy Till (London: Taylor & Francis, 2005), 3–22.

20 Von Osten, "Architecture Without Architects—Another Anarchist Approach".

21 Nezar AlSayyad, "Urbanism and the Dominance Equation: Reflections on Colonialism and National Identity," in *Forms of Dominance: On the Architecture and Urbanism of the Colonial Enterprise*, ed. Nezar AlSayyad (Aldershot: Avebury, 1992), 1–26.

22 Yates McKee, "Haunted Housing: Eco-Vanguardism, Eviction, and the Biopolitics of Sustainability in New Orleans," *Grey Room*, no. 30 (Winter 2008): 84–113.

"white-washed" by the construction of ecological parks (backed up by the argument that it was time to finally build "with nature"). What then emerged, instead of rebuilding the black neighborhoods, was a rhetoric of ecologically motivated "technically necessary" measures, which, in effect, made it impossible for many who had lost their homes to return to their neighborhoods.[23] In a critical study on the range of ideologies of the different projects, art critic Yates McKee differentiates a few critical projects as dissent-friendly, such as "Mobilizing Shame," an activist project by the Yes Men, or Laura Kurgan's "Justice Mapping." Kurgan and her students at Columbia University had already begun mapping New Orleans before Katrina. Their "Million Dollar Maps" survey and illustrate how much (or little) budget is spent on public infrastructure per city block and set this in relation to the total amount spent on the incarceration of residents living on a given block. In the maps, by overlaying physical parameters (topography, city planning traits, volumetry, figure-ground ratios, public functions and infrastructure, etc.) with otherwise invisible data, it becomes clear that an interrelation exists between the neighborhoods' location and design and the parameters mentioned above, and that there is a direct correlation between a lack in infrastructure and an increase in incarceration—providing a starting point for thinking about "justice reinvestment." Here, cartography is the tool that enables a critical assessment. This is one current example of social engagement through architecture which, from a postcolonial (self-)critical approach, demands that a just distribution of means be a fundamental part of postcolonial planning, in the sense of deconstructing existing conditions—before and after the disaster, before and after colonialism. To return to the *Model House* web-based data-map: Where parameter "North Africa" crosses parameter "Theory," we find Jean-Louis Cohen's text "Architectural History and the Colonial Question: Casablanca, Algiers and Beyond." His credo reads: "The first condition of any fruitful work in this domain [analysis of colonial territories] is mistrust vis-à-vis any political narrative, consisting of idealizations still bearing an imprint of colonialist relics, whether of the superiority of imposed models or of a natural suspicion of anti-colonialist discourse against all forms of cultural imposition."[24] Acknowledging suspicion in this way is a fruitful point of departure for numerous other (self-)critical inquires; for this paper, it is a (provisional) conclusion.

Literature

AlSayyad, Nezar. "Urbanism and the Dominance Equation: Reflections on Colonialism and National Identity." In *Forms of Dominance: On the Architecture and Urbanism of the Colonial Enterprise*. Edited by AlSayyad, Nezar, 1-26. Aldershot: Avebury, 1992.

Brecht, Bertolt. "Questions from a worker who reads [Fragen eines lesenden Arbeiters] (1935)." In *Poems 1913–1956*. Translated by Michael Hamburger, 252-53. New York: Routledge, 1979.

Cohen, Jean-Louis. "Architectural History and the Colonial Question: Casablanca, Algiers and Beyond." *Architectural History*, no. 49 (2006): 349–68.

De Carlo, Giancarlo. "Architecture's public. [1970]" In *Architecture & Participation*. Edited by Peter Blundell Jones, Doina Petrescu, and Jeremy Till, 3-22. London: Taylor & Francis, 2005.

Koolhaas, Rem, and Edgar Cleijne. *Lagos: How it Works*. Baden: Lars Müller Publishers, 2008.

Leubolt, Bernhard. *Staat als Gemeinwesen. Das Partizipative Budget in Rio Grande do Sul und Porto Alegre*. Vienna: Lit Verlag, 2006.

McKee, Yates. "Haunted Housing: Eco-Vanguardism, Eviction, and the Biopolitics of Sustainability in New Orleans." *Grey Room*, no. 30 (Winter 2008): 84-113.

Smithson, Alison (ed.): *Team 10 Primer*. Cambridge, MA: MIT Press, 1968.

Teyssot, Georges. *Die Krankheit des Domizils. Wohnen und Wohnbau 1800–1930*. Vieweg: Braunschweig, 1989.

Von Osten, Marion. "Architecture Without Architects—Another Anarchist Approach," *e- flux*, #6 (May 2009). Accessed May 2009. http://www.e-flux.com.

http://www.e-flux.com.
http://www.koolhaashouselife.com.
http://sarch.twoday.net.
http://www.transculturalmodernism.org.

23 Cohen, "Architectural History and the Colonial Question," 356.
24 Ibid.

Biographies

Fahim Amir is currently visiting professor for philosophy at the University of Art and Design Linz (Austria) and finishing his PhD "Pigeon Visions," which deals with modernist aesthetics, urban practices, and visions of posthumanist critique. Amir's last publications include: *Die Arbeit der Form/losigkeit. Ein ästhetischer Einwand gegen die Affirmation der ›Unsichtbarkeit‹ oder ›postrepräsentationaler Politiken* (with Johanna Schaffer, 2012) and *Animals and/in/on Alcohol* (2013). Furthermore, Amir was scientific director of the Live Art Festival 2013 "ZOO 3000" in Hamburg, Germany.

Zvi Efrat, architect and architectural historian, was head of the Department of Architecture at the Bezalel Academy of Arts and Design, Jerusalem (2002–2010). He has taught at the Technion Institute of Technolgy, the Tel Aviv University, and the Hebrew University, among others. He has lectured worldwide, published extensively in various periodicals and books, and curated numerous exhibitions in Israel and in Europe. His book *The Israeli Project: Building and Architecture 1948–1973* was published in 2004.

Eva Egermann is an artist based in Vienna. She is currently a PhD candidate at the Academy of Fine Arts Vienna, and was involved in the *Model House–Mapping Transcultural Modernisms* project, researching relations of urbanism and disability/crip theory. Her most recent publications include the *Crip Magazine* (2012) and *Regime. Wie Dominanz organisiert und Ausdruck formalisiert wird* (co-edited with Petja Dimitrova, Tom Holert, Jens Kastner, and Johanna Schaffer; Edition Assemblage, 2012).

Nádia Farage is senior lecturer at the Department of Anthropology, Institute of Philosophy and Human Sciences, University of Campinas, São Paulo, Brazil. She specializes in North-Amazonian ethnohistory and correlates aspects of social memory and rhetoricity. She is the author of *As Muralhas dos Sertões: os povos indígenas no Rio Branco e a colonização* (1991, Paz e Terra/ANPOCS) and articles on North-Amazonian Amerindian history and ethnography. In the last decade, she has been coordinating research on animality in various ethnographical and historical contexts in Brazil. Her current research targets antivivisection ideas in modern Brazil; partial results were published in "De ratos e outros homens: resistência biopolítica no Brasil moderno" (In C. Lépine et alii (orgs.) *Manuela Carneiro da Cunha: O lugar da cultura e o papel da Antropologia*. RJ: Ed.Beco do Azougue, 2011.)

Gabu Heindl is a Vienna-based architect, urbanist, and architecture theorist. She graduated in Vienna and Princeton and has been teaching at universities in Delft, Graz, and Vienna. Her building work focuses on public buildings/infrastructures ranging from schools and kindergartens, to repertoire cinemas (e.g. Austrian Film Museum, Vienna) and urban public space. Her research deals with spatial aspects of work/education under neoliberalism and with approaches to critical urban planning (involving insights from feminism, left-wing modernisms, and radical democracy theory). She is, among other things, guest editor of *Just Architecture!*, ERA 21 #1 (2012), and the editor of the volume *Arbeit Zeit Raum*, which deals with images and built structures of labor in post-Fordism (2008).

Moira Hille is a Vienna-based artist, performer and researcher with a focus on the relationship of space/architecture, body/movements, camera/film, and the critique of representation. Currently she works at the Academy of Fine Arts in Vienna at the PhD in-Practice program as artistic research staff and as a lecturer at the Institute of Art Theory and Cultural Studies. Since 2009, she has been performing at the queer feminist show *Club Burlesque Brutal*.

Rob Imrie is professor of geography at King's College London and principal investigator of a European Research Council funded project (2013 to 2016) about the significance of universal design in shaping designed environments. His most recent publications include *Accessible Housing: Quality, Disability and Design* (Routledge, 2006) and *The Knowledge Business: Critical Perspectives on the Commodification of Urban Research* (Ashgate, 2010).

Monica Juneja is professor of Global Art History at the Cluster "Asia and Europe in a Global Context" at the University of Heidelberg, Germany. Before her assignment in Heidelberg, she was visiting professor at Emory University, Atlanta, USA. She has been professor at the University of Delhi, India, and has held visiting professorial positions at the Universities of Vienna and Hannover. Her areas of research span the fields of European and Indian studies. They include practices of visual representation, the disciplinary trajectories of art history in South Asia, the interface between Christianization, religious identities and cultural practices in early modern South Asia. Monica Juneja is editor of *Transcultural Studies*, an electronic journal of the Cluster Asia and Europe.

Christian Kravagna is professor of Postcolonial Studies at the Academy of Fine Arts Vienna. He is the editor of the books *Privileg Blick. Kritik der visuellen Kultur*, Berlin 1997; *Agenda. Perspektiven kritischer Kunst*, Vienna/Bozen 2000; *The Museum as Arena: Artists on Institutional Critique*, Cologne 2001, and *Routes: Imaging travel and migration*, Frankfurt 2006. His curated exhibitions include "Living Across: Spaces of Migration," Academy of Fine Arts Vienna, 2010; "Planetary Consciousness," Kunstraum der Leuphana Universität Lüneburg, 2008, and "Migration: Globalisation of Cultural Space and Time," Max Mueller Bhavan, New Delhi, 2003 (with Amit Mukhopadhyay). He is artistic director (with Hedwig Saxenhuber) at Kunstraum Lakeside in Klagenfurt, Austria.

Christina Linortner studied architecture in Vienna and Delft, and Research Architecture in London. She is based in Vienna and works transdisciplinarily within the fields of art/ architecture, urbanism, and theory with a focus on housing culture and migration, transcultural studies, and haunted houses, among others, in Nigeria, the United States (California), and China. She has been involved in the artistic research projects *Model House–Mapping Transcultural Modernisms* at the Academy of Fine Arts Vienna and, *Eden's Edge* at the University of Applied Arts Vienna.

Duanfang Lu is associate professor and associate dean of education in the Faculty of Architecture, Design and Planning at the University of Sydney. She holds a BArch from Tsinghua University, Beijing and a PhD in architecture from the University of California, Berkeley. She has published widely on modern Chinese architectural and planning history. Her recent publications include *Remaking Chinese Urban Form* (2006, 2011) and *Third World Modernism* (2010). She serves on the editorial boards of *Traditional Dwellings and Settlements Review* and *Architectural Theory Review*, and chairs the International Committee of the Society of Architectural Historians.

Anoma Pieris is an associate professor at the Faculty of Architecture, Building and Planning at the University of Melbourne. Her most recent publications include *Hidden Hands and Divided Landscapes: A Penal History of Singapore's Plural Society* (Honolulu: University of Hawaii Press, 2009) and *Architecture and Nationalism in Sri Lanka: The Trouser under the Cloth* (Routledge, 2012).

Vikramāditya Prakāsh is professor of architecture and adjunct professor of landscape architecture and of urban design and planning at the University of Washington in Seattle and the Director of the Chandigarh Urban Lab. His published books include *Chandigarh's Le Corbusier: The Struggle for Modernity in Postcolonial India* (University of Washington Press, 2002), *A Global History of Architecture* (with Francis DK Ching & Mark Jarzombek, John Wiley & Sons, Inc., 2006) and *Colonial Modernities: Building, Dwelling and Architecture in British India and Ceylon* (co-edited with Peter Scriver, Routledge, 2007).

Susan Schweik is a professor of English and associate dean of Arts and Humanities at UC Berkeley. Her most recent book is *The Ugly Laws: Disability in Public*, published in 2009 by New York University Press. She is now working on a book tentatively titled *Lost and Found: How a Ward of Women in a State Institution Taught Us to Teach to the Test*.

Felicity D. Scott is associate professor of architecture and director of the program in Critical, Curatorial and Conceptual Practices in Architecture (CCCP) at Columbia University's Graduate School of Architecture, Preservation and Planning. She is also a founding co-editor of *Grey Room*, a quarterly journal of architecture, art, media, and politics published by MIT Press since Fall 2000. In addition to publishing numerous articles in journals, magazines, and edited anthologies, her book, *Architecture or Techno-Utopia: Politics After Modernism*, was published by MIT Press in 2007, and *Living Archive 7: Ant Farm*, appeared on ACTAR Editorial in 2008. She recently completed a book manuscript entitled *Cartographies of Drift: Bernard Rudofsky's Encounters with Modernity*, and is working on a book entitled *Outlaw Territories: Environments of Insecurity/Architectures of Counter-Insurgency, 1966-1979* to be published by Zone Books.

Marion von Osten is an artist, writer, and exhibition maker. She is a founding member of the Center for Postcolonial Knowledge and Culture (CPKC), Berlin, the media-collective Labor k3000 Zurich, and kpD-kleines post-fordistisches Drama, Berlin. Together with Kathrin Rhomberg she was the artistic director of the research and exhibition projects "Projekt Migration" (2003–2006) and "In the Desert of Modernity. Colonial Planning and After" (2007–2009), and co-edited (with Serhat Karakayll & Tom Avermaete) the reader *Colonial Modern: Aesthetics of the Past, Rebellions for the Future*, 2010. She was a curator at Shedhalle Zurich (1996–99), professor for Artistic Practice and researcher at the ZHdK, Zurich (1999–2006), and professor for Art and Communication at the Academy of Fine Arts Vienna (2006–2012). Since 2013 she has been teaching at the Universities for Art and Design in Geneva and Lucerne, and at the Center for Curatorial Studies CCS at Bard College. She was the head of the *Model House–Mapping Transcultural Modernisms* research project funded by WWTF (2010–2012) and worked on the case study *From/To Casablanca - Be'er Sheva*.

Chunlan Zhao received her bachelor's degree in architecture and master's degree in architectural design and theory from Tianjin University, China, in 1995 and 1998 respectively. She received the VLIR scholarship from the Flemish government and obtained her advanced master degree in architecture of human settlements with the thesis titled "Fengshui's Impact on Traditional Settlements in China: Case Study of Beijing in Its Form, Shape & Meaning" at PGCHS at K.U.Leuven, Belgium, in 2000. With the help of the IRO scholarship from K.U.Leuven in 2002, she completed her doctorate dissertation titled "Socio-Spatial Transformation in Mao's China: Settlement Planning and Dwelling Architecture Revisited, 1950s–1970s." In May 2011, Dr. Zhao started teaching as an associate professor at the Department of Architecture, College of Architecture and Environment, Sichuan University and was appointed the assistant dean of the college in September 2012.

Acknowledgments

Arya Amir, Isabella Amir, Tom Avermaete, Anette Baldauf, Mark Crinson, Ashley De Vos, Helga de Silva, Karel Dudesek, Noam Dvir, Zvi Efrat, Michaela Glanz, Michael Gross, Gabu Heindl, Ute Hölzl, Kumari Jayawardena, Ma Jia, Feng Jiang, He Jintang, Serhat Karakayali, Johannes Köck, Eduard Kögel, Matthew Kohrman, Kateřina Kolářová, Elke Krasny, Susanne Leeb, Tarun Mathur, Ralo Mayer, Kobena Mercer, Robert McRuer, Vikramāditya Prakāsh, Ariane Sadjed, Madhu Sarin, Hadas Shadar, Susan Schweik, Susil Sirivardana, Gang Song, Daniel Weiss, Ashley de Vos, Ye Yanfen, Shmuel Yavin, Lu Yuanding sen., Lu Yuanding jun., Zhao Xintien Vida, Zhang Fuhe, Zhang Jie, Zhang Qiushi, Zhi Heng.

]a[academy of fine arts vienna

Sternberg Press